T0414081

UTILIZING FORENSIC TECHNOLOGIES FOR UNIDENTIFIED HUMAN REMAINS

Death Investigation Resources, Strategies, and Disconnects

UTILIZING FORENSIC TECHNOLOGIES FOR UNIDENTIFIED HUMAN REMAINS

Death Investigation Resources, Strategies, and Disconnects

George W. Adams

NamUs Director, 2011–2015
(National Missing and Unidentified Persons System)
Hurst, Texas, USA

CRC Press
Taylor & Francis Group
Boca Raton London New York

CRC Press is an imprint of the
Taylor & Francis Group, an **informa** business

CRC Press
Taylor & Francis Group
6000 Broken Sound Parkway NW, Suite 300
Boca Raton, FL 33487-2742

Printed on acid-free paper
Version Date: 20150417

International Standard Book Number-13: 978-1-4822-6347-3 (Hardback)

Library of Congress Cataloging-in-Publication Data

Adams, George W., 1947-
 Utilizing forensic technologies for unidentified human remains : death investigation resources, strategies, and disconnects / George W. Adams.
  pages cm
 Includes bibliographical references and index.
 ISBN 978-1-4822-6347-3 (hardcover : alk. paper) 1. Identification. 2. Dead--Identification. 3. Forensic pathology. I. Title.

RA1055.A33 2016
614'.1--dc23   2015006596

Visit the Taylor & Francis Web site at
http://www.taylorandfrancis.com

and the CRC Press Web site at
http://www.crcpress.com

Our dead are never dead to us, until we have forgotten them.

George Eliot

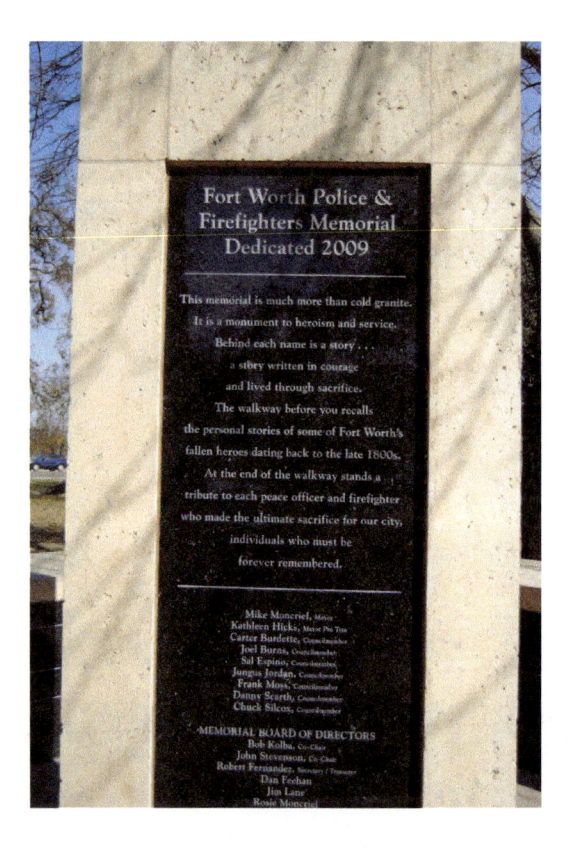

To my brother in blue, Eddie Belcher of the Fort Worth Police Department—struck down October 29, 1971 by an assassin's bullet while serving the citizens of Fort Worth, Texas—you will always be remembered.
To Jan Smolinski and Vicki Kelly, my inspirations.
To all the mothers, fathers, wives, husbands, sons, daughters, brothers, and sisters.
To all the investigators who give all they have for victims and families.
To all of the amazing volunteers who are forever searching to identify the missing among the thousands of John and Jane Does.
Within these pages, may you find hope and comfort along with understanding and knowledge.

George W. Adams

Contents

Testimonials

George Adams taught me about DNA identification when I was supporting the Model State Policy for Investigating a Missing Child/Adult & Identification of Unidentified Human Remains that eventually passed the Oregon legislature. He held Tommy in his hands, gave Tommy his identity, and sent Tommy home to me. I have been blessed to have him in my life, and I would like to thank one of my heroes.

Vicki Kelly

Photo courtesy of Vicki Kelly.

I reached out to George Adams after finding him on the Internet when my son Billy went missing. Through the years we have seen his compassion, commitment, and determination. He taught us about NamUs, a valuable investigative tool for authorities and the general public alike. George has spent hours on the phone to console family members and has helped tremendously. He took an oath to serve and protect and has upheld it daily. He is a real advocate who has helped teach us the real meaning and value of life. I am sure that this book is full of knowledge, compassion, and dedication from a person who gets it and understands. I think law enforcement and families will have better understanding and sensitivity after reading it.

Jan Smolinski
Jan, Bill, and Billy Smolinski. Photo courtesy of Jan Smolinski.

Foreword

I was thrilled when George Adams requested that I write the foreword to this book, which focuses on the identification of human remains. I am impressed with his forensic protocol, having recognized and acknowledged his work for many years and having shared his passion to provide the families of unidentified murdered victims some closure by having their loved ones identified at last. In many cases, his protocol for the identification of human remains has resulted in an arrest and conviction of the person or persons responsible for the death. The success of his protocol motivated me to ask him to contribute a section on identification of unidentified human remains to my newly revised textbook, *Practical Homicide Investigation: Tactics, Procedures, and Forensic Techniques* (5th ed., published by CRC Press).

Most homicide victims are killed by someone they know. Therefore, the identity of the deceased may provide motive and establish a clue to the identity of the killer. Even in stranger homicides, the identity of the victim will furnish information about his or her movements, which may establish time of death and other information about the crime. But knowing the identity of the deceased allows the investigator to do so much more to establish the victimology.

George Adams is the former Director of Financial Operations for the National Missing and Unidentified Persons System (NamUs), a national centralized repository and resource center for missing persons and unidentified decedent records. NamUs operates under the Forensic Services Unit of the University of North Texas Center for Human Identification (UNTCHI), with support from the National Institute of Justice (NIJ), and has become a recognized national center that provides forensic services and technical support about missing and unidentified person cases to public safety agencies, medical examiners, coroners, and crime labs throughout the country. In 2011, the UNTCHI Forensic Services Unit, located at the University of North Texas Health Science Center in Fort Worth, began operational control of NamUs on behalf of NIJ.

NamUs, in collaboration with criminal justice agencies, offers families with missing loved ones the opportunity to register a case and submit biological family member reference samples or direct reference samples from the missing loved one for mitochondrial, STR, and Y-STR DNA analysis. Criminal justice agencies, including medical examiners and coroners, may coordinate with NamUs to facilitate DNA and anthropological analysis for unidentified human remains as well as other forensic services (currently, dental and fingerprints). DNA profiles may be entered directly into the FBI's CODIS database and submitted to the National DNA Index System depending upon the DNA technology required to obtain viable profiles.

Ironically, the work of George Adams through UNTCHI was connected with a consultation I had with local investigators from Missoula, Montana in 1986 regarding unidentified human remains referred to as "Debbie Deer Creek." These remains were connected with suspected serial killer Wayne Nance, who is thought to have murdered five people in Missoula, Montana. In 2006, Debbie Deer Creek was finally identified through UNTHCI as Marci Bachman, who had been reported as a runaway from Vancouver, Washington in 1984. The Marcie Bachman case was a watershed case that verified the power of CODIS to make associations with innovative DNA technologies.

George Adams has written this book specifically for families seeking closure and identification of their loved ones as well as for the many law enforcement officers who have never worked an unidentified human remains case. He opens the black box of forensic science and improves investigative outcomes by dispelling the myths perpetrated by TV's "CSI effect." In a nonscientific format, Adams explains how, why, and when to use various forensic science resources. He focuses on improving unidentified human remains cases with law enforcement and communities working together.

The first section of this book addresses some of the complacency and biases that result in many of the errors that throw law enforcement off the trail. This section instructs the reader to be very cautious about accepting opinion evidence, and to rely on empirical reasoning rather than gut feelings or coincidences. In unidentified human remains cases, investigators are dealing with rare occurrences under the most adverse conditions. In this book, George Adams lays the groundwork for a multimodal biometric mindset, rather than the current and common assumption that DNA contains the most information with which to make identifications. In reality, DNA must be considered along with other metadata and biometrics, as well as the contributions of the investigators and personnel from other agencies.

Section II covers forensic resources and how they actually function in the context of developing and changing investigative strategies. For investigations, which are dependent on design and protocols, George emphasizes multimodal biometrics and widening investigative focus from local to regional/state to surrounding states to national. Ideally, investigators should access all available databases in a comprehensive and efficient manner.

Section III covers the uses and limitations of emerging technologies such as rapid DNA technology, next generation sequencing, facial-tattoo and scariation imaging, and stable isotope analysis. The studies George discuss document the importance of understanding what software can and cannot do with facial images, affirm the ability of family members to recognize a loved one under most adverse conditions, and reveal the very poor ability of strangers to link facial images even under the very best of conditions.

Section IV describes and illustrates an overall conceptual and foundational strategy that George developed from deconstructing hundreds of cold hit identifications.

Overall, this book is a masterful blend of theory and practice. It is the most comprehensive presentation I have yet seen of practical investigative protocols and the latest scientific forensic technology for the identification of unidentified human remains.

Vernon J. Geberth, M.S., M.P.S
Homicide and Forensic Consultant
Author, *Practical Homicide Investigation*
Series Editor, Practical Aspects of Criminal and Forensic Investigations

Preface

Over the past 45 years, I have attended hundreds of funerals in Texas for law enforcement officers who have died in the line of duty. I have also been one of the principal historians who has researched line-of-duty deaths in Texas for the National Law Enforcement Officers Memorial Foundation, the Texas Peace Officers Memorial, the Lost Lawmen's Memorial of the Sheriff's Association of Texas, the Officer Down Memorial Page, and the Texas Prison Museum. I have learned that although each case may have a different set of facts and circumstances, ultimately each is the same. It does not matter whether the person killed was a volunteer Texas Ranger during the days of the Republic of Texas or a police officer in 2015. Each man or woman who pinned on the badge took an oath to enforce the laws of the state and the Constitution. Each officer sacrificed his or her life to protect the lives and property of our citizens, and every officer in the state and nation has first-hand knoweldge of the sacrifice a fellow officer has made. The author of this book, George Adams, has served on the front lines as a police officer. Yet he is still impacted by the death of a friend and fellow officer, Fort Worth police officer Edward M. Belcher, 44 years ago. Here is the story of this young man's sacrifice.

On Thursday, October 28, 1971, Fort Worth police were dispatched to a shooting incident outside a nightclub called The Electric Circus, at the intersection of South Riverside and East Berry. A patron had fired 14–15 shots with a .22 caliber Saturday night special, critically wounding a man and slightly wounding a woman. Three suspects were immediately arrested.

Shortly after midnight on October 29, Officer Edward M. Belcher, 24, was one of the officers at the scene trying to clear out bystanders. He was standing in the parking lot when he was struck in the head by an armor-piercing bullet fired from a high-powered rifle. He died instantly. Officer Ronald G. Turner, also at the scene, received a minor injury that was at first believed to have been a bullet wound. It was later learned that pieces of Officer Belcher's skull, as well as metal fragments, had struck Turner in the neck.

The shooter had fired from behind a hamburger stand about 200 feet away. He was seen dropping a 30.06 military-issue rifle with a telescopic sight and fleeing on foot through the Riverside Village Apartments. A security guard fired twice at him, but he escaped in a car.

On November 1, 1971, homicide detectives arrested and charged David Nelson, an 18-year-old male on probation for burglary, with the murder of Officer Belcher. Without knowing the identity of Officer Belcher, Nelson had simply fired "at a uniform" that night. He was convicted and sentenced to death, but when the state death penalty was overturned his sentence was commuted to life in prison. He has been released from prison.

One random act by a teenager ended the life of a young officer. There is no evidence that they ever knew each other. Officer Edward M. Belcher reported to work that night and was trying to maintain the peace outside a nightclub. We can only speculate about the life and career he might have had. The number of lives he might have saved will never be known. His name is included on national, state, and local police memorials. Many citizens visiting those memorials will just see a name engraved on a wall, but we know as officers that his wife, family, friends, and fellow officers will never forget him.

I attended a police memorial service in Austin many years ago at which the chief, Jim Everett, gave an address that has been seared into my mind and heart. He said, "We do not pay the police for what they do, we pay the police for what they are willing to do." Officer Belcher was willing to give his life to protect the citizens of Fort Worth.

Ron DeLord*

* Ronald G. DeLord, MA, JD, is a distinguished and widely-published community servant who is currently in private law practice and public sector labor relations consulting. He specializes in assisting public employees, firefighters, and police officers. Mr. Delord began his career in 1969 as a patrol officer in Beaumont, Texas, and served in Mesquite as well. From 1977 to 2013, Mr. DeLord was associated with the Combined Law Enforcement Associations of Texas (CLEAT) as Founder/President (1977–2006), Executive Director (2007–2008), and Special Counsel (2009–2013). Since 1993, Mr. DeLord had served as guest faculty at Harvard University Law School's Labor and Worklife Program.

Acknowledgments

A work of this magnitude would not have been possible without the encouragement and support of many people. I thank Sue, my wife, for her patience and support. For well over a year, my seclusion and absence from normal family obligations on evenings and weekends have been graciously tolerated by my family. The results of working until the wee hours have been more than obvious; although I tried never to miss my grandson's baseball ballgames and other family gatherings, the sunglasses did not hide my more-than-occasional naps. I would like to thank my editor, Mark Listewnik, for believing in my work and for providing guidance and encouragement, as well as everyone at Taylor & Francis.

I would never have considered writing a book without the encouragement of Dr. Alex del Carmen of Tarleton State University. During my graduate studies at the University of Texas at Arlington, Dr. del Carmen was my teacher, my mentor, and my road map to a fuller life. Under his tutelage, I learned how to teach myself and study the greatest minds of history. Rhetoric abounds about the need for lifelong learning; however, it takes someone like Dr. del Carmen to plant the seed, nurture the crop, and bring it to harvest.

Three men who have devoted their lives to my own first love, police work, deserve special thanks. They are: Ronald G. Delord, PLLC; Det. Mark J. Czwornik (ret.); and Lieutenant Commander Vernon J. Geberth, M.S. (ret.).

Author

George W. Adams, national director of National Missing and Unidentified Persons System (NamUs) (October 2011 to January 2015), has devoted his efforts to understanding investigations of unidentified human remains and study of criminal justice. These efforts resulted in his obtaining a master of arts degree in criminology and criminal justice in 2013, and winning the National Institute of Justice NamUs competitive solicitation for its operation. This was under a three-year competitive agreement award, which totaled $7.55 million for award years 2011 through 2013. Prior to NamUs, George was the program coordinator for the UNT Center for Human Identification beginning February 2005. He also holds an active Texas Commission on Law Enforcement's Advanced Peace Officers Certification.

George's love for criminal justice and community began with his first permanent job as a patrol officer with the Fort Worth Police Department. While working as a patrol officer with the FWPD (Fort Worth Police Department—Texas) from 1968 to 1972, he earned a bachelor's degree in business administration. It was on the streets of SE Fort Worth where George developed a respect and commitment for community service through the inspiring efforts of local residents who worked multiple jobs to support their families and educate their children in hopes of a better life. In the blue-collar neighborhood in which George grew up and later patrolled, one had to earn everything on his or her own merit and effort—regardless of media's current false perceptions—nothing was or is easy in this struggle for a better life. Funny thing, when one works for something, that something becomes more cherished. It was the love and dedication of families and investigators that inspired the development of a comprehensive resource to bring families and law enforcement closer together, namely, this book, *Utilizing Forensic Technologies for Unidentified Human Remains.*

The sinews of law enforcement—transparency, loyalty, comradery, independence, and a fiduciary dedication to community—became part and parcel of George's being. In 1971 when his academy classmate, Eddie Belcher, was assassinated, George would be forced to choose between a career he most dearly loved and the commitment and responsibility to his family. In August 1972, George accepted a position with Mobil Oil, which provided the resources and stability for his family. After a successful 23-year career and retiring from Mobil's U.S. Marketing and Refining, he took on a new career with AMF Worldwide as the international financial manager, and later, joint venture chief financial officer in Brazil and Argentina. Little did George know that Mobil and AFM were training fields for his life's purpose. In 2005, George returned to his preordained destiny in criminal justice with the UNT Center of Human Identification as its program coordinator. It was not until George was invited to become a member of the NamUs advisory group and relink with community and law enforcement values that he understood his purpose for being. In the advisory group meetings of the development stage of NamUs, George began to discover the multiple disconnects related to cold cases of unidentified human remains, and saw the tremendous ability of NamUs to facilitate law enforcement's effort to resolve these cold cases that should have been solved much earlier. In 2011, as the main originator, George developed the logic and field organization structure that won the original solicitation: National Missing and Unidentified Persons System (NamUs) OMB No. 11121-0329 (SL# 000951). NamUs had the potential to become the educational catalyst for advancing empirically-based investigations across all law enforcement—not just cold cases (sentinel events). George realized the power of NamUs would center on fostering relationships between nongovernmental organizations (NGOs), families, and law enforcement. State-based NGOs and missing person clearinghouses were key, as they provided the needed coordination of local and national efforts for social services support to families in crisis that law enforcement was ill-equipped to deliver. George, as the former national director of NamUs, authored *Utilizing Forensic Technologies for Unidentified Human Remains: Death Investigation Resources, Strategies, and Disconnects* as a go-to resource for families, NGO, law enforcement, volunteers, activists, and the public, as well as state and federal legislators.

Introduction

On August 1, 2004, I lay in an emergency room cycling through chills, fever, and spasms. During a brief moment of lucidity, I heard a physician loudly tell some parents to keep their unruly son quiet: "There are some really sick people here!" Then the cramps started again, and they felt like a dull knife through my abdomen. All I wanted was for the pain to stop. I did not care how. A few days later, I understood that I had contracted sepsis. Each period of fever and cramps had been signaling that the bacteria was redividing.

During my recovery, I began to wonder why I had been taken to death's doorstep, pummeled with pain, and snatched back against the odds. Was it to teach me empathy for the families I would meet in the years ahead who must deal with missing someone they love—someone who has left them without explanation, possibly involuntarily? As I encountered families with missing parents, children, siblings, and/or spouses, their pain, and their experience of having no control over the situation, no glimpse of resolution, and no clue as to when resolution might be achieved, I realized that their pain is much worse than I had experienced with sepsis. I was blessed in that my situation was resolved in a few months; by contrast, many families suffer for decades. The purpose of this book, which has grown out of this realization, is to help bring resolution to such families in the most expedient manner and to help develop collaborative relationships between them and the investigators assigned to their cases.

On February 1, 2005, my first day at the Center for Human Identification, I received the first FedEx package of unidentified human remains submitted for DNA analysis and entry into the Combined DNA Indexing System (CODIS). This first (of what would eventually be hundreds of boxes) did not contain a package neatly sealed with evidence tape, or detailed chain-of-custody papers as seen on TV. Rather, a dirty pink hand towel was stuffed into the narrow cavity, with something hidden among its folds: a weathered lower jaw with empty tooth sockets. The submission papers stated that this jaw was from a young girl's dismembered body found in the sands of West Texas. As I gently placed the bone in a paper evidence sack, I could feel the pain she must have experienced in her last moments of life, as well as the loneliness of the years and days she waited to be found. At that moment, I understood my experience of surviving sepsis: It had opened up my heart to the nameless victims forgotten in back rooms and evidence lockers, and/or buried as John and Jane Does, but waiting to be returned to their loved ones.

The first calls were from investigators seeking assistance and information about submissions for DNA analysis. But it was not long before families started calling; some wanted help in finding their missing loved ones, others just needed an understanding ear. These people confided fears and frustrations that had been pent up for years or even decades. Soon, more family members started calling in ever-increasing numbers. Because each call and case were unique, I listened to each family member as long as it took to provide reassurance that someone *did* actually care and *would* try to help them find answers. Often these family members then informed investigators about new resources.

To improve awareness and knowledge about the resources available to victims, families, and agencies that seek to resolve missing and unidentified person cases, a series of four national training conferences (two on each coast) were held in 2008 and 2010. The approximately 150 attendees per conference ranged from law enforcement, medical examiners, and coroners, to families and activists. Top forensic subject matter experts in numerous disciplines were recruited as presenters. However, the technical/scientific language of some presenters clearly drove away many in the audiences; afternoon sessions were much more sparsely attended than the morning ones. It was then that I recognized the disconnect among forensic subject matter experts, law enforcement, and families. Not only the language, but also the air of self-importance that flowed from the dais were alienating.

In the first national training conference, held in Fort Worth, the Texas Department of Public Safety (TXDPS) gave a presentation in which TXDPS' first 15 CODIS DNA cold cases were highlighted to show the effectiveness of DNA for human identification. By my estimation, nearly 30% of the cold case identifications contained an investigative disconnect that prevented the cases from being resolved—in some instances, for several years. After that presentation, I began to deconstruct cold cases in order to understand the reasons that cases might take years to resolve. My efforts uncovered a number of disconnects in most cases, such as lack of knowledge about available resources, unquestioning acceptance of critical information, and poor-to-nonexistent investigative strategy design. For me, the TXDPS presentation brought to light the pervasive lack of accurate knowledge about forensic resources, the need to acquire such knowledge, and the need to design effective and efficient investigative strategies.

This book is written for the benefit of families, advocates, investigators, volunteers, activists, and the public, with the goal of advancing human identification of trafficking victims, those missing, and the unidentified deceased. I pray that readers use this knowledge to develop and empower their own use of current and future forensic resources in a complementary manner, rather than in the isolated and disconnected ways that seem to dominate the field of unidentified human remains investigations at this time. Only through feeling the pain and suffering of families can we inspire ourselves to develop and maintain the motivation necessary to make a real difference for them, and for their loved ones who are waiting to go home.

The profession of law enforcement is like no other calling in the world. Upon being commissioned, an officer voluntarily embraces a code of ethics that pledges his responsibilities to mankind. In investigations that involve missing and/or unidentified persons, dissonance between law enforcement officers and the communities they serve may create wounds that never heal. *Utilizing Forensic Technologies for Unidentified Human Remains: Death Investigation Resources, Strategies, and Disconnects* is written to bridge that abyss and avoid such dissonance through understanding and transparency. I was privileged to take the following oath in August 1968, in which I subscribed to the IACP's (International Association of Chiefs of Police) Code of Ethics:

> As a law enforcement officer, my fundamental duty is to serve mankind; to safeguard lives and property, to protect the innocent against deception, the weak against oppression or intimidation, the peaceful against violence or disorder, and to respect the constitutional rights of all men to liberty and justice.
>
> I will keep my private life unsullied as an example to all; maintain courageous calm in the face of danger, scorn or ridicule; develop self-restraint; and be constantly mindful of the welfare of others. Honest in thought and deed in both my professional and private life, I will be exemplary in obeying the law of the land and the regulations of my department. Whatever I see or hear of a confidential nature or that is confided to me in my official capacity will be kept forever secret unless revelation is necessary in the performance of my duty.
>
> I will never act officiously or permit personal feeling, prejudices, animosities, or friendships to influence my decisions. With no compromise for crime and with relentless prosecution of criminals, I will enforce the law courteously and appropriately without fear or favor, malice or ill will, never employing unnecessary force or violence, and never accepting gratuities.
>
> I recognize the badge of my office as a symbol of public faith, and I accept it as a public trust to be held so long as I am true to the ethics of the police service. I will constantly strive to achieve these objectives and ideals, dedicating myself before God to my chosen profession…law enforcement.[*]

Understanding the different circumstances that affect families and investigators, as well as the resources, strategies, and disconnects discussed in the following chapters, will help both groups work together in the crisis that surrounds unidentified human remains investigations—a national "silent mass disaster."

---

[*] Ritter, N. 2007. *Missing Persons and Unidentified Remains: The Nation's Silent Mass Disaster.* Department of Justice, Office of Justice Programs, National Institute of Justice, *NIJ Journal* No. 256, January 2007.

Unidentified human remains (UHR) investigations are sentinel events. NIJ's visiting fellow James M. Doyle defines a sentinel event as a "significant, unexpected negative outcome such as a wrongful conviction, an erroneous release from prison, or a cold case that stayed cold too long."* Sentinel events signal an underlying weakness in a system or process. They are damaging to a country's criminal justice system and to the worldwide forensic technology community. Databases such as CODIS and NamUs provide agencies with the ability to link and resolve UPs (unidentified persons) and MPs (missing persons) cases after decades, expose spurious practices associated with traditional forensic technology (based on human reasoning), and demonstrate the superiority of biometric (machine-based) forensic technology. Unfortunately, many forensic experts disapprove of biometric dominance in criminal investigations. However, as British statesman Harold Wilson (1916–1995) memorably stated: "He who rejects change is the architect of decay. The only human institution which rejects progress is the cemetery."†

According to the National Institute of Justice, "The investigative process has not changed much over the last 40 years."‡ Thus, my preparation of this book could not be completed until forensic databases and resources developed such that it became possible to affect a sufficient number of identifications. Enough cold cases had to be deconstructed and resolved for the profession to understand the contribution of rapidly developing forensic resources and databases in order to design effective investigative strategies and protocols.

Families, new investigators, and investigators who have little experience in (MPs), (UPs), unidentified decedents (UDs), or unidentified human remains (UHRs) investigations may not understand how important it is for an investigator to conduct and document his or her due diligence. New evidence, at any time, may cause a criminal investigation to be launched. In addition, failure to identify and address potential inconsistences, whether real or constructed, may prevent resolution and/or cause liability risks for investigators and agencies. MP investigations are often associated with UP, UD, or UHR investigations; this book contains information about MP cases but is focused on UP, UD, and UHR cases. When MPs are referred to herein, it is with the understanding that most of them are absent voluntarily and that great care must be taken to protect their privacy and security; many have "gone missing" to escape domestic abuse, gangs, or human traffickers.

---

* Doyle, J.M. 2013. *NIJ's Sentinel Events Initiative: Looking Back to Look Forward.* Office of Justice Programs; National Institute of Justice. *NIJ Journal* No. 273, November 2013. NCJ 244145. http://nij.gov/journals/273/pages/sentinel-events.aspx, p. 3. (Accessed October 12, 2015).

† Speech to the Consultive Assembly of the Council of Europe, Strasbourg, France, Jaunary 23, 1967.

‡ Sabol, W.J. 2015. *Policing Research: Dear Colleague Letter from William Sabol, Fiscal Year 2015.* Office of Justice Programs: National Institute of Justice. http://www.nij.gov/funding/Pages/fy15-dear-colleague-policing.aspx (Accessed August 1, 2015).

The contents of this book are presented in a way that blends conceptual and nonfictional narration so that it may be maximally useful for students, educators, investigators at all levels, families, and the general public. The material is presented in a nontechnical manner as much as possible. It offers abstract thoughts and concepts that are couched in ambiguously-related subject matter; here, actual cases and events are used to help the reader link concept to practice in real situations.

Many volunteers donate their time to search the Internet and use social media resources to help resolve UP cold cases. Other dedicated members of the public share their free time with local law enforcement agencies' Volunteers in Police Service (VIPS) MP divisions. This book is designed to guide these volunteers so that they may be better able to effectively assist law enforcement personnel in their communities. It may also be useful for educators who, due to the expansion of criminal justice programs in secondary schools, are asked to develop interesting, relevant, and timely courses.

Readers should not be concerned that information that seems to be the same is repeated in different places throughout this book. In fact, this information is presented slightly differently each time because it is discussed in different contexts. Key facts, conditions, practices, and other elements are also repeated because they are relevant to the discussion at hand as well as in their own right. The chapters in this book can be read in order, or consulted separately.

It is my hope that those who consult this book will come to know the work and hearts of many people in the investigative community, as well as the hearts and minds of families who have transformed adversity into advocacy. Hopefully, this book will be a celebration of their generous efforts to aid those who can no longer speak.

Concepts

I

There are many families out there who are needlessly going without an identification and slipping further and further into a state of despair … There should never be a cold case involving a missing person.[*]

George Adams

In Section I, complacency and bias—issues that are well documented and systemic in investigations of missing persons and unidentified decedents—are illustrated with actual cases. These issues, which stem from human perceptions of the world that are learned through sensory and personal experiences, are the sources of many problems in these investigations.

Understanding the forensic tools, resources, strategies, and disconnects that comprise investigations of missing persons (MPs), unidentified decedents (UDs), and unidentified human remains (UHRs) is a bit like opening a black box—a device, process, or system whose inputs/outputs and relationships to other systems are known, but whose internal workings are not easily understood, irrelevant to the purpose at hand, and confidential in any case.[†] In an airplane crash investigation, authorities search furiously for the black box because it contains unique information that might explain what happened. Similarly, when the black boxes of forensic and observational science are opened, cases can be solved. However, peering into these black boxes may reveal surprise contents such as previously undisclosed biases or errors in human judgment. When these weaknesses are recognized, they can be significantly improved.[‡]

It is difficult to say when forensic science's black box of sequestered knowledge was first cracked; however, considerable credit must go to Barry Scheck, Peter Neufeld, and Dr. Eric Lander. In *People v. Castro* (1989), these men successfully demystified information that had been assumed to be too complex and confidential to share with the general public. According to an eyewitness account: "In a piercing attack upon each molecule of evidence

---

[*] Scharpe, J. 2007. Relatives of Missing Turn to DNA. *The Baltimore Sun*, June 5, 2007. http://articles.baltimoresun.com/2007-06-05/news/0706050211_1_missing-people-dna-missing-persons.

[†] BusinessDictionary.com. 2014. http://www.businessdictionary.com/definition/black-box.html (Last viewed May 22, 2014).

[‡] Jasanoff, S. 2006. *Transparency in Public Science: Purposes, Reasons, Limits.* http://scholarship.law.duke.edu/cgi/viewcontent.cgi?article=1385&context=lcp.

presented, the defense was successful in demonstrating to this court that the testing laboratory failed in its responsibility to perform the accepted scientific techniques and experiments in several major respects."[*]

DNA evidence remained largely unchallenged until *Castro*. In this case, it was shown that the Lifecodes company failed to follow its own protocols, made multiple errors in identifying sources of control samples, and used contaminated probes in the analysis of forensic samples. Expert witnesses who met outside the court issued a joint statement that declared this evidence to be scientifically unreliable.[†]

In the wake of *Castro*, DNA testing improved so much that it is now the gold standard for most of the other forensic science evidence disciplines. In 2009, the National Academy of Sciences took on these other disciplines in the report *Strengthening Forensic Science in the United States: A Path Forward* (The National Academy Press, Washington, D.C.). Without this knowledge, UD investigations might continue to waste untold millions in investigative funds and untold hours of human effort without achieving resolutions. Not only would families and communities continue to suffer, communication gaps between families with missing loved ones and police would grow ever wider.

The information presented in the following chapters is not esoteric or mystical, although some of it has not commonly been public knowledge. Presenting this information clearly and openly is a demonstration of transparency, which is necessary if estrangement and suspicion between families and forensic service providers, as well as between families and police investigators, are to be alleviated. As a professional with many years of experience in UD and UHR investigations, it is my hope that sharing this information will not only help families through the ordeal of waiting for a loved one to return home but also help remove undeserved blame of police investigators for delays and dead ends.

I agree with the philosopher John Locke (1632–1704), who argued that there is no such thing as innate knowledge. He believed that human knowledge, understanding, and actions result from life experiences.

> The senses at first let in particular ideas, and furnish the yet empty cabinet, and the mind by degrees growing familiar with some of them, they are lodged in the memory, and names go to them. Afterwards, the mind proceeding further, abstracts them, and by degrees learns the use of general names. In this manner the mind comes to be furnished with ideas and language, the materials about which to exercise its discursive faculty.[‡]

---

[*] Scheindlin, G. 1989. The People of the State of New York, Plaintiff, *v*. Joseph Castro, Defendant (144 Misc.2nd 956).

[†] Aronson, J. 2007. *Genetic Witness: Science, Law and Controversy in the Making of DNA Profiling*. New Brunswick, NJ and London: Rutgers University Press.

[‡] Locke, J. 1690. *An Essay Concerning Human Understanding*. First published in 1689.

I believe that Locke's words apply to all of us, and that we all may be influenced in the same way—through our senses, and then through our experiences. In terms of UD and UHR cases, it is essential for families and investigators to use knowledge, but not to depend solely on their own senses and prior experiences. Instead, they must look at each case objectively, on its own terms.

Two of the main challenges to objectivity are complacency and bias. To avoid these problems, each UD/UHR case or MP report must be seen as a unique incident that requires its own strategy, forensic tools, and subject matter experts. It is also essential for families to remember that forensic subject matter experts are just human beings, even though they deal with information that may seem very complex and very mysterious, and even though their expertise may come to naught (in the form of unsolved cases). All people, no matter how highly educated they are or how good their intentions, are liable to succumb to complacency and/or bias.

Many obstacles hinder medical examiner/coroner (ME/C) investigations of UD and UHR cases (most of which are assumed to be victims of violent crime). The need for forensic tools to address such cases, which are estimated to number in the tens of thousands nationwide, attained national prominence on January 21, 2010 at a meeting of the Judiciary Subcommittee on Crime, Terrorism, and Homeland Security. At this meeting, Rep. Christopher Murphy (D-Connecticut) stated that "... according to the Bureau of Justice Statistics, there are over 100,000 unsolved missing persons cases open at any given time. Approximately 4400 unidentified human remains are also found in an average year. Those numbers are too high, but just as intolerable are the roadblocks that family members face when trying to help law enforcement find a missing loved one."[*]

At the same hearing, Jan Smolinski stated that

> Everything changed on August 24, 2004 when [our son] Billy vanished at the age of 31. Our search [...] unleashed the nightmare plaguing the world of the missing and the unidentified dead ... After waiting the three days [as advised by police], we filed [a missing persons] report, and expected the police to launch an aggressive investigation. When the police did nothing we organized our own search with family and friends. We even hired a private investigator.
>
> Yet we still couldn't get the attention of the local police department. They dismissed Billy as a voluntary runaway case ... they also didn't properly report the case. It took four years for a report to be correctly filed with the National Crime Information Center. Moreover, not only did they lose seven separate DNA samples, but they also didn't know about the National DNA Index System. In fact, it wasn't until the FBI took over the investigation—two years

---

[*] Murphy, C. 2010. *Testimony by Representative Christopher Murphy: H.R. 3695, The Help Find the Missing Act (Billy's Law)*. January 21. http://judiciary.house.gov/_files/hearings/pdf/Murphy100121.pdf.

after Billy vanished—that the proper reports and DNA samples were collected and filed. Eventually we uncovered information that led us to believe Billy had been murdered in Woodbridge, Connecticut and buried in Seymour.*

Bill and Jan Smolinski, advocates for families of the missing.
(Photo courtesy of the Smolinski family.)

The information in this book is intended to help police and communities work together in the often complicated and highly emotional environments that surround missing and unidentified persons investigations. Policing, which is an integral part of community life, is funded in the United States by tax revenues. In return, law enforcement can provide a feeling of security that allows communities to thrive. In order for this relationship to succeed, "the values on which the police department operates, as well as the practices it follows, must be known to all members of the community as well as to all members of the police department … [In addition], these values must incorporate citizens' expectations, desires and preferences."†

It is essential for communication between police and the communities they serve to be based in transparency and trust. Stephen Covey may have provided a roadmap to this relationship in his book *The Speed of Trust: The*

---

* Smolinski, J. 2010. *Testimony by Janice Smolinski: Subcommittee on Crime, Terrorism and Homeland Security.* http://judiciary.house.gov/_files/hearings/pdf/Smolinski100121. pdf.
† Community Relations Service. 2003. *Principles of Good Policing: Avoiding Violence Between Police and Citizens.* U.S. Department of Justice. p. 6.

One Thing That Changes Everything.[*] According to Covey, transparency and trust, which he refers to as credibility, are built on (1) integrity, (2) intent, (3) capabilities, and (4) results. Here, integrity means acting in congruence with personal values, even when doing so incurs personal risk. Intent is the willingness to be open and straightforward, in clear and candid language. Capabilities means knowledge, skills, and strengths. The results of integrity, intent, and capabilities are good results: the right things have been done, at the right time, and for the right reasons.

In law enforcement investigations of missing and unidentified persons, the best results are achieved when investigators know why, when, and how to use innovative forensic resources. Of course, this technology is rapidly changing. Just since 2005, several versions of the combined DNA index system (CODIS) have been released with new algorithms that allow searches of offender DNA and UP indexes; mitochondrial DNA testing is being replaced by next-generation sequencing that can produce multiple different types of DNA profiles (including mtDNA) during the same process at the same time; familial searching has become available in many states; several new DNA databases have been compiled to manage DNA samples that are ineligible for CODIS; and rapid DNA technology has been implemented statewide in at least one state (Arizona; acceptance by NDIS began in January 2015[†]). In addition, next-generation sequencing (NGS) is being introduced into law enforcement by the National Institute of Justice to replace current legacy DNA technology; NGS provides better interpretation of forensic DNA mixtures and simultaneously performs multiple types of DNA analysis in crime laboratories. In September 2014, the FBI's integrated automated fingerprint identification service (IAFIS) was replaced with next-generation identification (NGI), an approach that complements human identifications with multimodal biometrics. These advances in technology provide investigators with more ability than ever to resolve MP and UP cases—provided that law enforcement can design and implement investigative strategies that take advantage of them.

Application of forensic resources and investigative designs begins with the idea that crime, including MP/UP incidents, is local and expands outward. This premise has been confirmed by Great Britain's Home Office Research and Development and Statistics Directorate (2000), which found offenses to be overwhelmingly local; when longer-range travel was involved, the crimes were mainly committed in places that had strong connections to

---

[*] Covey, S. 2006. *The Speed of Trust: The One Thing That Changes Everything.* New York, NY: Free Press, p. 56 (e-Book).

[†] National DNA Index System (NDIS) Operational Procedures Manual: FBI Laboratory Version 3, Effective January 1, 2015. https://www.fbi.gov/about-us/lab/biometric-analysis/codis/ndis-procedures-manual. pp. 41–42.

the offender's home location.* This book builds on this discovery by exploring strategy design and utilization of forensic resources in an outward direction, from local to regional/state to surrounding states to national. It will be assumed throughout that all strategy related to UHR is developed in the local context and expanded from there.

When police and communities can practice empathy (that is, when they are able to acknowledge, understand, and respect each others' points of view), they have a much easier time avoiding the complicated and often highly emotional environments that surround and may even derail MP/UP investigations. Today, all too often, these environments destroy trust and divide communities. When families practice empathy, they are able to understand that law enforcement is obliged to look beyond the incident(s) at hand; likewise, empathetic police realize that families may have no one else to turn to for help or answers.

The strategy designs and developmental concepts presented in this book are applicable to all investigations. The transparency and candor within this book as well as its graphic images may be upsetting for some readers; however, I believe it is not only important but also necessary to honestly convey the environment in which investigators work every hour of every day in MP, UP, and UHR investigations. In addition, I believe that it is important for the public to realize that, under such stress, investigators develop the same health issues that families with missing loved ones know all too well. If this book helps to bring resolution in a case or relief to a family in crisis 1 day earlier, or helps one investigator clear a case, I will welcome criticism with open arms.

---

* Wiles, P., Costello, A. 2000. *Road to Nowhere: The Evidence of Traveling Criminals.* Great Britain Home Office Research Development and Statistics Directorate. Information and Publishing Group, London, UK. Abstract, NCJ 187255.

Complacency 1

Once a human intellect has adopted an opinion (either as something it likes or as something generally accepted), it draws everything else in to confirm and support it.

Sir Francis Bacon (1561–1626)

The conceptual stage of this book began in August 2008, at the Texas Department of Public Safety presentation at the Forensic Science Forensic Training Workshop in Fort Worth, when the first 16 TXDPS cold DNA hits were presented. Most of the workshop presentations seemed to be both laborious and esoteric, with little attention paid to the development of investigative strategies. Other conferences, although their presentations may have been deeply moving, were essentially based upon series of stories that were meant to elicit emotional reactions (e.g., the Identify the Missing Conference held in Philadelphia in 2005, which became a model for many future conferences). Developments in MP/UD/UHR investigations other than the launching of the National Institute of Justice's (NIJ) National Missing and Unidentified Persons System (NamUs) in 2009 have been scarce, and nearly none have occurred in the area of investigative strategies.

This book is not a research project or study, or a how-to checklist. Instead, it is a tool that is designed to educate investigators, families, and public about databases, resources, strategies, disconnects, and knowledge of innovative forensic technologies so that MP/UD/UHR cases may be resolved more successfully, and more quickly. The first obstacle to resolution, and one of the most damaging, is complacency.

The definition of complacency has long been a contextual construct in law enforcement, the military, business, and medicine. In terms of policing, much of the current literature may be so confusing or esoteric that families and investigators set it aside. When the law enforcement tasks involve investigating unidentified human remains (UHR), decades of frustration may be in store unless one can recognize the difference between a complacent construct and a considered thought. Dictionary definitions of "complacency" seem to include previous experience, perception, or assumption of reality.

Webster's definition is "self-satisfaction, especially when accompanied by unawareness of actual dangers or deficiencies."[*]

A culture of complacency is pervasive in UHR investigations that are conducted when better (i.e., easiest or quickest) is more valued than best.[†] Herein, I will be defining complacency as "speculative justification or belief based on previous events, including limited experience and training, masquerading as empirical reasoning." Unlike theoretical reasoning, empirical reasoning is based on sufficient observation of and experimentation with quantitative or comparative phenomena.[‡] Speculative justification refers to beliefs that are not observable or quantifiable, but are assumed or perceived to exist. Theory, speculation (assumptions and presumptions), and lack of knowledge have long been the driving forces UHR investigations, as opposed to critical inquiry and/or discussions.

> **Key point:** Criticism is a part of the critical thinking process that helps to differentiate complacency from empirical reasoning. Criticism is therefore necessary if one is to elicit facts rather than find comfort and expediency in assumptions and presumptions.

In 2004, when human remains were discovered in a field near Alice, Texas, presumptions rooted in local anecdotes may have influenced the thoroughness of the initial investigation. The complacent view held by investigators, namely that the remains were those of an undocumented immigrant, also meant (to them) that identification would be difficult if not impossible. Sure enough, the remains were not identified until 2007, when reference samples were submitted by the grandparents of April Ann Repka, who had disappeared in 1991.[§]

Why did it take 3 years to obtain reference samples? According to Texas statutes, law enforcement must notify appropriate persons regarding provision of a voluntary sample no later than the thirtieth day after a missing person report is filed.[¶] Many states have similar statutes. Unfortunately, agencies and investigators may be unaware of such statutes about MP/UD

---

[*] Merriam-Webster. merriam-webster.com. 2014. http://www.merriam-webster.com/dictionary/complacency.

[†] Rosene, F. 2003. Complacency and service quality: An overlooked condition in the GAP Model. *Journal of Retailing and Consumer Services Series* 10, 52.

[‡] The Free Dictionary by Farlex. 2014. http://www.thefreedictionary.com/empirical.

[§] Kassabian, D. 2008. Bones Solve 17-Year-Old Missing Person Case. *Corpus Christi Caller Times*. http://www.caller.com/news/2008/jun/26/bones-solve-17-year-old-missing-person-case/.

[¶] Texas Code of Criminal Procedure, Chapter 63.

investigations. Such systemic problems of complacency can plague both families and investigators.

In another case, in 1963, remains that were assumed to have female characteristics (features and clothing) were found in a remote part of Tarrant County, Texas, but languished in a crime lab for the next 42 years. An anthropologist reanalyzed the bones and determined that in fact they had belonged to a man; full identification was made after comparing DNA from a cousin.* Unfortunately, it is normal for investigators to accept the opinions of forensic service providers without doing anything to ascertain the accuracy of the information.

Herbert Packer (1925–1972) invented a simple two-question determination of the truth in any inquiry: (1) How reliable is the data? and (2) How well-adapted are the processes used to elicit and test the data?† Packer's second question is probably more crucial to the UHR investigator because answering it requires not only previous knowledge about forensic services and capabilities of the provider, but also a proactive effort to obtain such knowledge. Knowledge, which drives the critical thinking process for both families and investigators, is necessary if the fog of complacency is to be avoided.

People learn of the world through our senses and experiences. The human mind combines instinct, experience, training, and acquired knowledge to form perceptions and assumptions. For expedience, we use previous knowledge in response to unexpected situations—doing so speeds up the processes of making decisions and formulating responses. It is only natural when people use this approach in daily affairs and professions. The more repetitive events become, the more they may be absorbed into a customary or complacent attitude; the more intense the experience, the more the outcome becomes ingrained in our psyche, to the point that it may become difficult to separate current experience from previous ones. However, in law enforcement, it is necessary to separate the circumstances of a current case from previous ones. Each MP or UD/UHR investigation is unique.

Complacency is a naturally occurring state of mind that can affect our lives every day. For example, behind the wheel of a car, it is not unusual for the driver to begin a lane change after looking in the rear-view and side-view mirrors (as he or she may have done thousands of times before) only to hear a horn honk. Such drivers assume, from past experience, that both the rear-view and side-view mirrors would reveal the presence of other vehicles that might impede a safe lane change, and that because the mirrors are reliable for this purpose, it is not necessary to actually turn the head and look.

---

* Boyd, D. 2005. Man's Body Found 42 Years Ago Is Identified. Fort Worth, TX: *Star-Telegram*, June 2, 2005. http://www.baldonart.com.
† Packer, H. 1962. *Ex-Communist Witnesses: Four Studies in Fact Finding*. Stanford, CA: Stanford University Press, p. 3.

Good drivers routinely adjust mirrors and check both the rear-view and side-view mirrors, but do not routinely observe and experiment to see whether a blind spot exists either behind or next to their vehicles.

Similarly, people have a strong tendency to seek supporting evidence (e.g., mirrors) and to weigh evidence based on our experiences and expectations (e.g., how a mirror is positioned). Repeated experiences that result in similar outcomes may produce custom behavior, also known as complacent behavior.[*] It was this practice, along with years of driving experience, that lead an acquaintance to change lanes into the side of a tractor/trailer. When we are aware of the possibility of complacency, we can control and counter its influence through thinking critically and forming independent opinions.

All too often, families seeking a missing loved one and expecting help from law enforcement enter a world of complacency instead, as Jan Smolinski discovered when she attempted to locate her beloved son. Her story, unfortunately, is not atypical. Overworked investigators, who routinely deal with revolving-door runaways and family members trying to escape abusive relationships, may discourage families from making a report or may openly refuse to take an MP report. Or, families may assume that their MP report will be entered into multiple databases, and that police will continue the search until the case is resolved, when neither of these assumptions are valid. It is only through frequent and open communication that families and police can establish trust and cooperative, mutually beneficial relationships.

In 2012, 661,593 missing person records were entered into the National Crime Information Computer (NCIC); during the same period, 659,514 records of missing persons were cleared or cancelled. Law enforcement located the subjects; they returned home; or the records were found to be invalid.[†] Based on these facts, could argue that the vast majority (99.7%) of missing person reports concern people who are voluntarily absent. Law enforcement agencies are not only obligated to locate absent individuals; they are also obligated to ensure the safety and privacy of individuals who choose to be absent, because they may be escaping domestic and intimate partner violence or other threatening/dangerous situations.

As bureaucratic organizations, law enforcement agencies manage personnel through volumes of policy, procedures, and general orders and accomplish these tasks with a tremendous amount of discretionary power. In 2011, the FBI counted 14,633 law enforcement agencies with more than 1,001,984

[*] Wang, X., Kapucu, N. 2008. Abstract—Public Complacency Under Repeated Emergency Threats: Some Empirical Evidence, *Oxford Journals Social Sciences*, 18(1), 57–78. http://jpart.oxfordjournals.org/content/18/1/local/front-matter.pdf.

[†] Federal Bureau of Investigation. *NCIC Missing Person and Unidentified Person Statistic for 2012*. http://www.fbi.gov/about-us/cjis/ncic/ncic-missing-person-and-unidentified-person-statistics-for-2012.

personnel (698,460 sworn officers).* Considering the numbers of law enforcement personnel and MP cases entered and removed, it may be easy to see how complacency can influence an investigation, and how investigators may find it difficult to assess a particular case independently of a "typical" one.

When MP investigations are tainted by complacency, the relationships that communities and families may have with law enforcement agencies suffer. Investigators often end up trying to ameliorate the frustrations of the families, frequently by apologizing for forensic service providers' delays. For example, a new officer from a small agency in South Carolina called me for information about submitting a sample for DNA analysis from decomposed remains found in a vacant lot. The investigator explained that she had replaced a previous investigator after family members voiced dissatisfaction. She was meeting regularly with the family, often in their home, and had developed what seemed to be very good rapport with them. As our conversation moved from DNA samples to case management, I cautioned her about the likelihood of experiencing the same criticisms—if not worse—from the family because an association report of inclusive (positive), exclusive (negative), or inconclusive (unable to determine) could take 4–6 months or even longer. In a rough timeline, for the first 30 days the family might view this new investigator as the best ever; after 60 days they would begin to question her abilities; and after 90 days, they would decide that she was the most uncaring and incompetent officer ever.

This frustration is not mysterious. At the beginning of an MP investigation, the investigator represents the family's only hope for resolution. As the situation drags on, the investigator becomes an easy target for the family's anguish and disappointment. This reaction, which is common in MP investigations, is brought on by the family's stress and the CSI effect (i.e., the family's unrealistic expectations).

About 60 days later, the young investigator called me again. She explained that the family, accompanied by out-of-town relatives, had visited the station the day before and that a very loud disturbance had ensued, during which senior officers began considering whether to arrest family members. Fortunately, she interceded on their behalf by explaining to command staff that such a reaction was to be expected, and that the best response would be to show empathy until the family members had vented their frustrations. If she had not intervened, the confrontation could easily have escalated, with adverse consequences for all. When they arrived at the station, the family saw law enforcement as complacent and uncaring; when the family began to cause a disturbance at the station, the agency saw the family as hostile and ungrateful for all the agency had done on their behalf.

A few months after this second phone call, a positive association was made between the reported MP and a UD. As the agency worked to transmit this information to various parties and maintain control of a possible homicide investigation, they also took care to apologize to the family for the forensic lab's lengthy analysis process. To do otherwise would have incited more anger from the family, who would have seen avoiding the issue or excusing it as attempting to shift blame. But by showing empathy for the family's frustration, and apologizing for the circumstances (without taking responsibility for them), the agency was able to preserve a harmonious working relationship with the family.

In the course of my career in law enforcement, outreach activities related to MP investigations have provided me with many opportunities to address audiences across the country and to share knowledge about resources and investigative strategies that can breathe life into decades-old cold cases. At every conference, at least one or two family members with long-term missing family members have approached me privately. For most of them, life had been twisted into a physical, emotional, and financial wreck (a "roller coaster of emotions" or "a living hell") due to complacency they had encountered. Also at these conferences, recently assigned MP investigators would ask me about "typical" MP cases. Here, the word "typical" strongly indicates the presence of complacency. Every missing or unidentified case is unique, which means that investigators should expect to use different strategies and different forensic tools as needed.

For police, controlling complacency presents serious challenges because so many MP cases turn out to be voluntary absences. It takes a disciplined and honest individual to admit that past events do affect their perceptions of current events. A thorough and competent officer will accept circumstances as presented and work with them as they are. According to Jeffrey Hawkins, founder of the Redwood Neuroscience Institute, "If you look at the history of big obstacles in understanding our world, there's usually an intuitive assumption underlying them that's wrong."[*] Hawkins's remark seems very constructive as we delve into disconnects involving the forensic services tools used for UD investigations.

In April 2005, I was invited to attend the Identify the Missing Conference in Philadelphia. John Bish, the father of Molly Bish, spoke about her disappearance and the recovery of her remains. Even some of the most experienced G-men in the audience were moved to tears, which dispelled the common portrayals of an investigator's stoic façade. Eventually, I came to know many

---

[*] Hawkins, J. 2014. *Machines Like Us.* https://machineslikeus.com/biographies/jeff-hawkins.

of those people for their strength, compassion, and empathy. But their dedication is not unique. As mentioned in the foreword to this book, investigators across the country worked and collaborated for decades as they attempted to identify "Debbie Deer Creek" (Marcella Bachmann) by scouring the Internet and running NCIC searches. Ms. Bachmann was removed from the NCIC in 1986, 2 years after being entered as a missing juvenile.*

In another long-term case, after two decades the remains of Donna Lisa Williamson were identified via a cold DNA hit. Her remains were found in 1993 but remained unidentified because she was excluded by dental records early in the investigation.† Had this crucial error not been made, thousands of hours of investigative labor, untold amounts of investigative resources would not have been wasted, and years of a family's suffering would have been avoided.

In cold cases, which I consider to be sentinel events, coincidences seem to abound and complacency is often the reason that they go unchallenged. For example, what are the chances that a dental records error 1 day would result in an investigation going cold for two decades, thousands of dollars being wasted, and a family remaining in anguish unnecessarily? If a correct identification had been made that day instead of an incorrect exclusion, would it have been more likely for the murderer to be caught? Did others lose their lives because a murderer remained at large? The answers to such questions cannot be known; however, we do know that failure to control complacency can be very costly. Perhaps Tomas Gilovich phrased it best when he said, "Many of the mechanisms that distort our judgments stem from basic cognitive processes that are usually quite helpful in accurately perceiving and understanding the world."‡ In the case of Donna Lisa Williamson, a failure of basic cognitive processes (comparing two dental charts) distorted someone's judgement—with serious consequences.

This book is not meant to provide families, investigators, and forensic service providers with an investigative checklist, but rather to provide a framework within which these people may visualize the component parts and anomalies of their cases as unique occurrences that require individualized investigative strategies and forensic tools. It is the small anomalies that must be questioned and resolved in order to reconcile the truth with available data. In this sense, the work of investigators to create investigative strategies

* Scott, T. 2006. The billings gazette. *Cold-Case Research Yields ID of 1984 Murder Victim.* http://billingsgazette.com/news/state-and-regional/montana/cold-case-research-yields-id-of-murder-victim/article_a01dbe0d-5c2d-5181-9927-460950a1ddd1.html.

† Warner, B. 2006. philly.com via DNA Labs International. *How ID'ing Texas Remains Could Aid Phila.* http://www.dnalabsinternational.com/email_newsletter/vol_9_jan_06/vol9_ref02.html.

‡ Gilovich, T. 1991. *How We Know What Isn't So: The Fallibility of Human Reason in Everyday Life.* New York, NY: The Free Press, Simon & Schusrer, p. 10.

is similar to the alchemical goal of changing a cold case (straw) into a resolution (gold). The difference is that gold was never created from straw, but cases thought to be unsolvable are closed every day.

As I debriefed a multitude of cold hit cases (cases without any investigative leads), I encountered numerous weaknesses in forensic evidence that rested only on the judgment of experts—which, despite education and experience, remains human and flawed. Biometric evidence, which involve machine- or program-derived data, must underpin forensics, which involve the human decision making process. The National Academy of Science's seminal report on the state of forensic science in the United States—*Strengthening Forensic Science in the United States: A Path Forward*[*] confirmed my impressions. A wide variability is found across forensic disciplines in regard to reliability, error rates, reporting, research foundations, general acceptability, and published material.[†]

Cooke and Rohleder,[‡] paraphrasing Sagan,[§] identified restrictions that prevent organizations from successfully learning to avoid normal accidents. These are

- Ambiguous causation
- Politicized environments
- Human tendencies to cover up mistakes/errors
- Secrecy within and between competing organizations

I find these observations to be very relevant to UD/UHR investigations and related forensic services, because law enforcement and other agencies often believe that any exposed anomalies may negatively affect future funding. In such an atmosphere, complacency can run wild. In turn, the inability to soften the impact of complacency on long-term UD investigations may result in the permanent loss of important resources, families suffering needlessly for years, and communities remaining at risk.

As I have reviewed decades-old cold hit cases (to help improve investigate strategies and police efficacy as well as in preparation for writing this book), the main anomaly I have pondered has to do with why UD are not identified earlier. I also wondered why a comprehensive study has not been done to answer this question. Lists of individual anomalies in separate cases have been compiled, for example by the Texas Department of Public Safety

---

[*] National Academy of Science. 2009. *Strengthening Forensic Science in the United States: A Path Forward*. National Institute of Justice funded 2006-DN-BX-0001. Washington, D.C.: The National Academies Press.
[†] *Ibid*. p. 188.
[‡] Cooke, D.L., Rohleder, T.R. 2006. Learning from incidents: From normal accidents to high reliability. *Systems Dynamics Review* 22(3).
[§] Sagan, S.D. 1993. *The Limits of Safety: Organizations, Accidents and Nuclear Weapons*. Princeton, NJ: Princeton University Press.

(TXDPS) in 2008. At the NIJ-sponored Forensic Training Workshop in Ft Worth, TXDPS presented 16 DNA cold hit cases;[*] with nearly a third having major errors in forensic reports that may have negatively impacted the investigations.

> No. 1: Donna Williamson (6/8/2004)—dental records transposed (reversed).
> No. 2: Maria Solias (2/7/2005)—remains identified as a Black female; were actually an Hispanic female.
> No. 4: Cory White (11/14/2006)—remains identified as a Black female; were actually a Black male.
> No. 6: Terri Reyes (6/6/2007)—remains identified as White/Black admixture; were actually White.
> No. 11: April Repka (11/5/2007)—remains identified as Mestizo or Amerindian admixture based on the anthropological report;[†] were actually White.

More recently, a criminal justice forensic support provider ordered tests of UHR that had been in storage for many years because they had not been thought to have significant forensic value. However, when the DNA analysis was completed on the first set of remains, a cold DNA hit was produced to a recent MP. Evidently, some of the remains were in fact forensically significant! Again, humans tend toward complacency as we gain knowledge and work with ambiguous data. In UHR investigations, this tendency can become a fatal flaw. The reliability of data depends not only on measurable factors having to do with the data itself, but also on the expertise of those who evaluate it as well as the degree to which human judgment is involved in the evaluation.[‡]

Even veteran law enforcement and other personnel can succumb to complacency, which "seems an especially common and troubling vice... Complacency does not cause evil or mediocrity; it is a vice that allows these to exist."[§] A truly objective (empirical) investigative strategy does not include complacent practices such as accepting test results or expert opinions without

[*] University of North Texas Forensic Services Unit. 2010. http://www.untfsu.com/wp-content/uploads/2010/07/UNT-August-2008-Baltimore.pdf (Accessed May 14, 2014).
[†] Texas Department of Public Safety. 2008. *Texas Department of Public Safety: Cimingal [sic] Law Enforcement Bureau of Information Analysis: Unidentified Persons & DNA Unit. (Updated September 26, 2013).* http://web.unthsc.edu/downloads/file/3967/texas_department_of_public_safety_cimingal_law_enforcement_bureau_of_information_analysis_unidentified_persons_and_dna_unit.
[‡] Risinger, D.M. et al. 2002. The Daubert/Kumho implications of observer effects in forensic science: Hidden problems of expectation and suggestion. *California Law Review* 20(1).
[§] Kawall, J. 2006. On complacency. *American Philosophical Quarterly* 43(4).

question. Particularly when ambiguous forensic data are involved, evaluations and conclusions must be challenged from a detached perspective.

It is not uncommon for forensic subject matter experts to consult one another and to ask each other to confirm opinions. Such collegial discussions can be very useful, but groupthink may result if the practice becomes complacent (expected and unchallenged). Groupthink is a pattern of thought characterized by self-deception, forced manufactured of consent, and conformity to group values and ethics.[*] (For example, I cannot count the times I have questioned a procedure, only to be told that this is "our customary" or "typical" practice.) In MP/UP investigations, it might be wise to consider Sir Francis Bacon's quote, at the beginning of the chapter, when he refers to people acting according to "custom"; each case is unique in every aspect—there is no such thing as a "typical" case.

According to Victor Tan, "One of the greatest dangers of complacency is that it creates blind spots in people towards the need for change and growth."[†] People may start off with the concept of complacency as a natural human phenomenon, but if progress is to be made in any human endeavor (science, the military, business, medicine, law) controlling strategies must be developed. This is particularly so if the goal is to bring earlier resolutions to MP and UD/UHR cases in the criminal justice system.

Unfortunately, many people assume that through sheer force of will, one can control the forces of complacency. But this is not so. Self-evaluation is required, as are inquiries into anomalies, requesting and accepting help, and—as we will see—the savvy use of forensic tools.

It might have been complacency that left one family in anguish for more than 30 years, thinking that their daughter had run away.[‡] On August 1, 1974, Ima Jean Sanders disappeared from Warner Robins, Georgia; in 1976, UHR were found in a wooded area not far away.[§] In June 2011, a detective from a Texas sheriff's office asked me to enter the case into NamUs, after the family had contacted him about this Jane Doe situation. The National Clearinghouse for Missing and Exploited Children (NCMEC) immediately began to work on the case, and coordinated resources for the detective. The detective, NCMEC, and the FBI staff who processed the Jane Doe remains were able to identify them as Ima Jean Sanders, but they are conspicuously

[*] Merriam-Webster. merriam-webster.com. 2014. http://www.merriam-webster.com/dictionary/groupthink.

[†] Tan, V. 2004. *The Dangers of Complacency*. KL Strategic Change Consulting Group.

[‡] Lewis, K. 2011. Cold Case Solved: Family Members Learn Girl, 13, Killed by Serial Killer in 1974. *Atlanta Crime Examiner*.

[§] Georgia Bureau of Investigation. 2011. *1974 Disappearance and Murder of Teenaged Warner Robins Girl Solved*. Decatur, GA: Press Release. December, 2011. https://gbi.georgia.gov/press-releases/2011-12-21/1974-disappearance-and-murder-teenaged-warner-robins-girl-solved.

absent from news releases about it—as are the personnel who may or may not have tried to keep the case from going cold.

In the drive to impress an agency's local community (i.e., its funding source), it is not unusual for public information officers to spin their involvement or fail to acknowledge the work of other agencies. Thomas (1991) refers to such practices as "sharpening" and "leveling." [*] When people deliver messages, they are completely accurate only rarely and are often delivered in a manner most favorable to the messenger(s). The message is sharpened to emphasize its favorability to the messenger; it is leveled when the messenger does not emphasize these aspects.[†]

Below is a timeline of the Ima Jean Sanders case.

June 13, 2011: I received a telephoned request for help from a detective in Texas who was trying to help a family locate their missing daughter. They had been searching for decades. The family had hoped that unidentified remains originally listed in NamUs UP belonged to their daughter, but they were not. At first, the sheriff's office in Texas had refused to enter Ima Jean Sanders into the NCIC system because she was missing from Georgia; this meant that a Georgia agency would have to handle inquiries. If the Texas office entered her data, all inquiries would be directed to them, instead of to Georgia, by their ORI (original agency identifier) number.

State missing persons clearinghouses will often "shop" a case (most area of the U.S. have some form of concurrent jurisdiction—local/municipal, county, state or federal) to try and help families get their missing loved ones into NCIC. For example, I have entered cases into NamUs at the request of an officer/agency from out of state, and have facilitated entry into NamUs through still other agencies. For a commissioned police officer, it is considered a professional courtesy to assist other officers and agencies with case requests. Many law enforcement officers have done this for me when a local agency could not or would not process a long-term MP report.

June 13, 2011: I entered the case into NamUs as requested,[‡] and NCMEC automatically began to investigate it.

June 21, 2011: Family reference samples of DNA previously secured by a Texas sheriff's office received a designation of "association," which means that UHR entered into the system had a high probability of belonging to someone biologically related to that family.

---

[*] Gilovich, T. 1991. *How We Know What Isn't So: The Fallibility of Human Reason in Everyday Life*. New York, NY: The Free Press, Division of Simon & Schuster, Inc. p. 81.

[†] *Ibid*. p. 94.

[‡] www.namus.gov (2014).

June 26, 2011: NCMEC contacted the author and explained that they were trying to get a police department in Georgia to make an MP report; NCMEC also asked that the detective who had contacted me receive training about NamUs protocols for DNA submissions in adult MP cases.

June 29, 2011: The requested training was completed.

September 2011: An association between DNA in the FBI's National Missing Persons DNA Database (NMPDD), better known as the Combined DNA Index System (CODIS) was made at the NDIS (National DNA Index System) level was confirmed.

December 21, 2011: The Georgia State Bureau of Investigation announced in a press release that a positive identification had been made.[*]

I cannot help but wonder if complacency was part of the reason that this case had several anomalies that persisted for decades. For example, why was an MP report not filed when Ms. Sanders was originally reported missing by her family? Why did NCMEC have difficulty getting an agency to upload the case into NCIC when it was already in NamUs? Why did no agency in Georgia voluntarily conduct any follow-up on the Sanders case? Why was the family reduced to contacting law enforcement officials in another state (Texas)?

I am sad to report that such anomalies are not uncommon in the world of MP/UD/UHR investigations. To manage them requires insight. Families, and investigators, must be aware that occurrences that are not only unexpected but also, possibly, simply wrong may cripple investigations.[†] Effective leadership, which can correct and—ideally—prevent such occurrences thinks proactively instead of struggling to manage the unexpected after the fact. In this case, a sheriff's office in Texas faced with the unexpected incident of an out of state resident seeking investigative assistance, led to resolution.

No complacency was involved. The investigator from the Texas sheriff's office accepted the circumstances presented by the family as true, even though the case was out of his agency's jurisdiction. He then initiated actions that would confirm or refute the family's story. When the story was confirmed, he sought help for the family.

---

[*] Georgia Bureau of Investigation. 2011. *1974 Disappearance and Murder of Teenaged Warner Robins Girl Solved.* Decatur, GA: Press Release. December, 2011. https://gbi.georgia.gov/press-releases/2011-12-21/1974-disappearance-and-murder-teenaged-warner-robins-girl-solved.

[†] Sutrcliffe, K.M., Christianson, M.K. 2013. *Managing for the Unexpected.* Ann Arbor, MI: Michigan School of Business, Center for Positive Organizational Scholarship.

The timeline and circumstances of the Ima Jean Sanders case provide a realistic picture of the amount of time involved, and complacency that may be encountered, in the process of identifying a sentinel event concerning a UD. It may be necessary to extend timelines, depending on the difficulty of extracting a profile from remains, the search capability of the DNA service provider, the availability of suitable DNA samples, or simply by the limitations of legacy DNA technology. Unfortunately, the timeline of DNA analysis is usually consumed with waiting for administrative, technical, and peer reviews rather than by actual physical processing or review processes. At this time, legacy DNA technology is not able to produce the expedient DNA analyses that UHR investigations require.

In this book, the term "complacency" refers to speculative justification or belief based on previous events—including limited experience and training—that masquerades as empirical reasoning. Used correctly, and kept under control, complacency (along with the assumptions presumptions that underlie it) allows us to move through life efficiently and efficaciously. Complacency is inappropriate, however, when assumptions and presumptions prevent an MP report from being filed or cause investigators to accept inaccurate forensic service analyses.

Repeated exposure to complacency may cause an otherwise good investigator to form biases, particularly when there are no negative consequences. Later, contradictory revelations may simply be explained away or even ignored. Transparency removes ambiguity, allays the political environment, encourages discovery of mistakes and errors, and encourages openness and cooperation from all parties. Transparency is necessary to effect change[*] and to allay the vice of complacency.

Let us repeat the two questions that can be used to eviscerate the destructive influence of complacency in UHR investigations: How reliable is the data? and How well-adapted are the processes used to elicit and test the data?[†] Perhaps the transparency and understanding provided by Herbert L. Packer's two rules of inquiry are best summed up by the words of novelist Émile Zola (1840–1902): "If you shut up truth and bury it under the ground, it will but grow, and gather to itself such explosive power that the day it bursts through it will blow up everything in its way."[‡]

[*] Swensen, J.S., Cortese, D.A. 2008. Transparency and the "end result idea." *Chest* 133(1).
[†] Packer, H. 1962. *Ex-Communist Witnesses: Four Studies in Fact Finding.* Stanford, CA: Stanford University Press.
[‡] Zola, Emile (1840–1902). http://en.wikiquote.org/wiki/Emile_Zola. *The Truth Hurts.* LinkedIn.

Bias

2

I know that most men, including those at ease with problems of the greatest complexity, can seldom accept even the simplest and most obvious truth if it be such as would oblige them to admit the falsity of conclusions which they have delighted in explaining to colleagues, which they have proudly taught to others, and which they have woven, thread by thread, into the fabric of their lives.

Leo Tolstoy (1828–1910)

Today, all types of media seem to obsessively cover stories that supposedly feature objective forensic science. However, even the most scientifically rigorous investigative tools, approaches, and techniques may cause problems as well as solve them in UP investigations. For example, statistics released by different entities may include identity confirmations achieved by secondary modalities. Such contradictions, which are confusing to the public and which give false impressions of how such investigations are conducted, must be countered by the development of effective investigative strategies—but not from the perspectives of research scientists or subject matter experts who function as expert witnesses.

Instead, police and other investigative bodies must create and improve strategies to more rapidly resolve the large numbers of UD/UHR investigations that remain open nationwide. Despite the existence of massive databases and swift advancements in forensic science technology, it is still the investigative leads from families and friends, the hard work of investigators, and the support of the public that, in the vast majority of cases, lead to resolutions.

The fraudulent practices by rogue scientists that are occasionally revealed in newspapers and research reports cause public alarm and may even cause previously closed cases to be reopened; however, follow-up investigations and sanctions do not guarantee that all will be fine when these few bad actors have been removed and additional controls installed. In reality, responses to such indiscretions do little to change the environment of UHR investigations because the very concept of "objective" forensic science masks an element that is more insidious and pervasive: cognitive bias. Until we get beyond blaming individuals, in both the forensic science and criminal justice communities, and consider operations as a whole, we will not be able to understand how to improve the efficacy of UD/UHR investigations as a whole.*

Objectivity in UP investigations is a malleable concept. "Objective" does not necessarily mean "quantitative," as in measurements whose results are independent of observer influence; instead, the term "qualitative" refers to observers' judgments, interpretations, or opinions. But data that is quantitative (for example, measurements that are described in distinct, unchanging units) can be converted to qualitative data—in other words, even hard figures can be interpreted in ways that vary by observer or subject. This conversion is particularly likely when multiple, conflicting, or ambiguous data/materials are involved.

A forensic subject matter expert works with hard data, but also formulates and offers an express opinion, in verbal and/or written form, about what that data may mean. In fact, forensics is composed of data developed by human judgment and opinion. This process differs greatly from biometrics, in which data is derived from machines or software that cannot attach biased alterations or cite subjective influences. Caution should always be used when evaluating human interpretations of any forensic data.

Although consultations are routinely scheduled between forensic subject matter experts and investigators, the language of forensic science is not familiar to most investigators. Inaccurate assumptions or feelings of confusion may result if all parties are not clear with each other about what they know, and what they need to know. When communication is unclear, investigators may be unsure of what a forensic report actually means and, as a result, may not take action. Other types of problems may arise when forensic subject matter experts are presumed by families and the public to be unwaveringly objective, concise, accurate, and impartial (an impression that has been aided and abetted by what I call "the CSI effect"). As I try to emphasize throughout this book, such people are as prone to error as anyone else.

Forensic reports should be provided to investigators without ambiguous or esoteric phrases and should include explanations of the methods that were used to derive the results. Full and complete disclosure that leads to understanding is important for investigators, so that they can decide if and when to reanalyze evidence with newer, more advanced technologies.† It is especially important for investigators to know the methods of measurement and indications of uncertainties in UP investigations, which may remain open for decades.

---

* Thompson, W.C. 2009. *Beyond Bad Apples: Analyzing the Role of Forensic Science in Wrongful Convictions: Chapter 1: Criminal Justice Through the Lens of Organizational Theory*, p. 1033. http://www.swlaw.edu/pdfs/lr/37_4thompson.pdf (Accessed September 23, 2015).

† Committee on Identifying the Needs of the Forensic Community, National Research Council. 2009. *Strengthening Forensic Science in the United States: A Path Forward.* Washington, DC: The National Academies Press, p. 21.

With advances in technologies also comes the burden of complexity; in other words, the more we know, the more we become aware of how little we actually know, and how much more we need to know. Education, in the form of clear communication, reduces our knowledge deficiencies. Biases, in the form of incomplete communication and/or subjective conclusions, make us think we know more than we actually do.

For example, many known collections of human remains are used for research. These include the Smithsonian's Terry Collection in Washington, DC; the George Huntington Collection at the National Museum of Natural History in Washington, DC; the Hamann–Todd Collection in the Cleveland (Ohio) Museum of Natural History; and the William M. Bass collection at the University of Tennessee in Knoxville.[*] Most such collections originated from the mid-1800s to early 1900s and consist of limited quantities of remains and limited ethnicities; with the exception of the Bass skeletons, they are largely undocumented as to source, ethnicity, and identification. Obviously, these collections—while valuable—are not representative of the world's population today.

Subject matter experts have a host of metric data from such collections that they can use to support their opinions. However, this data is not necessarily relevant for current cases in which ancestry is unknown. Moreover, few samples may be analyzed in supporting studies, which presents contextual concerns about generalized relevance to the population under consideration. Numbers that are based on such supporting studies cannot be considered truly relevant, let alone accurate, unless the context of their origins is known. In fact, context is the most significant consideration in evaluating any information in any investigative case. Not only does it allow more accurate identification, it also helps investigators identify potential sources of bias.

When a subject matter expert accepts a case, he or she may consciously or subconsciously express bias when considering various metadata, as well as ambiguous data contained in crime scene photos and reports. Therefore, the question of which data/studies are "safest" for the subject matter expert to use in justifying his or her opinions is highly relevant. Some subject matter experts state that they want to keep our reports thin to avoid fishing expeditions by the defense. However, it is through exactly this kind of questioning that anomalies are detected and appropriate resolutions are made possible. "The simple reality is that interpretation of forensic evidence is not infallible—quite the contrary... In addition, any testimony stemming from forensic science laboratory reports must clearly describe the limits

[*] Chunn, B.L. 2008. *A Study of Non-Metric Traits Using the William M. Bass Donated Skeletal Collection.* University of Tennessee Honors Thesis Projects.

of the analysis; currently, failure to acknowledge uncertainty in findings is common."*

One of the major classes of biases that influence forensic science opinions, known as confirmative bias, may include observational effects, anchoring bias, or types of circular reasoning that range from preexposure to circumstantial familiarity with a particular inquiry. Observational effect errors are included in this category, for example when an observer modifies his or her behavior after exposure to previously unknown stimuli or data. Circular reasoning errors result when experts interpret data or events by deductively affirming extraneous knowledge or observations.† Anchoring bias is a well-known tendency of examiners to rely too heavily on one piece of information when that information is the first to be encountered.‡

Errors that result from confirmative bias may occur at any time or stage of an inquiry. The true values of the underlying observations may be so vague, ephemeral, and mired in interoperational dynamics (manipulations, calculations, and explanations) that they are effectively masked in the interpretative statements/conclusions.§ Professionals and nonprofessionals alike can be easily influenced if they are not well-grounded in the fundamentals of forensic science; in such cases, confirmative bias may be rampant. Subject matter experts understand that errors may be resolved during plea bargaining, which occurs in more than 95% of criminal cases.¶

In 1991, the remains of an unidentified homicide victim found in the Upper Midwest were identified as an adult female of indeterminate race; the head was not recovered. An anthropological analysis in 2011 "definitely" confirmed the remains as female (the original anthropological analysis had been provided to the second forensic subject matter expert). However, after DNA results were obtained in 2012, the sex determination was changed to male.**

In this case, the crime scene photos, reports, and information that had been requested by the first two investigators before their forensic examinations may have unconsciously influenced them. However, such requests are common and even expected, because time is of such critical importance in

† The National Academies. 2009. 'Badly Fragmented' Forensic Science Needs Overhaul; Evidence to Support Reliability of Many Techniques is Lacking. *News from the National Academies*. February 16, 2009.

† Office of the Inspector General. January 2006. *A Review of the FBI's Handling of the Brandon Mayfield Case*. p. 7.

‡ Committee on Identifying the Needs of Forensic Science Community, National Research Council. August 2009. *Strengthening Forensic Science in the United States: A Path Forward*. p. 146.

§ Risinger, D.M., Saks, M.J., Thompson, W.C., Rosenthal, R. 2002. The Daubert/Kumho implications of observer effects in forensic science: Hidden problems of expectation and suggestion. *California Law Review* 90(1), 26.

¶ Mergler, M., Durocher, C. 2011. *The "Right-to-Counsel Term."* American Constitution Society for Law and Policy. p. 1.

** www.namus.gov. 2013. NamUs UP #4765.

homicide investigations. Individual memories are malleable; witnesses vanish or die; evidence degrades or disappears; and the ability to obtain DNA reference samples become more difficult. In this case, investigators could not effectively investigate the remains for more than 20 years because they were searching for a missing female.

The above case exemplifies later stage confirmation bias. The Brandon Mayfield case, by contrast, shows early stage confirmation bias (circular reasoning). After a bomb explosion in Madrid, Spain on March 11, 2004 killed 200 people and injured 1400, the FBI responded to an INTERPOL request for assistance in identifying a fingerprint found at the scene. On March 19, the FBI's latent fingerprint unit (LPU) identified a U.S. citizen, Brandon Mayfield, as the source. This identification was made by searching the FBI's automated fingerprint identification system (IAFIS), the precursor to next-generation identification (NGI). A second LPU examiner concurred with this finding, as did a court-appointed independent fingerprint examiner. But on May 19, Spanish authorities informed the FBI that the identification was in question because the same fingerprint had been positively identified as originating from an Algerian national.

Upon reviewing the Algerian national's prints, the FBI withdrew its identification of Brandon Mayfield. FBI fingerprint examiners had initially found as many as 10 points of similarity between the print image stored in IAFIS and the reference print taken from the bombing site. However, they also interpreted ambiguous or murky details as additional points of similarity, even though these were not clear but only "suggested." When a panel met at the FBI laboratory to review the case in June 2004, some panelists concluded that multiple positive verifications had been "tainted" by the knowledge of the original examiner's findings.*

This type of conflict became more frequent as IAFIS continued to grow. NGI, the newest repository for fingerprints, is not immune from such confusion. NGI, which is even larger than IAFIS, incorporates publicly and privately imaged fingerprints and is linked with some international databases; the presence of fingerprints that show very close similarities may thus become even more perplexing for examiners who must differentiate between reference candidate prints and the prints they are trying to identify. NGI/IAFIS produces a list of candidate fingerprints that most closely resemble a questioned fingerprint and then examiners individually include or exclude them.

Even though forensic subject matter experts are not detectives, they are routinely portrayed as such on popular TV shows that greatly influence public perceptions. The truth is that forensic science provides tools to be used by investigators, who are the ones to actually bring resolution to a case. When

---

* A Review of the FBI's Handling of the Brandon Mayfield Case. US Department of Justice, Office of the Inspector General. March 2006.

forensic subject matter experts are exposed to, rely on, or are influenced by information that originates outside their sphere of expertise, even if they believe that this information will make their conclusions more reliable, they are abusing their position and failing to serve the public in the most professional way. The remains and fingerprint identification cases discussed above, in which subject matter experts overreached their spheres of knowledge, illustrate confirmative bias. In both situations, the investigations were negatively affected and investigators and agencies were placed at risk for lawsuits.[*]

In late summer 2010, after a human torso was discovered in a Midwest river, several subject matter experts were consulted and contributed to descriptive metadata (e.g., race, age, height, and weight) about the unidentified decedent. Although their age range estimates varied widely, all agreed that the decedent was a Black male. But when a cold hit investigative lead was developed, it produced an association to a White male. Without this reliable lead, investigators would not have been able to develop viable investigative strategies but instead would have only searched for associations to a Black male.

The point of this story, as with the previous ones, is that multiple different forensic experts from different forensic disciplines can be wrong—and are wrong more often than the public believes. Why there was a wide range of opinions about the decedent's age in this case, and how the various forensic disciplines developed consistent "opinionated" evidence that nonetheless produced an incorrect race identification, remain unknown. Whether investigators debriefed the case to learn how these discrepancies and consistencies developed also remains unknown. Nonetheless, until forensic science researchers increase their transparency and begin to publicly disclose failure analyses and estimation uncertainties, investigators, families, and the public must realize that the formulation of investigative strategies may include numerous errors.

In spring 2011, an unidentified decedent was said to have been identified on the basis of circumstance and a DNA association with other than first-order biological relatives; however, in winter 2012, this person (who had been missing and presumed dead) was reported found alive. Although it is well known that DNA statistical likelihood ratios for second-order biological relatives (such as an aunt or uncle) are usually lower than for first-order biological relatives (such as parents), particularly when only one physical modality of identification is used, this error occurred. Even with strong circumstantial

---

[*] U.S. Code, Title 42, Chapter 21. Section 1983: Every person who, under color of any statute, ordinance, regulation, custom, or usage, of any State or Territory or the District of Columbia, subjects, or causes to be subjected, any citizen of the United States or other person within the jurisdiction thereof to the deprivation of any rights, privileges, or immunities secured by the Constitution and laws, shall be liable to the party injured in an action at law, suit in equity, or other proper proceeding for redress, except that in any action brought against a judicial officer for an act or omission taken in such officer's judicial capacity, injunctive relief shall not be granted unless a declaratory decree was violated or declaratory relief was unavailable. Legal Information Institute at Cornell University Law School.

evidence, making DNA associations on the basis of second-order relatives must be done with caution. Biological family member reference samples are the poorest samples for ascertaining identity because they rely on probability analyses and familial comparisons.

Numerous inconsistences and errors in the identification of MP and UD indicate that commonalities derived from ancestral biological markers are far more widely dispersed than is generally known. In other words, as cold hits in UHR investigations have shown, the emphasis that has been placed on DNA associations other than first- or second-order ones has over-influenced the opinions of forensic subject matter experts—and continues to do so. The National Academy of Sciences acknowledged this problem in its report, *Strengthening Forensic Science in the United States: A Path Forward*: "It was clear that some members of the forensic science community will not concede that there could be less than perfect accuracy either in given laboratories or in specific disciplines."[*]

Of course, forensic subject matter experts may be partly or fully employed as consultants or expert witnesses. If an expert cannot provide a definitive opinion that is convincingly based on what seem to be objectively derived facts, his or her livelihood may be at risk. Worse, an admitted error may incur liability. In 1989, Novack et al. reported the results of a questionnaire that was sent out to 407 physicians. One-third of the 211 respondents indicated that they would offer incomplete or misleading information after a patient's death resulted; simply put, when forced to make ethical decisions that might implicate their own knowledge or skill, they indicated a willingness to deceive.[†] All too frequently, equivocal responses are given in order to reduce or avoid adverse repercussions—or experts simply do not concede that errors were made at all.

In 2005, *The Texas Prosecutor* (the official journal of the Texas District and County Attorneys Association) attracted international attention with an article about a "grave robbery." Inside a flaming car at the bottom of a gulley next to a road in rural Burnet County, a charred body consisting of 12 pounds of remains with no head was found. Two women who arrived at the scene said that they knew the car and its driver, Clayton Daniels; one woman claimed to be his mother and the other claimed to be his wife. These women and other untrained viewers could not discern any genitals in the remains; however, the medical examiner (a pathologist) stated that

---

[*] Committee on Identifying the Needs of Forensic Science Community, National Research Council. 2006. Op. cit. [note 3] p. 69.
[†] Novack, D.H., Barbara, B.J., Arnold, R., Forrow, L., Landisky, M., Pezzullo, C. 1989. Physicians' attitudes toward using deception to resolve difficult problems. *The Journal of the American Medical Association* 261(20).

he could see part of a penis and listed Clayton Daniels as the deceased in his autopsy report.[*]

Despite this supposedly positive identification, investigators sought confirmation and therefore submitted reference samples for DNA analysis and comparison to DNA samples from the burned remains. Months later, it was confirmed that the remains in the vehicle were not those of an individual biologically related to the mother of Clayton Daniels; moreover, investigators followed Clayton Daniels' wife and arrested Clayton himself when he arrived at a restaurant to meet her. The burned body in the car turned out to be an 81-year-old female who had been exhumed from her own grave earlier that day.[†] In this case, it is quite possible that the ME treated the case with bias, due to the presence and input of Daniels' mother and wife when the burning car was discovered.

Thirteen Texas counties have MEs, and 239 counties use a Justice of the Peace (JP) as coroners. Counties without a medical examiner must pay for an autopsy if one deemed necessary, at an average cost of $1248 to $1640.[‡] Of course, in the light of budget cuts, these revenues are welcomed by public and private medical examiners alike. DNA testing, which is far more expensive, must also be publicly funded; accordingly, on April 28, 2005, the Department of Justice's Office of Justice Programs announced that $14,200,000 would be allocated to law enforcement agencies to resolve cold cases and identify UHR using DNA.[§] Competition for funding dollars means that any investigative strategy logic is vulnerable to bias: a particular method, even if it only gives the impression of greater relative success, may generate more funding and thus be more widely used.

Another factor that influences choice of analytical method is grant funding, which is temporary at best and therefore may cause agencies to be reluctant to add permanent staff, even though increased staff means that workloads can be managed more quickly and efficiently. Heavy workloads, competition for funding allocations, and the pressure to secure additional funds through external fees for services all increase the pressure on forensic subject matter experts who work in fixed-revenue governmental environments.

The Clayton Daniels "grave robbery" case was the first well-known case involving an unidentified decedent in which the initial forensic opinion was challenged as part of the investigative confirmation process. Clearly, this

---

[*] Stames, J. 2005. Woman digs up corpse to fake husband's death. *The Texas Prosecutor* September/October, 23.

[†] *Ibid.*

[‡] Emerson, P. 2006. *Autopsy Costs in Various Counties: The County Information Project.* Austin, TX: Texas Association of Counties.

[§] Department of Justice, Office of Justice Programs. 2005. *Justice Department Awards $14 Million to Law Enforcement to Solve "Cold Cases" at 1st Conference on Identifying the Missing.*

investigative strategy was successful. Further discussions of strategy development and initial critical thinking concepts that raise awareness of possibly unsupported or inaccurate forensic opinions appear in Chapter 13.

Motivational bias becomes easier to understand when one considers the concept of heuristics, which is not only common to human thought processes but also may play a significant role in the development of complacency, which was discussed in Chapter 1. Heuristic thinking affects all human beings and is very difficult to control or avoid when making decisions or judgments. We've all heard expressions such as "Experience is the best teacher there is," or "in my experience." When such phrases are used in MP/UP investigations, they indicate heuristic thinking.

> **Key point:** Heuristics is experience-based knowledge gained from past observations, exposure to circumstances, and/or trial-and-error experimentation. Heuristic thinking produces "mental shortcuts" that allow decisions and judgments to be made as efficiently as possible. It does not guarantee that these decisions and judgements will be sound or correct.[*]

When investigators or forensic subject matter experts are faced with circumstances that resemble previous events, mental associations may be made that produce assumptions and presumptions about the case at hand. When those memories, assumptions, or presumptions (e.g., a certain sex or race for UHR), the tendency toward such reinforcements is not only affirmed through the effect of heuristics but also may be unnoticed. Each confirming outcome of initial assumptions related to previous cases may affect the cognitive process and judgment; in such situations, the event under investigation functions to reinforce previous assumptions and presumptions and thus and increases the influence of heuristic thinking. Individuals who work in law enforcement, despite their training and motivations, may find it very difficult to objectify and isolate their involvement to a single case. Just being present at the scene of an UD recovery may provide a circumstantial cognitive connection to a previous case(s) that influences what the subject matter expert sees or not see, or how much weight he or she places on ambiguous data, observation, and so forth.

Situational pressures (e.g., time, reputation, and ego) may increase the effect of heuristic thinking about data. Ambiguous data (for example, the knowledge that a UD was found wearing what appeared to be women's clothing) may cause a subject matter expert to draw an inaccurate conclusion even though such experts also know that the human skeletal frame may carry both

---

[*] Correia, V. 2011. Biases and fallacies: The role of motivated irrationality in fallacious reasoning. *Cogency* 3(1).

male and female characteristics and that both males and females may dress in recognizably female attire. Similarly, knowledge that human remains were found in a location that is highly populated by Black residents may affect the subject matter expert's opinion about the race of the decedent. Or, reviewing investigative reports that contain witness identifications of the decedent may influence a pathologist. Investigative errors have been recorded under such circumstances.

Determining the exact degree of correlation of error to causation by circumstance is not important. The objectives are to help investigators design strategies that reduce such systemic errors in UHR investigations and to help families understand how such errors may occur. It is the awareness of the possibility of errors, not their causation, that is important. It is also important to reduce such errors, which are common in UHR investigations and may not only cause cases to remain unresolved for decades, but also cost communities thousands to millions of dollars that may be desperately needed elsewhere.

It is difficult to understand why investigative errors impact some cases so negatively and others not at all. Perhaps, there are so many events and uncertainties in our world that establishing causation is the exception rather than the rule. As it happens, the complexities of solving that particular mystery are beyond the scope of this book. What we know is that errors are a result of inconsistencies in rationalization processes used by subject matter experts when formulating articulated opinions. In general, experts support their opinions with a combination of personal experience and selected research; very seldom are contradictory positions stipulated in expert reports. The essential problem is that the difference between rationally and relatively derived opinions are not clear cut, but rather a matter of degree. In MP, UP, UD, and UHR investigations, ambiguous information and data may dominate; this pattern is systemic, as the case histories throughout this book demonstrate.

In forensic science, as in all other human endeavors, various types of bias can modulate the influence of both rationality and relativity. However, reality (in the form of accurate, reliable data, and rational decisions that result from the unbiased consideration of such data) tends to correct investigative errors.

Motivational biases are present in all of our daily lives, but their definitions may vary according to context. In that respect, all definitions of motivational bias may be relevant and appropriate though they may differ widely. In the context of MP and UD/UHR investigations, motivational bias refers to events and circumstances, as well as the individual characteristics of investigators and/or examiners, that impact their formulation of opinions.

As previously stated, each UHR investigation is unique. The key to successful resolution of a case, if serendipitous intervention does not occur, depends on the ability of investigators and examiners to objectively handle the investigation. To do so, they must disregard previous cases and also strive to develop empathy with present victims, families, and communities. According to one researcher, "The assumption of discernible uniqueness that resides at the core of [the forensic sciences] is weakened by evidence of errors in proficiency testing and in actual cases."[*]

As discussed in Chapter 1, in *People v. Castro* (one of the first major cases that involved the science of DNA in a double murder), the court found that the "testing laboratory failed in several respects to use the generally accepted scientific techniques and experiments for obtaining reliable results, within a reasonable degree of scientific certainty."[†] (Fortunately, in this case the accused confessed to the murders.[‡]) Before *Castro*, most DNA evidence went unchallenged in court—much as identification opinions presented at the investigation level by forensic subject matter experts are unchallenged today in most unidentified decedent cold cases. The inability of experts to treat cases with unconditional objectivity may be the reason that as of July 19, 2014, NamUs listed 9721 open UP cases.

As we expand our understanding of MP and UD/UHR investigations that may involve motivational bias, case studies reveal similar patterns which indicate that the problems of forensic science may be systemic in the criminal justice system. As stated in a report by the National Academy of Sciences, "...some members of the forensic science community will not concede that there could be less than perfect accuracy either in given laboratories or in specific disciplines."[§] Motivational biases, in particular, may be based in situational factors. For example, the costs of autopsies (which may or may not include anthropological analyses) can significantly influence unidentified remains investigations. Jurisdictions that lack a medical examiner's office or coroner's office with a qualified pathologist may spend more than $2000 per necessary autopsy (Table 2.1) for an unidentified decedent.[¶]

In Texas, where (as previously noted) only 13 counties have medical examiners and 239 counties use JP as coroners, smaller counties and counties in which undocumented migrants expire near the border must contract with either a public or private medical examiner's office for UD/UHR identifications. Such offices may or may not have a board-certified forensic pathologist or anthropologist with sufficient experience in the forensic identification of

[*] Saks, M.J., Koehler, J.J. 2005. The coming paradigm shift in forensic identification science. *Science*, August, 398, 892.
[†] *People v. Castro*, 144 Misc. 2nd 956—NY: Supreme Court, 1989.
[‡] King, J. 1989. DNA forensic testing industry faces challenge to credibility. *The Scientist*. November 13, 1989.
[§] Committee on Identifying the Needs of Forensic Science Community, National Research Council. 2006, [note 3] p. 69.
[¶] Emerson, P. 2006. *Autopsy Costs in Various Counties: The County Information Project*. Austin, TX: Texas Association of Counties.

Table 2.1　Autopsy Costs in Some Texas Counties

County	Data Year	Average Cost
Andrews	2005	$1582
Bexar	2004	$1545
Borden	2005	$1450
Crane	2005	$1655
Dallas	2004	$1580
Dawson	2005	$1744
Denton	2004	$1200
Ector	2005	$2029
El Paso	2004	$550
Gaines	2005	$1384
Galveston county (UTMB[a])	2004	$2000
Glasscock	2005	$1633
Howard	2005	$1720
Johnson	2004	$1100
Lubbock	2004	$2500–$3000
Martin	2005	$1818
Midland	2005	$1497
Nuecces	2004	$1200–$1850
Parker	2004	$1200
Pecos	2005	$2184
Reeves	2005	$1734
Tarrant	2004	$1200
Travis	2004	$1600
Upton	2005	$2065
Ward	2005	$1909
Wichita	2004	$975–$1575
Winker	2005	$1887

Note: Costs include transportation cost when available; in addition, testimony fees can range from $1500 to $3500 or more.
[a] UTMB: University of Texas Medical Branch.

degraded or skeletonized human remains. These uncertainties, along with the inherent ambiguities of the cases themselves, in combination with motivational bias may cause tremendous difficulties for contracted subject matter experts. Some end up reporting a determination of "unknown" as to the race and sex of decedent remains. Other subject matter expert reports contain the term "admixture" (meaning a combination of two or more races) that is presented as opinion without a scientific basis.

> **Key point:** Because race is a social construct rather than a scientifically-based category, associated biases may be reflected in the findings of subject matter experts in numerous forensic disciplines.

Racial designations are not derived from clearly defined scientific delineations; instead, throughout human history race has been defined by human observers in ways that are ambiguous, subjective, and heavily subject to political, religious, and economic factors. For example, the term "Hispanic" is associated not with the biological or physiological attributes of individuals but rather with countries in which Spanish is the dominant language. Thus, even indigenous peoples who live in countries that were conquered by Spain may be referred to as Hispanic when in fact they are members of native tribes and do not speak Spanish at all. The flawed logic of continuing to rely upon racial designations continues to produce wide-ranging consequences, however, as this quotation illustrates: "Although the typographical race concept is obsolete in present-day systemic biology and anthropology, the idea that human populations and individuals are classified into separate races (Blacks, Whites, Native Americans, etc.) persists in government census data and mass media sources as well as forensic science."[*]

Current legacy forensic DNA technologies (e.g., capillary electrophoresis or CE) provide rudimentary capabilities to identify ethnicity; despite their lack of complexity, such identifications are helpful to anthropologists for estimating descriptors (not including sex) of UD. Emerging DNA technologies such as NGS that depend on a greater use of biometrics may be more helpful to anthropologists and pathologists in terms of determining accurate geographic origins or ethnicities for UD.

Although subject matter experts give their clients and investigators the impression of having used definitive facts in their opinions, the error rates are simply too high for these opinions to be taken as single sources of definitive facts in UD/UHR investigations. Even when clients and subject matter experts alike are content with the conclusions of a forensic report, a decedent may not be accurately identified until a cold hit provides more accurate information about race or sex. For families who are in anguish as they wonder where their loved ones are, and whether they are even still alive, identification delays caused by current legacy DNA technology and protocols may be unbearable.

---

[*] Kennedy, K.A.R. 1995. But professor, why teach race identification if races don't exist? *Journal of Forensic Science, Abstract*, 40, pp. 797–800.

The Tommy Kelly Story

On January 26, 1999, 17-year-old Tommy Kelly went missing in Oregon. Eighteen months later, a skull and 25 bones were recovered in a nearby blackberry patch. According to his mother, Vicki Kelly:

> To experience having a missing murdered child is to experience physical, emotional, psychological, and spiritual pain beyond imagination. No parent should have to bring their child home bone by bone. We had been told by law enforcement we were just going to have "to take their word for it" that the skull was Tommy's. When we asked for a 10-min meeting with the coroner to show us how the identification had been made, we were told that he was a busy man and didn't have time for our "silly" questions, and that we would just have to take their word that it was Tommy. [This insensitivity added] to our trauma and plac[ed] our lives in an ambiguous reality.
>
> In 2007, my husband and I advocated for the passage of the Model State Policy for Law Enforcement Best Practices in investigations of a missing children and adults and the identification of unidentified human remains, which was passed by the Oregon legislature. In 2008, Tommy was positively DNA identified; our son was given his identity and returned home to us.

I had the honor of returning Tommy Kelly's remains to his mother on Mother's Day, 2008. Unfortunately, Tommy's father had died not long before.

In the criminal justice sphere, both prosecution and defense may have very defensible arguments. However, in unidentified decedent investigations, the system is not set up to be adversarial. The opinion of a single forensic subject matter expert may be all that is available to an investigator, who may in turn assume that this opinion is factual. Second opinions are rarely sought, but may be requested by the original subject matter expert (rather than the investigating agency) in ambiguous situations or under challenging circumstances. This second expert must endure tremendous pressure, even though he or she has the referral and has been apprised of the first consultant's opinion. One result of this pressure is off-the-record conversations that increase influence on the second subject matter expert and allow bias to enter the investigation. There may even be a professional or personal relationship between the first and second subject matter experts that promotes motivational bias. If the second forensic contractor reports findings that differ from those of the first forensic contractor, their relationship or even their careers could be damaged. Therefore, it is possible that motivational bias could contribute to the subconscious formulation of a confirming opinion offered by the second contractor.

In 2006, an audit of the FBI was conducted by the Office of the Inspector General (OIG) in reference to the investigation of Brandon Mayfield, the U.S. citizen wrongly implicated by fingerprints after the Madrid bombing.

This audit highlighted "circular reasoning" based in motivational bias as a possible contributing factor to the confirming opinions, which were in fact erroneous, that were contributed to the case by several subject matter experts. Not only has the CSI effect given the public false confidence about the ease with which criminal cases are resolved by forensic science, but some subject matter experts in UD cases also appear to believe in their own abilities to ferret out the truth from ambiguous and nebulous circumstances.

Every time a subject matter expert offers a confirming but erroneous opinion that is based on a misinterpretation of ambiguous data, if the error is not found, he or she is more likely to make a similar mistake in future cases. This overconfidence, also called hubris, may over time become the defining professional characteristic of some subject matter experts. Hubris builds in subject matter experts when their opinions are praised by families and investigators who have no way of knowing that the opinions are deeply flawed.

Since 2005, inspired by people such as Jan Smolinski and Vicki Kelly, I have been studying and deconstructing cold hit cases with the goal of developing effective strategies for UD/UHR investigations. During this time, I have had many opportunities to attend forensic conferences, meet with advisory groups, and listen to forensic experts from various disciplines. I've come to know people who overreach their abilities and people who practice professional reserve and transparency. These experiences have taught me that whether the parties interested in a case are investigators or families of the missing, all they have to work with are ink on paper and images on a computer screen; usually they do not know the ability, history, track record, or even the names of people who have provided this forensic data.

Similarly, we cannot definitively know the reasons that any particular case remains unresolved for decades; we only know that waiting for serendipity to provide the key to resolution is the worst possible strategy. In fact, the actual causes of investigative errors in UD/UHR cases may not be important. What is important, what we must understand, is the potential for errors to be made and how to design strategies that prevent them.

Section I of this book describes the main contributors to investigative errors and which errors cause cases to remain unsolved well into the future. If effective investigative strategies are not implemented as early as possible, and if they are not continuously monitored and adjusted, there is little hope of keeping UD/UHR investigations free of error. The impact of such errors can only be mitigated through the effective design of appropriate investigative strategies.

By the Numbers

3

If you get all the facts, your judgment can be right. If you don't get all the facts, it can't be right.

Bernard Baruch, 1870–1965

Long-term UHR investigations may span multiple jurisdictions across the country over multiple decades, and involve all ages, sexes, and ethnicities. Use of the term "race" is strongly discouraged in such investigations because cold hit associations have revealed numerous inconsistencies between the race of an individual in life and analytical information about his or her remains after death. A cold hit is an association (usually via CODIS or NGI) between a missing person's DNA profile or a biological family member DNA profile and a DNA profile or fingerprints from unidentified remains that has been made without any investigative link between submitting agencies. Most DNA identifications are warm hits that result from investigators' diligence or from leads (usually) provided by family members.

Warm hits, which are commonly referred to as body identifications, may be conceptualized as likely confirmations of anticipated identifications. Some examples would be a body found in his or her residence or automobile, a body found with identification papers or licenses, or a body that has been visually identified. Many leads are pursued with great enthusiasm by investigators in hopes of a getting warm hit, but results of the DNA analysis, fingerprints, or dentals exclude the anticipated association.

According to the DNA Identification Facts section of the UNT Center for Human Identification's website (9/13/2013), since 2005 the Center "has assisted in the identification of almost of 890 missing person cases: 215 'cold' hits [2004 to 2013] and 673 'warm' hits." Still, more than 14,000 identification cases are open in Texas. These 14,000 UHR, which are located in multiple jurisdictions, may be decedents who migrated from other countries and differ by ancestry/ethnicity as opposed to race. Without knowing the ancestry/ethnicity of UHR, it is difficult to ascertain accurate metadata about physical attributes (age, sex, height, etc.).

> **Key point:** There is no way to consistently classify human beings by race. Racial groups are impossible to define in a stable and universal way, which means that scientifically valid generalizations cannot be made about them.[*]

This chapter describes contextual factors that contribute to the problems faced by investigators who perform UHR investigations. Designing effective strategies to avoid or eliminate these problems, which are also called anomalies, is an art that, when combined with scientific facts, may bring astonishing results never before thought possible. The key to success is the ability to discern fact from opinion.

Investigators are artisans who use forensic science as a sculptor uses the chisel and mallet. The search for resolution in the Kenneth Bennett Glaze case (one of the nation's first resolutions via DNA), which spanned nearly 42 years and numerous jurisdictions, ended in 2005 with his identification; the Marcella Bachmann case (one of the first interstate resolutions achieved by utilizing CODIS) was closed after nearly 22 years of investigative efforts. Both Glaze and Bachmann were homicide victims who are believed to have died from gunshot wounds.

The imbalance between the numbers of UHR cases listed in various sources contributes to the confusion and frustration of investigators, families, and the public. Because the amounts of investigative resources required to resolve such cases are so enormous, it is critical for investigators to have factual information about how such cases work. Incessant dedication is also required; a UHR investigation is not a *nolens volens* (willy-nilly) undertaking for any investigator. If families as well as investigators can develop an appreciation for the context of UHR cases (for example, in terms of number and frequency), knowing that their case—however tragic—is only one of many may help assuage possible frustrations and conflicts with various agencies, databases, and scientific disciplines that seem to impede their efforts to find resolution.

Inconsistencies between forensic descriptors of a UD and forensic descriptors related to the corresponding MP occur so frequently that they may reasonably be described as endemic, not just systemic, in UHR investigations. It is normal for investigators to remain unaware that they have been working with expert opinions that were incorrect, assumed to be factual, until a cold hit association is made or identification is confirmed by other means.

---

[*] Goodman, A.H., Moses, Y.T., Jones, J.L. 2012. *Race: Are We So Different.* Oxford, UK: Wiley-Blackwell, American Anthropological Association.

Law enforcement personnel who spend time listening to families hear heart-wrenching tales of complacency, as well as frustrating indications of bias, in our profession. Some reasons may be found by framing the investigative environment as it is experienced by the two main groups who are involved: investigators and families. For families, attempts to divine the truth are daunting. For their part, investigative agencies, subject matter forensic experts and support agencies, are constantly attempting to provide results in a manner most favorable to their own agendas, without allowing themselves to be held to time frames or compelled to provide complete details. Without understanding that they are sharpening and leveling facts rather than proving them, investigators may follow inefficient or even disastrous strategies.

The chapters in Section II present conceptualizations of the logical constructs for effective strategy development in UHR cases. The aim of these processes is not to prove hypotheses or test alternate ones. Nor is it to support the "hope and pray" investigative approach, which relies exclusively on chance and is the predominant method used by many UHR investigators. Figures 3.1 through 3.3 (courtesy of Courtesy Detective Mark Czworniak—retired—Chicago Police Department) represent typical evidence facing investigators in cold cases that may make resolution seem hopeless without sound investigative strategies. In this approach, it is hoped that the evidentiary samples (DNA profile, fingerprints, dental records, etc.) from the remains are of sufficient quality for database entry, and that a viable reference is already in the chosen database. This approach, in addition to its internal flaws, is likely to be defeated by serendipity.

The key to good strategy development is not to diminish the role or value of serendipity, but rather to enhance it by creating multiple entry points for

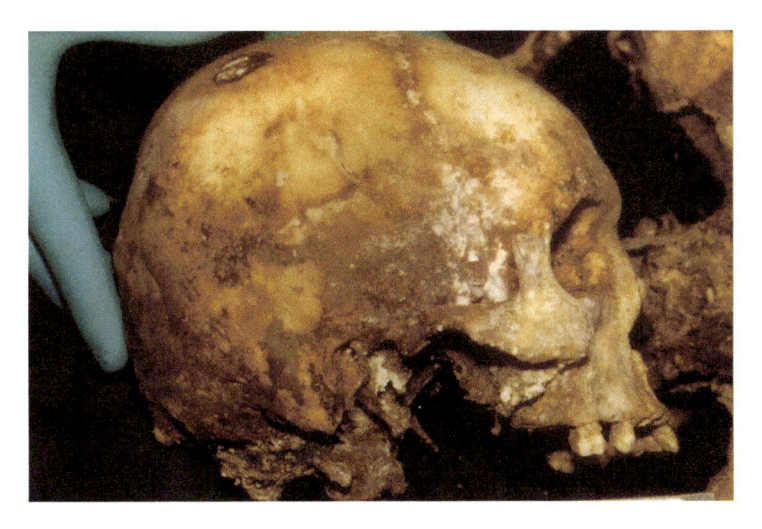

Figure 3.1 Typical case file image human skull—right side view.

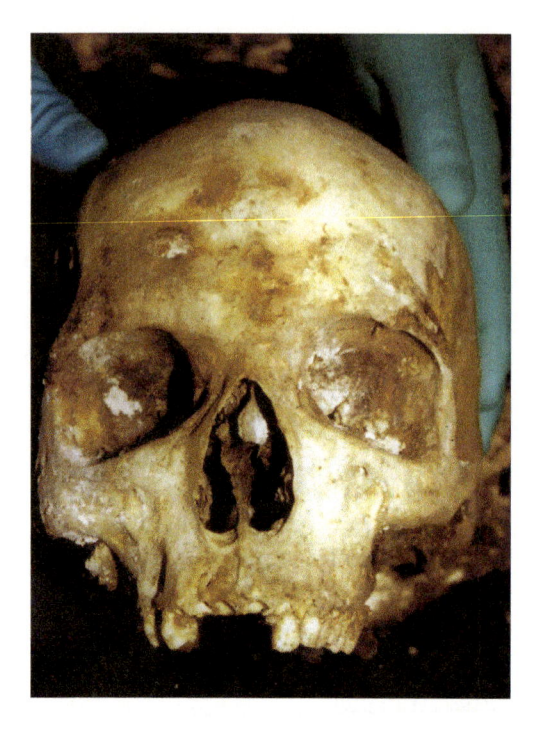

Figure 3.2 Typical case file image human skull—frontal view.

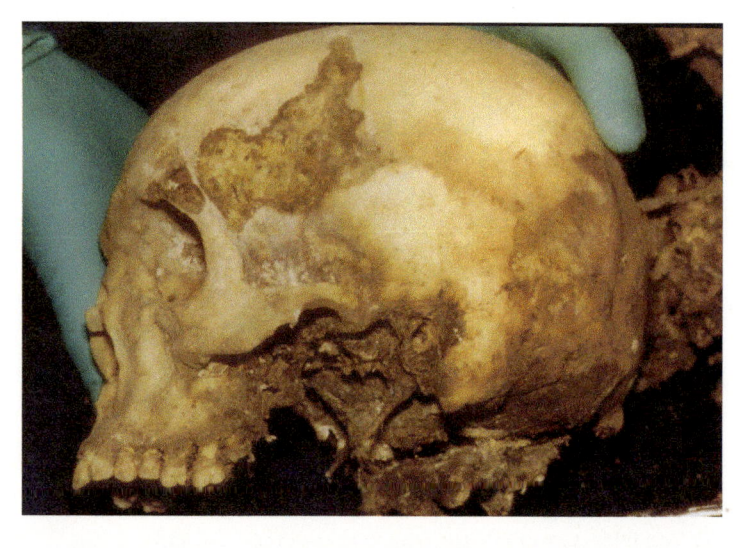

Figure 3.3 Typical case file image human skull—left side view.

the unexpected and unknown. Ironically, the reality sought by families and investigators may be discovered precisely through these avenues. Unless an investigator is aware of this possibility, and welcomes it, despite years of hard work and dedication, he or she may never be able to resolve UHR cases. The same is true for families and advocates who carry out their own parallel investigations.

In my experience, another distraction from the true context of UHR cases appears in the form of "experts" who ply their trade on websites and at conferences and training programs with a few celebrity cases. The celebrity success stories trumpeted by these people, which tend to be enthusiastically received by the public, function poorly as real examples of UHR investigations. The use of such celebrity cases in investigator training as illustrations of context are similar to the use of eyewitness testimony in court to counteract weak physical evidence. In both circumstances, vividness (for example, graphic allegations from alleged victims of satanic cults, or alleged eyewitnesses to lurid crimes who are really only seeking attention) tends to overwhelm the impact of less "sexy" information.* It is the nuts and bolts of sustained investigative work that resolves cases, even though the part played by serendipity is often a game-changer.

Investigators as well as families must also understand that, although each case should be considered unique by investigators and of course is already perceived as unique by each family or community, the annual numbers of MP/UP and UD/UHR cases nationwide are not only consistent but also low (Table 3.1). This rarity explains much about why UHR are among the least understood types of criminal investigations; this lack of understanding directly contributes to the communications issues between investigators and families, as well as between investigators and forensic matter experts and other parties who should provide reliable guidance and knowledge in UHR investigations but, as investigators know all too well, often do not.

Key point: Small numbers of events should not be construed as representative of a population or an accurate reflection of events under study.

I cannot count how many times I have heard statements from proclaimed subject matter experts such as, "If it [a DNA profile] is in CODIS, the profile is automatically searched, and if an association had been made, a notification would have been received by the submitting agency." Unfortunately,

---

* Rossmo, D.K. 2006. Criminal investigative failures: Avoiding pitfalls. *FBI Law Enforcement Bulletin.* September, p. 7.

Table 3.1   NamUs Unresolved UHR Cases as of December 17, 2014

Case Years	
1900–2014	10,013
1900–1996	5050
1949–1996	5042
1996–2014	4963
Average Numbers of Cases per Decade	
1949–1996	1073
1996–2014	2752
Average Numbers of Cases per Year	
1949–1996	108
1996–2014	276
Total U.S. Populations (from U.S. Census)	
1900	76.1 million
1950	152.3 million
2010	308.7 million

sometimes this statement is true but under some circumstances it is not. Understanding the difference between what should happen in forensics and what does happen is dependent upon understanding the context of each case; particulars alone are not enough. Accordingly, Chapter 3 contains descriptions of MP/UD/UHR investigative environments that are meant to introduce readers to the many obstacles encountered by families and investigators in their quests for resolution.

When UHR are located, either a medical examiner or a coroner is the customary legal authority responsible for identifying them; however, some states delegate this task to elected persons such as a justice of the peace, coroner, or district attorney. This lack of consistency from state to state, or even from county to county or city to city, is the very first obstacle faced by investigators in UHR cases. The National Association of Medical Examiners (NAME) recognized this problem in 2004, and described it in a report on the medico-legal death investigation system that was delivered at the National Institute of Justice Forensic Summit held in May of that year.[*] Key points included

1. The system is neither uniform or complete, but rather a "frayed patchwork" of agencies.

---

[*] The National Association of Medical Examiners. 2004. *Preliminary Report on America's Medicolegal Offices: Prepared for the National Institute of Justice Forensic Summit, May 18–19, 2004.* Washington, DC: National Association of Medical Examiners.

2. As of 2004, NAME had 1000 members (80% physicians and 20% lay death investigators).
3. Many physicians who conduct autopsies are not qualified to do so. They consist of (a) board-certified hospital pathologists, rather than forensic pathologists; (b) physicians who have failed forensic board certification; and (c) physicians who are not trained in pathology.
4. Of the 350–400 board-certified forensic pathologists, 40% reported conducting more autopsies per year than the recommended 250 maximum, and 9% reported doing more than 350 autopsies per year.[*]

According to the 2007 special report on ME/C offices published by the Bureau of Justice Statistics (BJS), in 2004 approximately 956,000 cases were referred to 1998 ME/C by medical and law enforcement personnel.[†] This number may seem enormous, but it represents less than half (40%) of all deaths in the United States that year. Of these referred cases, approximately 4400 involved UHR; an estimated 1000 cases remained unidentified after 1 year; and an estimated 600 received final disposition per year (cremation, burial, or other method). ME/C were not granted direct access to the NICIC for the purpose of entering cases until 2006.[‡]

This report indicates that 60% of the UHR in long-term cases are no longer available for testing or assessment with advanced investigative technology (because they have been cremated, buried, etc.). Thus, the case files of John and Jane Does who were recovered years ago may be missing critical definitive forensic identifiers (dental records, DNA, etc.). In 2004, when the report was published, the FBI's MP and UHR indices in CODIS were just beginning to be populated. This task was complicated by the fact that it was often difficult to obtain accurate biological demographic descriptors.

When elected officials such as coroners retire or fail to be reelected, they commonly remove not only such remains but also the associated case files. These practices add to the difficulty of obtaining biological descriptors for UHR and, despite the beginnings of significant funding allocations to MP/UD programs in 2004, are still obstructing the resolution of many cases.

Even when remains have been kept in state custody, identification may be next to impossible. One example involves the efforts of the North Carolina Medical Examiners' Office to identify the remains of 115 people found dead in the state since 1975; these remains, which are stacked on metal shelves, are either skeletal or in the form of "ashes." Intact but unidentified bodies are

---

[*] *Ibid.*
[†] U.S. Department of Justice. June 2007. *Medical Examiners and Coroners' Offices, 2004.* Office of Justice Programs, Bureau of Justice Statistics. NCJ 216756, p. 1–8.
[‡] *Ibid.*

kept for a month and then cremated;* the ashes are scattered in the Atlantic Ocean. Legacy technology has been of no use in resolving these cases, and limited funding, personnel, and facilities preclude the use of advanced technologies such as NGS, and stable isotope analysis. These new technologies, which are being more widely utilized across the country, may never be available in North Carolina.

According to *Missing Persons and Unidentified Remains: The Nation's Silent Mass Disaster*, a report produced in 2007 by the NIJ, 40,000 sets of UHR that could not be identified by conventional means (examples: Figures 3.1 through 3.3) were being held in the evidence rooms of ME and other medicolegal authorities.[†] However, vital information was missing from this report, such as how long these remains had been stored; in addition, statistics about these remains seem to have been gathered from a variety of sources. As a result, some of them were confusing or even conflicting. In reality it is not possible to accurately quantify the total number of UHR in the United States because (as the 2004 NAME report discussed) the system is plagued by fragmentation, inconsistent reporting, and wide discretionary powers in terms of reporting, investigating, and case tracking.

Inconsistent statistical information, even though its presentation may appear to be clear and concise, adds not only to the complexity of conducting MP/UD investigations but also to the frustration of families and the lack of accountability among investigating entities. An NIJ publication might state that "On any given day, there are as many as 100,000 active missing person cases in the United States,"[‡] but will not interpret the meaning of this number or explain the context in which such numerical values are used. In fact, 100,000 MP is a dynamic value because it changes according to the frequency of entries and removals of cases from the NCIC. Moreover, a significant portion of NCIC entries are cases of repeat runaways and their returns, cases that are not removed (deleted, cleared) after resolution, cases that are cleared when a juvenile reaches his or her majority but are not reentered in the category of emancipated juveniles, and cases that require validation but have not been validated (which are deleted as a result, even though they have not been cleared). When trying to interpret the meaning of any such numbers, it is necessary to consider both their context and relevance. Otherwise, families may experience unrealistic optimism or unnecessary despair.

---

* Wral.com. 2007. *'They're Like Puzzles:' Inside NC's Effort to Identify Nameless Dead.* http://www.wral.com/-they-re-like-puzzles-inside-nc-s-effort-to-identify-nameless-dead/12916155/. October 7.

† Ritter, N. 2007. *Missing Persons and Unidentified Remains: The Nation's Silent Mass Disaster.* U.S. Department of Justice, Office of Justice Programs, National Institute of Justice. *NIJ Journal* No. 256, JR216522.

‡ *Ibid.*

The unfortunate fact is that, at this time, there is no reliable way to assess the resolution (clearance) rate of UHR cases in the United States Estimates of the total number of such cases are subject to speculation and confusion, as are the rates themselves. We do know, however, that a large number of resolved cases involve decedents who had been at high risk for homicide. Therefore, homicide clearance rates—although they are very imperfect indicators—may be most reliable indicators of resolution rates in UHR investigations.

Between 2006 and 2010, homicide clearance rates in the United States consistently averaged in the 60% range.[*] By contrast, in 2014 NamUs reported a UP closed case rate of 12.86%.[†] As previously discussed, this discrepancy is the result of inconsistent reporting requirements, timelines that vary widely from case to case, and the fact that homicide investigative information and data are derived from investigators' accounts. By contrast, UD and UHR cases span years to decades with limited control by investigators, and difficulties with data verification are compounded by the inability to interview subject matter experts who provided opinions in the original investigations. In addition, even when causative factors are determined in long-term unresolved cases, these breakthroughs cannot be of value to other cases unless the concerned parties are immediately debriefed. In most cases, the best that can be hoped for is the revision or clearance of reports in various systems and databases.

Although the U.S. criminal justice system is composed of rules, policies, and protocols, the tremendous variation in the circumstances of criminal cases has caused a great deal of flexibility (i.e., discretion) to be built into the system. Accordingly, investigators and families must also be flexible by embracing investigative logic based on the real factors of investigations. But investigators and families must also vigilantly guard investigations against unthinking habits, outdated routines, customary ways of thinking and behaving, and that formidable nemesis of change, the status quo.[‡]

In developing effective UP investigative strategies, reliance on unsound arguments is mitigated by critical thinking. For the purposes of this book, critical thinking refers to investigators' self-directed, self-focused criticism and to their purposeful analysis, questioning, and verification of all data, opinions, and evidence.

In the introduction to this book, the definition of "sentinel event" was given as a significant, unexpected negative outcome. NIJ's Doyle, however, specified that a sentinel event is "a cold case that stayed cold too long [and]

---

[*] FBI's *Crime in the United States: Percent of Offenses Cleared by Arrest or Exceptional Means.* 2006–2010.
[†] *Unidentified Persons Database: UP Case Breakdown.* August 15, 2014. http://www.namus.gov.
[‡] Thayer, L. 2010. *Leaders and Leadership: Searching for Wisdom in All the Right Places.* E-book, pp. 714–716.

signals a possible weakness in the system or process."* In order to avoid this type of sentinel event, I agree with Rossmo that investigators must "[c]onduct routine systematic debriefings after major crime investigations [and] organize a full-scale 'autopsy' after an investigative failure [sentinel event]."† As previously explained, the reasons for investigative failures cannot always be found. Nor is it necessary to find them in all cases. The point is that all UHR investigations, whether or not they are successful, should be followed up with critical analysis and other measures that prevent sentinel events.

Key point: Through the debriefing process, investigators and learners (e.g., families) build their own knowledge bases and use them to develop effective strategies for resolving cases. Law enforcement personnel (and others) refer to this process as "constructivism."

Chapter 2 contained a brief explanation of the importance of context in UHR investigations. Context, which can also be thought of as the surrounding environment, includes a wide range of information that is relevant not only to a specific case but also to such investigations in general. Of course, awareness of context is crucial to the UP critical thinking process. For the purposes of constructing a critical approach to UHR investigations, illustrations of context will be taken from the state of California.

California is a good example of the reality of MP searches because it is the most populous state; according to the U.S. Census Bureau, in 2010 it had 38 million residents and comprised just under 12% of the U.S. population. It was the first state to pass laws that address the collection of DNA in MP/ UP cases; this has served as model legislation for implementation by other states. It is also the state that probably keeps the most detailed records about MP/UP and UHR cases.

According to the Director of Missing Persons DNA Program at California's Department of Justice, "There have been about 3000 long-term missing persons reported in California since 1972";‡ approximately 100 decedents cannot be identified each year in California; and a total of 2100 UHR cases dating back to 1959 have been reported. An expansion of these figures (which were published prior to the survey sponsored by the NIJ in 2004) as

---

* Doyle, J.M. March 21, 2014. *NIJ's Sentinel Events Initiative: Looking Back to Look Forward. NIJ Journal* No. 273.
† Rossmo, D.K. 2005. *Criminal Investigative Failures.* San Antonio, TX: Texas State University, p. 17.
‡ Applied Biosystems. 2003. California missing persons DNA program challenged with identifying thousands of human remains. *Applied Biosystems.* http://tools.thermofisher. com/content/sfs/brochures/cms_040170.pdf, p. 3. (Accessed September 5, 2015).

a generalization (i.e., not derived from a random sampling) of the MP environment, indicates that the annual number of UHR cases in California may range from 833 to 1000. To derive this range, one statement has been taken from a credible source (the 2004 NIJ survey of ME/C offices) and compared to statements from another credible source (the Director of Missing Persons DNA Program with the California Department of Justice). If necessary, the statements were evaluated in terms of national census data.

Here is how the calculation above was rendered, with the caveat that the goal was not to reach a definitive number but rather to increase general understanding of UP/UHR context. First, two reputable sources of data were consulted (the California DOJ and the NIJ). When the national census information about California's share of the total U.S. population (12%) is taken into account, we find that the 2100 sets of UHR reported in California since 1959 equal a national estimate of 17,500. According to the 2004 NIJ special report,* which did not need to be evaluated in terms of the national census, approximately 1000 UP nationwide are not identified within 12 months. Of this number, 600 are given final disposition (e.g., burial, cremation, or other means), which leaves an annual nationwide total of 400 sets of UHR. Therefore, between 1960 and 2004, approximately 17,600 sets of long-term UHR have accumulated nationwide.

This number is almost equal to the national projection of 17,500 based on the California DOJ figures, and is not much higher than the number of 14,000 calculated by the UNT Center for Human Identification.[†] It is also roughly comparable to the total of 11,233 UP published in August 2014 on the NamUs UP website[24] (https://identifyus.org/en) under "UP Case Breakdown." But all three figures (17,600; 14,000; and 11,233) are so much lower than the estimate of 40,000 UP sets of human remains that are supposedly being stored in ME evidence rooms throughout the United States[24] that we may conclude the figure of 40,000 is quite inaccurate.

At first glance, with no context for these numbers, they seem so daunting that they are likely to foment complacency, bias, and hopelessness among families, investigators, and subject matter experts. Further avoidance of contextual disclosures surrounding UD/UHR investigations fail to identify the major errors impacting the resolution of UD/UHR cold cases numbers. Through my experience of deconstructing cold hit resolutions, a significant level of error was observed in reported race and sex descriptors of the UD/UHR when compared to MP in life (Figure 3.4). Evaluating these figures by comparing them to other statistical sources is therefore essential, because doing so reveals how the lack of context may be misleading and thus function

---

* Bureau of Justice Statistics, U.S. Department of Justice, Office of Justice Programs. June 2007. *Special Report: Medical Examiners and Coroners' Offices*, 2004. NCJ 216756.
† UNT Health Science Center. September 13, 2013. *DNA Identification Facts*. http://web.unthsc.edu/info/20039/press_kits/17/dna_identification_facts (Accessed August 18, 2014).

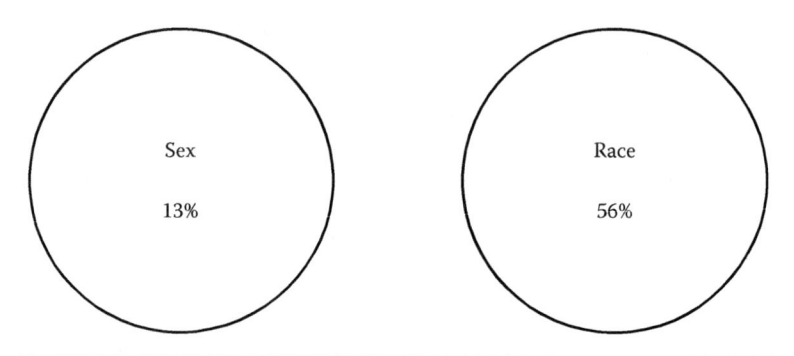

Notes on the 48 cases reviewed

1. An accurate association required the descriptors to be exact with the following exceptions:
   a. African American = Black
   b. Caucasian = White
   c. Hispanic = Latino
2. Unknown was considered as inaccurate, unable to classify thus inaccurate.
3. Admixtures between both missing person and unidentified had to match exactly.
4. Classification which were confusing and could be considered as several different classifications were considered as inaccurate.
5. Classifications were considered from the point-of-view of a recently assigned law enforcement officer or normal family member for whom this manuscript was developed.

Figure 3.4 Biological demographic inaccuracies in UHR investigations for sexing and race.

as a basis for erroneous beliefs.[*] Large numbers of events presented to families and investigators are really meaningless without the understanding of context surrounding the development and presentation of the numbers. The relevancy and reliability of large numbers for the listener's purposes are impossible without understanding the context, such as time span and categories. Tables 3.2 through 3.5 are presented to provide a feeling of context surrounding the large number of missing persons often espoused to support an agenda or cause that are not relevant to a unique individual case. Such large numbers may have a tendency to discourage families and investigators—as the "haystack" appears too large to find that one needle. In UD/URH investigations, investigators must remember that each case is a unique event separate from the "haystack" that is made up of mostly reported missing persons who are not deceased and may be voluntarily missing.

[*] Gilovbich, T. 1991. *How We Know What Isn't So: The Fallibility of Human Reason in Everyday Life.* New York, NY: The Free Press a Division of Simon & Schuster Inc., E-book, p. 90.

Table 3.2   California Adult Missing Persons 2011[a]

Category	Category Amount	Total Amount
Total all categories		32,711
Returned	16,694	
Located	10,502	
Voluntary missing	1350	
Invalid	321	
Emancipated	1	
Arrested	977	
Canceled—other	2488	
Canceled—unknown	38	
Found live	32,371	
Found deceased	340	
Balance		0

[a] California Department of Justice. http://oag.ca.gov/sites/all/files/agweb/pdfs/missing/adults/adults_11-13_status.pdf? (Accessed December 19, 2014).

National reports may be equally misleading if taken out of context. For example, in 2007 an NIJ report stated that "On any given day, there are as many as 100,000 active missing person cases... Viewed over a 20-year period, the number of missing persons can be estimated in the hundreds of thousands."[*] In Connecticut, the Office of the Victim Advocate proclaimed in

Table 3.3   California Adult Missing Persons 2013[a]

Category	Category Amount	Total Amount
Total all categories		36,372
Returned	17,104	
Located	12,171	
Voluntary missing	1601	
Invalid	354	
Emancipated	1	
Arrested	1141	
Canceled—other	3489	
Canceled—unknown	52	
Found live	35,913	
Found deceased	459	
Balance		0

[a] California Department of Justice. http://oag.ca.gov/sites/all/files/agweb/pdfs/missing/adults/adults_11-13_status.pdf? (Accessed December 19, 2014).

[*] Office of Justice Programs, National Institute of Justice. January 2007. *Missing Persons and Unidentified Remains: The Nation's Silent Mass Disaster. NIJ Journal* No. 256.

Table 3.4   California Missing Children Reports 2011[a]

Category	Category Amount	Total Amount
Total all categories		88,648
Returned	63,346	
Located	17,840	
Voluntary missing	104	
Invalid	496	
Emancipated	72	
Arrested	2467	
Canceled—other	4167	
Canceled—unknown	120	
Found live	88,612	
Found deceased	36	
Balance		0

[a] California Department of Justice. http://oag.ca.gov/sites/all/files/agweb/pdfs/missing/children/children_11-13_status.pdf? (Accessed December 19, 2014).

2014 that "Every day, 2300 people are reported missing in the United States. That's one person every 30 s. Of the 900,000 people reported missing each year in the United States, 50,000 are above the age of 18."[*] The harm caused by such scare stories, which are typical, does not stop with families, investigators, forensic matter experts, or the MP/UP themselves. These distortions

Table 3.5   California Missing Children Reports 2013[a]

Category	Category Amount	Total Amount
Total all categories		80,918
Returned	55,402	
Located	17,513	
Voluntary missing	140	
Invalid	549	
Emancipated	127	
Arrested	2622	
Canceled—other	4403	
Canceled—unknown	115	
Found live	80,871	
Found deceased	47	
Balance		0

[a] California Department of Justice. http://oag.ca.gov/sites/all/files/agweb/pdfs/missing/children/children_11-13_status.pdf? (Accessed December 19, 2014).

[*] The Office of The Victim Advocate (CT). 2014. *The State of Connecticut: Time is of the Essence!* http://www.ct.gov/ova/lib/ova/OVA_Missing_Persons_Brochure.pdf.

find their way into public perception through the media, and even into proposed federal legislation. Moreover, MP/UP figures that have not been transparently calculated or confirmed by multiple sources can be used to support agendas that do not help UHR investigations to be conducted more efficiently or effectively.

The subject of child abductions also well illustrates the conflict between public perception and actual numbers, as well as the importance of context. As with MP/UP reports in which the tendency is to publish large numbers of MP as well as large numbers of UHR—a practice that causes the public to equate the two types of cases—the public tends to assume that large numbers of missing children (presented out of context) must mean that there are also large numbers of unidentified deceased children. This perception, however, is quite false. In 2003, the director of the Missing Persons DNA Program (a department within the California DOJ) reported only 3000 long-term MP cases for the entire state*—which has, as stated above, a total population of more than 38 million. Similarly, a 2009 OIG reported the results of a federal study that found 99.8% of children reported missing nationwide were located or returned home alive (the other 0.2% did not return home or were never found).

A fact largely unknown to the American public is that most missing children reports involve runaways from juvenile detention centers. Many of these runaways flee again at the first opportunity after their return. Although many such runaways (especially teens) end up in the sex trade, as the findings in the previous paragraph demonstrate, the per capita rates of both child abductions and murders in the United States are low.[†]

The OIG findings support the 2003 statements of the Director of Missing Persons DNA Program with the California Department of Justice. Additional confirmation comes from the California Attorney General's Office; in 2013 and 2011 reports indicate 0.06% of 80,918 and 0.04% of 88,918 total.

Cases of missing children are similar to adult cases, although most jurisdictions require missing children to be entered immediately into NCIC. Nearly every state has passed MP legislation that places adult MP cases on par with juvenile cases, in accordance with federal statutes, by eliminating the traditional waiting periods before a report can be filed. In fact, NCIC entry may be required immediately or in as short a time as 2 hours. Nationally, USC Title 42, Section 5780, specifies that "states reporting under this title shall (1) ensure that no law enforcement agency within the state establishes or maintains any policy that requires the observance of any waiting period

[*] Applied Biosystems. 2003. California missing persons DNA program challenged with identifying thousands of human remains. *Applied Biosystems.*
[†] Office of the Inspector General. January 2009. *Audit Report 09-08: The Federal Bureau of Investigation's Effort to Combat Crimes against Children.* http://www.justice.gov/oig/reports/FBI/a0908/chapter3.htm.

before accepting a missing child or unidentified person report." Section 5779 states that "In general, each federal, state, and local law enforcement agency shall report each case of a missing child under the age of 21 to the National Crime Information Center of the Department of Justice."[*]

As previously stated, the numbers of missing person cases reported to NCIC are dynamic; that is, cases are constantly being entered and cleared. One week there may be 100,000 MP/UP cases (the stereotypical number that appears the media) but another week that number could be much higher or lower. The point, also as previously stated, is that the vast majority of reported MP cases do not turn out to be long-term or to involve high-risk individuals. In addition, a high percentage of the touted missing person numbers that have been in the system for a year or longer may include reports that were not cleared from NCIC even though the cases were resolved.

The context of MP/UP and UHR cases, which involves varying rules, procedures, discretion, and other factors, means that investigators must comb through haystacks of reports and other data that have been compiled by others, change by the day, and are subject to errors that may be difficult if not impossible to discern. Some of these errors are listed below.

- No MP report was ever made. This usually applies to runaways, MPs from dysfunctional families, foreign nationals, and convicted offenders.
- An MP report was not validated by state authorities, so the NCIC record is deleted.
- An MP report was not accompanied by proper documentation during an audit, so the NCIC record is deleted.
- An MP report has been removed because its status with the original complainant cannot be verified within a particular time period.
- An original MP report, for a juvenile, was deleted but not reentered when the juvenile reached his or her majority. This problem has supposedly been corrected in most states.
- An MP report was not deleted after the subject was located.
- An MP report remains active because the MP is a frequent runaway.

These problems affect juvenile as well as adult cases; in addition, if they have manifested in a juvenile case, they may continue when that juvenile ages into adulthood. However, all of them can be addressed by effectively designed investigative strategies, particularly if investigators and families accept that bureaucratic rules, policies, and procedures may not be reflected in actual practice. At this time, UHR investigations are all too likely to be

---

[*] *Federal Register.* U.S.C. Title 42 Section 5779–5780.

caught in a paradox: The numbers of MP cases are routinely overstated, but many MP cases are never successfully reported.

Another problem for investigators is that most MP are alive and have gone missing voluntarily. Although their families, friends, and associates may be worried, may be eager for police to take action, and may become very angry if police do not do so, calling attention to a live person who seems to be missing but is in fact only hiding may place his or her life at risk. An abuser or trafficker may even arrange for an MP case to be filed in order to enlist the police find a victim or force a victim to return.

My years of investigating complex financial frauds and then deconstructing cold hit associations have taught me that failures are caused by anomalies (in the form of data errors or discrepancies among data), and that locating these anomalies is absolutely essential. However, investigators must be aware that the direction of the investigation, rather than the anomaly, may be the actual problem. Because the vast majority of anomalies in MP/UP and UHR cases involve human error, opinions must be suspect—especially our own.

Key point: *"Nothing exists except atoms and empty space; everything else is human opinion."* (Democritus of Abdera).[*]

When a sentinel event is recognized in a UHR investigation, however, it is not enough to go through the process of acquiring the knowledge that is needed to learn how human failures contributed to creating it. Instead, thorough deconstructing or debriefing must be done immediately, and must also be done after each case is closed. As John Dewey (1933–1998) stated: "If you have doubts about how learning happens, engage in sustained inquiry: Study, ponder, consider alternative possibilities and arrive at your belief grounded in evidence."[†]

[*] Lederman, L.M. 2013. *The Beginning....* American Physical Society. http://www.physics central.com.
[†] UCD Dublin. 2014. *Educational Theory: Constructivism and Social Constructivism.* Open Educational Resources of UCD Teaching and Learning, University College Dublin. http://www.ucdoer.ie/index.php/Education_Theory/Constructivism_and_Social_ Constructivism.

Resources, Strategies, and Disconnects

Facts are stubborn things; and whatever may be our wishes, our inclinations, or the dictates of our passion, they cannot alter the state of the facts and the evidence.[*]

John Adams (1735–1826)

In September 2014, the National Institute of Justice released a special report, *Mission Justice: Sentinel Event Reviews*. Its opening paragraph states that

> Confidence in our nation's criminal justice system rests on several core beliefs: First, that most justice work is routine, following a fairly prescribed path that renders error a rarity. Second, that in the rare instance when a mistake does occur, it is typically a clear case of negligence or misconduct, and "the system" readily detects and fixes it through its many separate (and characteristically adversarial) components, which "backstop" each other. Finally, when an error occurs, we believe that there are processes in place to make sure that type of error will never happen again. The problem is that these beliefs may be largely unfounded.[†]

As previously stated, my intent in writing this book is to share knowledge and provide guidance that will help to ameliorate the harm of these errors in MP/UP and UHR investigations. Therefore, the subjects discussed herein are applicable to general criminal investigations as well and can be applied by law enforcement, families, advocates, and the general public. My observations, which are based on both research and experience, and the cases I discuss, are meant to help law enforcement construct effective strategies to improve investigations, regardless of the circumstances. It is my hope that readers of this book, whether they are law enforcement professionals, families of missing persons, students, or members of the general public, will be encouraged to engage in a constructive learning process that focuses on collaborative

---

[*] John Adams Historical Society. 1770. *Argument in Defense of the British Massacre Trials.* John Adams Historical Society. http://www.john-adamns-heritage.com/quotes/.
[†] Holder, E.H., Mason, K.V., Sabol, W.J. 2014. *Mending Justice: Sentinel Event Reviews.* U.S. Department of Justice, Office of Justice Programs, National Institute of Justice. p. 1.

efforts to resolve MP/UP and UHR cases. As each case is unique, so must be the investigation strategy.

DNA analysis, the subject of Chapter 4, is of particular importance to police; in the twenty-first century, it should be a cornerstone topic of their educational programs. To do the best job, criminal investigators should not only provide proof that can be used to hold offenders accountable but do so in a manner that protects the rights of all individuals and avoids liability risks for themselves and the communities they serve. The information in this chapter comprises basic working knowledge of DNA reporting results, advice about when to seek an expert's opinion about interpretation of results and how to recognize the limitations of an expert's opinion, and warnings about the importance of privacy and confidentiality when handling DNA. In particular, entities that use professional health care providers for DNA and dental analysis should be sure that their agencies' policies, procedures, and general orders ameliorate liability risks for the investigators and their agencies and mandate compliance with all legal requirements, so that evidence and follow-up results may be used in investigations.

In the real world of investigative design, long-held beliefs must be challenged and even deconstructed. One can never rely upon the status quo, solid as it may seem, or dismiss new approaches out of hand. This conclusion becomes painfully obvious when one considers the difference between the reported clearance rates for homicides, which are in the 60% range, and the clearance rates reported for UHR cases by NamUs, which are approximately 25% for NamUs-aided resolutions and 13% for closed UHR cases registered with NamUs.[*]

In the 1990s, when I worked for Mobil Corporation, I developed a multi-phase process to understand and identify irregularities (fraud) in retail operations; this logical investigative process is very applicable to the design of effective MP/UP and UHR investigative strategies. Resources were extremely limited at that time for Mobil retail operations; retail units were scattered across the United States; audits were failing to discover irregularities; and a new electronic reporting system had just been installed. In addition, systems developers and senior management lacked sufficient retail experience to understand the operational environment. Now, it may seem as if the criminal justice system and the corporate environment are totally unrelated—but they are not. The same developmental logic can be used in both, because the same construction methods (actual learned experiences) and expansion approach (local to regional to national) can be applied.

At first, the idea that centralized national management is the most inclusive and efficacious way to improve results may sound plausible and

---

[*] National Missing and Unidentified System. 2014. https://identifyus.org/en.

appealing. This was the situation with Mobil. However, in practice, the opposite may be true—as Mobil and criminal justice agencies alike have discovered. Corporations with successful operations focus on customer service as the points of both service and sale, because their supposed reason for existence is to serve customers without trying to push their own agendas about what customers need, or to assume that they know customers' needs better than they do. In the same way, criminal justice agencies cannot assume to know the facts of a particular investigation or assume that handling an investigation according to the status quo is the best approach for every family that is missing a loved one. Although insensitivity toward families is not illegal, court judgments are frequent against criminal justice agencies that assume facts rather than critically questioning evidence.

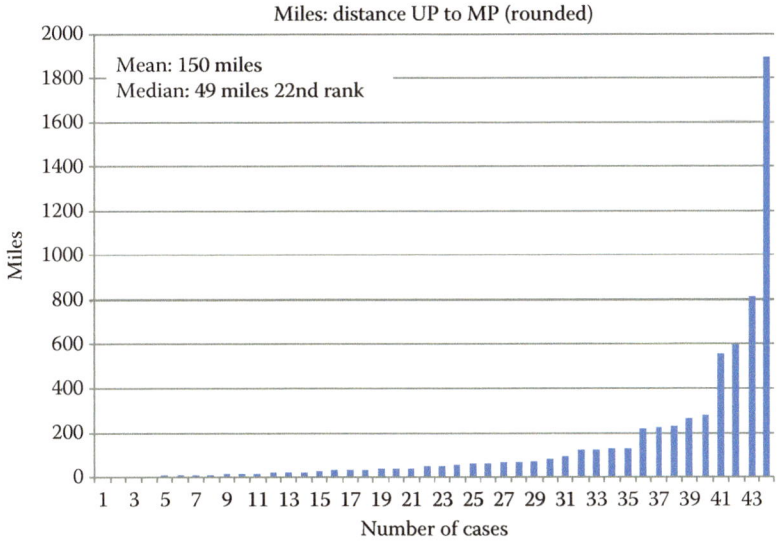

Distances between locations where MPs were last reported alive and locations where UD/UHR were found, based on 44 cold-hit case reviews.

The developers of the combined DNA index system (CODIS) designed it to first conduct local (LDIS) searches, then state (SDIS) searches, and finally national (NDIS) searches. It is my observation and opinion that approximately 80% of cold hit identifications of UD/UHR investigations are affected at the local or LDIS level. Such national programs and resources are made to address needs at the farthest distance from individual crime scenes; local resources and programs have the most impact near the incidents; and state programs and resources provide linkage between the two.

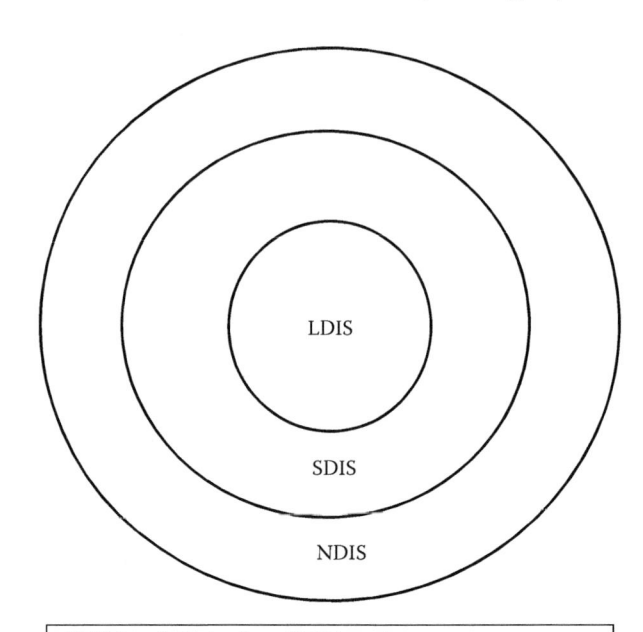

LDIS (local): Uploads to SDIS (state)
SDIS: Uploads to NDIS (national)
LDIS lab cannot search another LDIS lab, LDIS can only
search internally or upload to SDIS

CODIS searching order.

Tools to help investigators challenge the status quo in UHR case investigations were not available until DNA testing improved drastically in 2004–2005, as a result of the findings in *People v. Castro* (1989) that DNA could be used for exclusions and required extensive discovery requirements, and that pretrial hearings would be required to determine if laboratories' methodologies were in conformance with scientific standards.[*] Before these findings, as previously mentioned, DNA evidence had mostly gone unchallenged; afterward, DNA testing rapidly progressed and moved from the realm of soft science (i.e., opinion based) to the realm of hard science (i.e., supported by facts and verified statistical probabilities). As a result, the dangers of relying on the results of soft forensic research, which "have little or no basis in actual science,"[†] have steadily decreased.

---

[*] Connors, E., Lundregan, T., Miller, N., McEwen, T. 1996. *Convicted by Juries, Exonerated by Science: Case Studies in the Use of DNA to Establish Innocence after Trial.* U.S. Department of Justice, Office of Justice Programs, National Institute of Justice. p. 5.
[†] Saks, M.J., Faigman, D.L. 2008. Failed forensics: How forensic science lost its way and how it might yet find it. *Annual Review of Law and Social Science* 4, pp. 149–171.

The August 2009 report by the National Academy of Sciences succinctly stated the problem, and its solution: "With the exception of nuclear DNA analysis...no forensic method has been rigorously shown to have the capacity to consistently, and with a high degree of certainty, demonstrate a connection between evidence and a specific individual or source."[*] According to the NAS, the "simple reality" is that discrepancies exist within and between various forensic disciplines related to evidentiary interpretation, and that scientific studies may flatly disprove the validity of those interpretations.[†] Nonetheless, despite the honesty involved in pointing out these problems in the forensic science and technology environment, those whose reputations may be at risk may passionately defend their agendas and opinions, along with the status quo. The question, for investigators, then becomes one of designing effective strategies under such conditions.

Investigators can undertake the design process in four phases: (1) identifying the subject, (2) recognizing the environment, (3) selecting strategies and tools, and (4) execution of the design. I have developed and extensively tested this process with Mobil Corporation and AMF Bowling Worldwide; in both circumstances, as in my experience as a law enforcement professional, these steps have proven to be flexible and effective.

Here, subject refers to the case. As much as possible, the investigator's focus should be free of bias and centered on the subject or event. Environment refers to everything about the surroundings, physical and nonphysical, that influence the case investigations. Conceptual knowledge of each of the forensic science fields is necessary to design and adjust an effective investigative strategy; at this time, in-depth knowledge is difficult to sustain because the development of forensic science is accelerating at such a rapid pace. Advances in rapid DNA technology (hands-free analysis) and next-generation sequencing (NGS) is moving rapidly to upgrade legacy DNA technology that currently dominates MP/UD/UHR investigations.

Strategy design/tool selection refers to choosing among the available tools, systems, databases, and subject matter experts. Execution/resolution refers to the application of the selected tools and resources. Investigators must be flexible enough to change strategies as new circumstances become known. There is no such thing as a one-stop resource or single strategy in MP/UP and UHR investigations.

---

[*] Committee on Identifying the Needs of the Forensic Sciences Community, National Research Council. 2009. *Strengthening Forensic Science in the United States: A Path Forward*. Washington, DC: The National Academy Press, p. 7.
[†] *Ibid*. p. 8.

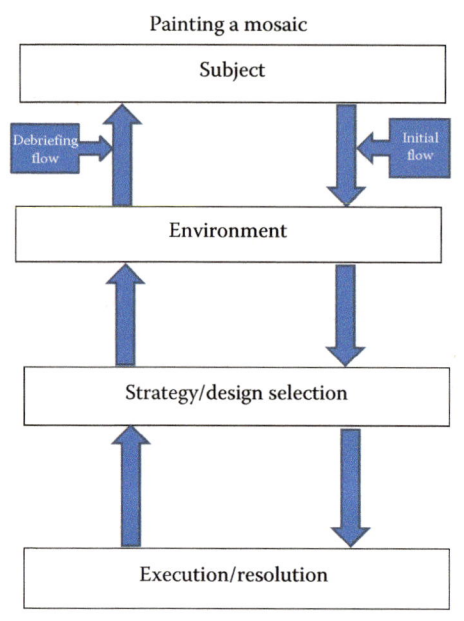

Four phases of the investigative process.

Finding resolution in terms of identifying a victim, however, does not mean that an investigation has come to an end. Debriefing/deconstruction must be undertaken so that errors can be located that may improve future investigations. This approach, known as constructivism, involves teaching ourselves based on our actual experiences.

DNA

4

Practitioners in an adversarial system that probes, refutes, and defends do not, in general, concede fault readily. Yet we are missing a chance to improve outcomes if we ignore the opportunity for growth that an honest assessment of error provides. Some errors are the result of careless omission or even willful commission by a single individual or group. In those cases, the ones responsible should be held accountable. But other mistakes stem from decisions that were well intentioned, were consistent with customary practice, and seemed sound at the time. The problems that arise could have been avoided had the system been better equipped with safeguards... If we truly hope to get to the bottom of errors and reduce the chances of repeating them, then it is time we explore a new system-wide way of responding, not by pointing fingers, but by forthrightly assessing our processes, looking for weaknesses in our methods, and redesigning our approach so that the truth will be more attainable.[*]

Eric H. Holder, Jr.

DNA (deoxyrbonucleic acid) is one of the most widely sought sources of evidence in UHR investigations, yet obtaining and comparing DNA profiles may be among the least understood research procedures. The accuracy of DNA identification in UHR investigations is heavily dependent upon the capabilities and policies of the analyzing laboratory and its status (local, state, national, or private), differences among search protocols, frequent changes to search protocols, the influence of historical practices, and differences and advances in the actual procedures of obtaining and comparing DNA profiles. In the United States, DNA analysis for the purposes of law enforcement is conducted at approximately 190 public CODIS laboratories, but analysis can also be done at private facilities. Searches are also conducted at these laboratories.

All living organisms contain DNA. The following descriptions and explanations of human DNA are not meant to be exhaustive. For fuller details, many of which are important but not immediately relevant here, readers are encouraged to consult reference works in the subject areas of anatomy, botany, genetics, physiology, zoology, etc. These can be found in bookstores and libraries, or in online resources such as the National Institute of Health's Genetic Home Reference Handbook (http://ghr.nlm.nih.gov/handbook/illustrations/chromosomallocation), the National Human Genome Research Institute's

---

[*] Holder, E.H., Sabol, J.S. September 2014. *Mending Justice: Sentinel Event Reviews*. National Institute of Justice. *NIJ* 247141. p. 1.

website (http://www.genome.gov/Glossary/), and NIJ's DNA for the Defense Bar publication (https://www.ncjrs.gov/pdffiles1/nij/237975.pdf).

DNA manifests in strands or chains within the nuclei of cells. Individual DNA strands, called chromatids, connect in pairs that cross each other in an X shape; the connector between them is called a centromere and the entire X shape is called a chromosome. The general biological instructions that dictate basic traits, known as heredity, are contained in sections of DNA along each chromatid; these are called genes and their instructions are often referred to as genetic codes. The particular, specific biological instructions that make each organism different from every other, known as hereditary variation, are contained in alternate gene forms called alleles. Most alleles develop naturally and spontaneously, but genetic mutations of alleles may occur as a result of exposure to certain chemicals, radiation, or errors in replicating DNA within the body as part of the normal biological process. Alleles (frequen cies) are the preferred genetic material in forensic DNA testing at this time and stage of technological development.

DNA is present in the nuclei of all human cells, with two exceptions. One is red blood cells, which have no nuclei; however, blood samples are preferred for DNA analysis due to sufficient number of other cells in the blood and ease of DNA extraction. The other exception is hair shafts, whose nuclei are populated with mtDNA (mitochondrial DNA) but whose roots (follicles) contain limited amounts of viable nuclear DNA. Therefore, any hair submitted for nuclear DNA testing must contain one or more shafts that are attached to the root(s). Hair shafts without roots can only be tested for mtDNA. While hair may often be the easiest to acquire, it should probably be the last in line as a source of viable DNA analysis, depending on the contextual circumstances surrounding the case. It is probably more common than not that a DNA lab will not accept hair for DNA analysis without a certified hair examiner's report that the hair is human in origin. I have found from experience that often times it is difficult to find a certified hair examiner. Many investigators strive to find alternate sources, other than hair, for DNA testing material due to the nature and history of hair analysis by top certified hair examiners. In April 2015, newspapers around the world carried a headline similar to the following: "FBI admits that ALL its forensic experts exaggerated hair evidence at every criminal trial for nearly 20 years." The stories go on to state that reviews of 268 trials suggest 95 per cent may have been affected."[†]

---

* Robinson, W., 2015. FBI Admits That ALL Its Forensic Experts Exaggerated Hair Evidence at Every Criminal Trial for Nearly 20 Years. Dailymail http://www.dailymail.co.uk/news/article-3045293/FBI-Justice-Department-admit-forensic-experts-gave-flawed-evidence-nearly-criminal-trials-20-years.html (Accessed August 15, 2015).
† Ibid.

In order to help understand forensic DNA applications, we need to first cover some basic concepts. The goal is to provide the nongeneticist with a common base of knowledge in order that a meaningful discussion may take place with DNA labs and to understand DNA association and match reports. There are many variations and infrequent occurrences that happen because of the genetic makeup of an individual or chemicals during the typing process that only a highly skilled analyst may explain. However, any unusual finding or occurrence experienced during the DNA typing process should be fully disclosed in any forensic DNA association or match report.

Human body cells contain 46 chromosomes: 22 pair of autosomal chromosomes (autosome refers to other than sex chromosomes), and 1 pair of sex chromosomes (occasionally referred to as allosomes or allosomal). Each of the autosomal chromosomes is made up of two chromatids (a chromatid is either of two strands—each containing the double helix of DNA—formed when a chromosome duplicates itself as part of the early stages of cell division) that are joined together by a centromere (see Figure 4.1). The customary terms "autosomal DNA," "nuclear DNA" (nDNA), and "STR" are a reflection of this circumstance. During reproduction, the nuclei of the egg and sperm fuse together. As a result of the fusing process during reproduction, each parent contributes half of its DNA to the offspring, and it is the same for multiple births (twins, triplets, etc.). At this time, it is not possible to determine which allele frequency from the DNA typing process is from the father

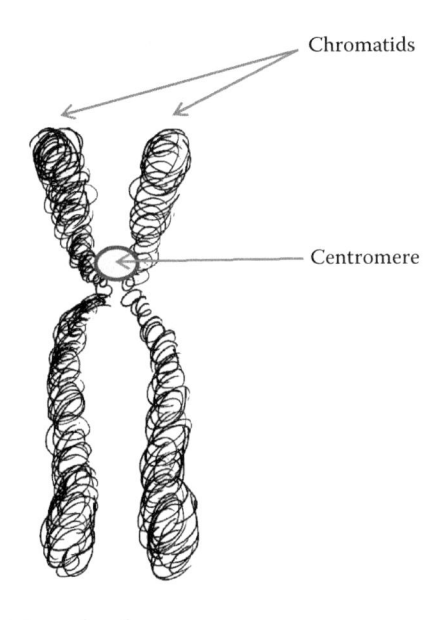

Figure 4.1 Composition of a chromosome.

or the mother. During the reproduction process, the male's mitochondrial DNA (mtDNA) from the sperm is not passed along to the offspring—only the female's mtDNA survives in both the male and female offspring.

Each chromatid in a pair is an approximate mirror image of the other—a matched set for all practical purposes. So every particular point on a chromosome (called a locus; the plural is loci) and every discrete section of DNA in a chromosome, actually appears twice—once on each chromatid. Each locus in a chromosome has been assigned a specific name by geneticists (TPOX, TH01, FGA, etc.).

The DNA sequences within the alleles at a particular locus on each chromosome, which appear in matching sections on each chromatid in a pair, are repetitive. The numbers of repetitions are highly variable, so the general term for them is variable number tandem repeats (VNTR—which you will seldom hear in forensic conversations); however, in the criminal justice environment, the common vernacular used is STR (short tandem repeat) for the loci of interest. STRs are individually distinguished in the DNA process by length. Short means that the locus takes up a minute portion of the length of a chromosome; tandem means that the sequence involves repetitions of various sequential patterns of specific combinations of pairs of four protein molecules; and repeat means that the sequence occurs more than once. The number of times a sequence appears is known as its frequency.

This repetitive quality of DNA sequences is the foundation of DNA profiling, because a number of alleles appear the same at the same loci in people who are closely related (e.g., a mother's allele sequence will be the same at one of the two alleles at all loci with the exception of one or, rarely, two possible mutations when compared to the mother's offspring)—and, of course, allele frequencies at all loci will be identical when samples originate from the same person.

Alleles, the so called sub-units of DNA that are examined at certain loci, are used to create STR DNA profiles. Alleles are made up of four protein molecules that join in specific paired combination of sequences that are repeated in a wide variety of sequential patterns relative to each locus. These combination molecules, called nucleotides, are composed of amino acid molecules that can only bind together with its specific partner molecule. The amino acids are adenine (A), thymine (T), guanine (G), and cytosine (C). A and T cannot directly bond with G or C.

An STR is described by the composition of its nucleotides; for example, ATGC means that one of the nucleotides is composed in order of AT (adenine + thymine), TA (thymine + adenine), GC (guanine + cytosine) and CG (cytosine + guanine). Or, it could be described in any number of combinations as AAGC, TTGC, ATGG, TTCC, ATAT, CGCG, etc. depending on the situation. (The example is for instructional purposes only, not to be considered as actual examples of any particular loci.) Each allele contains an orderly pattern of repeated combinations. The frequency of the combined paired of protein molecules is congruent with each other with the exception of mutations called a single nucleotide polymorphism (SNP), which cannot be detected with legacy DNA technology.

SNP (i.e., exceptions to such patterns) are relevant to DNA analysis in human identification. One of the most important mutations for forensic testing, SNP, is discussed later in this chapter. In an SNP, one nucleotide differs in a single repetitive pattern in the series (frequency) of repeated patterns (e.g., AAGC<u>C</u>TA may appear in all repetitive patterns of a frequency in an allele with the exception of one which is presented as AAGC<u>T</u>TA). The presence of an SNP at a particular locus may be useful as a means of additional variation/discrimination in establishing the probability of an association between comparative DNA profiles when less than a full profile is obtained from degraded UHR. SNP may be useful in determining membership in geographical or ethnic groups; however, as miscegenation increases between highly mobile populations, the utility of establishing relationship to a particular ethnic may be impacted.

A common occurrence that is not a mutation is heterozygous and homozygous allele frequencies at a particular locus. The appearance of multiple homozygous frequencies may be an indication of incest (this will be discussed later in the chapter) but may not be reflected in an association or match report from the analyzing DNA laboratory. As previously mentioned, the alleles of the loci are categorized by frequency. If the two frequencies of a particular allele at a specific locus are dissimilar (i.e., one frequency from the father and a different frequency from the mother), the occurrence is called heterozygous and is reflected by two different numerical frequency values in a DNA profile. If the frequencies are the same (i.e., both mother and father happen to have the same frequency at a particular locus), the occurrence is called homozygous, and is reflected, by convention, as one numerical value (e.g., Table 4.1 at locus D3S1358). Note that current legacy DNA technology cannot differentiate which allele is contributed by the father and which is contributed by the mother.

Think of each human cell as a U.S. state. The capital of each state (the nucleus) contains 23 pairs of nearly identical streets (chromosomes) that cross in 23 separate X shapes. Each strand (chromatid) in a pair is made up of blocks (loci). Each block only has duplex structures (two alleles) comprised of A, T, G, and C in various combinations. For the purposes of forensic DNA testing, the FBI has identified 13 core loci*: CSF1PO, FGA, TH01, TPOX, vWA, D3S1358, D5S818, D7S820, D8S1179, D13S317, D16S539, D18S51, and

* Federal Bureau of Investigation. N/A (2014). *Frequently Asked Questions (FAQs) on the CODIS Program and the National DNA Index System.*

Table 4.1   FBI 13 Core Loci and Amelogenin[a]

Locus	Allele Frequency (Female)	Allele Frequency (Male)
CSF1PO	11	12
FGA	20	22
THO1	6	8
TPOX	8	11
vWA	16	17
D3S1358	14	
D5S818	11	12
D7S820	8	11
D8S1179	12	15
D13S317	11	12
D16S539	11	12
D18S51	12	15
D21S11	28	31.2
AMEL	X	Y

[a] Nonspecific example.

D21S11. These loci are the most likely "addresses" for the specific STR alleles that are most useful in the identification of an MP, a UD, or UHR.

The human DNA profile is made up of the contribution by each parent of an individual; in other words, one of every pair of alleles at loci in all 22 autosomal chromosomes is contributed by the father and the other by the mother. The 23rd chromosome, which determines sex, is particularly important in forensic DNA testing because it contains a marker referred to as amelogenin (AMEL). AMEL is represented as XX for a female and XY for a male. (Some mutations may show up as XYX, XXX, or some other combination, that should be shown on DNA association and match reports.) In some cases, Y-STR (i.e., STR extracted from a male's Y chromosome) may be used for DNA analysis for purposes other than the determination of sex as helping to identifying a perpetrator of a sexual assault from a DNA sample from the female victim or investigative leads in a familial searching effort. It has been my experience derived by reviewing well over a thousand DNA profiles that AMEL can be obtained from most unidentified human remains that only produce a partial STR profile. AMEL is a tremendous benefit to investigators to have a definitive determination of sex, knowing the high error of sexing opinions by forensic service providers from skeletal or partial remains recovery.

In order to have a basic understanding of DNA reporting, it is not necessary to memorize much of the above information—doing so does not aid the development of investigational strategies although, of course, it is essential for trial or laboratory casework. However, understanding the logic of how nuclear DNA (also referred to as STR, nDNA, or autosomal DNA) analysis is described in forensic reports is absolutely necessary in order to understand what a DNA analysis is conveying, and what it is not conveying. Being able to recognize when information is missing, or when there are anomalies in a report, enables investigators, families, and subject matter experts to ask questions that, in turn, help to develop effective investigative strategies and/ or improve strategies already in place.

When an investigator reviews a DNA report and suspects that anomalies are present, he or she must be able to converse intelligently with the DNA analyst who worked the case. Families or members of the general public who achieve a good general understanding of the basics of DNA should also be able to have productive conversations with subject matter experts. Not only can they obtain information that may be valuable to the case under consideration, they will find it easier to recognize when subject matter experts who are not DNA analysts are overreaching their expertise. This is not to say that all subject matter experts who present their assumptions as fact are deliberately deceiving anyone; it is human nature to speculate, and to believe in our own speculations. The bottom line is that the investigator—not the family, and not the DNA subject matter expert—is obligated to understand every aspect of the case. This includes being able to infer information that a testing lab may not make explicit in a DNA report.

As will be discussed further in Chapter 5, the disposition report from a lab may not put important information into context—but that context may be very important to a case. For example, if a UHR profile indicates that up to 50% of the alleles are homozygous, it may be appropriate for the investigator to contact an independent genetic scientist to determine the likelihood of incest. In a case that involved a deceased expectant mother, "The observation of seven identical loci between the mother and the foetus with four homozygous loci in a foetal profile suggested that pregnancy might have been a consequence of incest... 25% of times a pair of alleles—for any gene being considered—is expected to be identical by descent."[*] One would hope that this quotation represents information provided by the testing lab; instead, it comes from research by a graduate student. If the investigator on this case already knew the percentages, however, he or she would have been alerted to likely criminal activity whether or not the expectant mother had been murdered or charges of fetal homicide could also be considered.

The goal of DNA searches is to come up with a hit, which means an exact or approximate match (referred to as an association in most forensic DNA laboratory reports) between two types of samples in two scenarios:

---

[*] Jankova-Ajanovska, R. et al. 2010. Case report: Inherited alleles revealing an incestuous paternity. *Biol. Med. Sci.*, XXXI/2, pp. 261–266.

one from an MP, a UD, or UHR, and one or more others from a family member(s); or one from a UD or UHR, and one or more others from an MP or family member(s). It is always best to have two or more FRS from first order relatives (ex. mother, father, child, or sibling) of an MP, to provide the highest statistical probability for a valid association. Therefore, DNA comparisons are based on a minimum of two profiles: one from a candidate (MP, UD, or UHR) whose identity is in question, and one or more from a target (an MP, family member, or other person in particular instances) whose identity is known. The target sample is also called the reference sample, because the identity of the donor is known. When the target (reference) sample has been taken from an MP who is suspected of also being the UP/UHR, it is called a direct reference sample (DRS). DNA profiles derived from biological family member samples are commonly referred to as family reference samples (FRS).

Table 4.2 shows DNA comparisons that include at least one allele match at all loci, as would occur in a comparison of an FRS profile with an MP, UD, or UHR profile. This kind of comparison can only produce an associated match (i.e., a match that indicates it is highly statistically probable that the donors of the two DNA samples are biologically related). The loci shown in Table 4.3 represent a direct or exact match (i.e., all allele frequencies at all loci are the same), as would occur in a comparison of a DRS profile with an MP, a UD, or UHR profile. This kind of comparison can produce a direct match (i.e., a match that indicates it is highly statistically probable that the donors of the two DNA samples are the same person). Again, an associated match indicates that the people who provided the compared DNA are likely

Table 4.2   FBI 13 Core Loci and Amelogenin (Relative Match or Association)

Loci	UHR Profile (Female)	Known Profile (Female)
CSF1PO	10, 12	11, 12
FGA	20, 25	20, 22
THO1	6, 7	6, 8
TPOX	8, 11	8, 11
vWA	16, 15	16, 17
D3S1358	14, 15	14
D5S818	11, 12	8, 12
D7S820	8, 12	12, 8
D8S1179	12, 15	13, 15
D13S317	11, 12	11, 12
D16S539	11	11, 12
D18S51	12, 16	12, 15
D21S11	28, 31.2	28, 31.2
AMEL	XY	XY

Table 4.3   FBI 13 Core Loci and Amelogenin (Exact Match)

Loci	UHR Profile (Male)	Known Profile (Male)
CSF1PO	11, 12	11, 12
FGA	20, 22	20, 22
TH01	6, 8	6.8
TPOX	8, 11	8, 11
vWA	16, 17	16, 17
D3S1358	14	14
D5S818	11, 12	11, 12
D7S820	8, 12	12, 8
D8S1179	12, 15	12, 15
D13S317	11, 12	11, 12
D16S539	11, 12	11, 12
D18S51	12, 15	12, 15
D21S11	28, 31.2	28, 31.2
AMEL	XY	XY

(perhaps very highly likely) to be biologically related. A direct or exact match indicates that the DNA in the two samples that have been compared may have come from the same person.

When two associated DNA samples are compared (one from an MP, a UD, or UHR, and one from someone who may be biologically related to that MP, UD, or UHR), if the MP, UD, or UHR is a member of that family, then the frequency of one or more particular alleles in each sample will be the same and those alleles (with the exception of one or two mutations) will be found at the same loci in both samples. When two DRS are being compared (one MP sample, which may have been obtained from a hairbrush or clothing—or, in certain cases, a sample from a living person such as an arrestee or convicted felon—and one from a UD or UHR), if the MP and the UD or UHR are the same person or identical twins, all of the frequencies of all the alleles will match exactly with legacy DNA technology for the same loci shown in the DNA match report.

The above information constitutes some of the black box referred to in Section 1 "Concepts." However, understanding it does not make anyone an expert overnight. Spheres of responsibility must remain separate during DNA testing (Figure 4.2). At no time is it recommended that investigators or families make any assumptions or presumptions about numerical probability (i.e., statistical) results, or try to "outguess" trained laboratory personnel. However, investigators should strive to be as familiar as possible with their case files. Doing so will help them spot errors or anomalies much faster, and may save families from prolonged suspense and heartache.

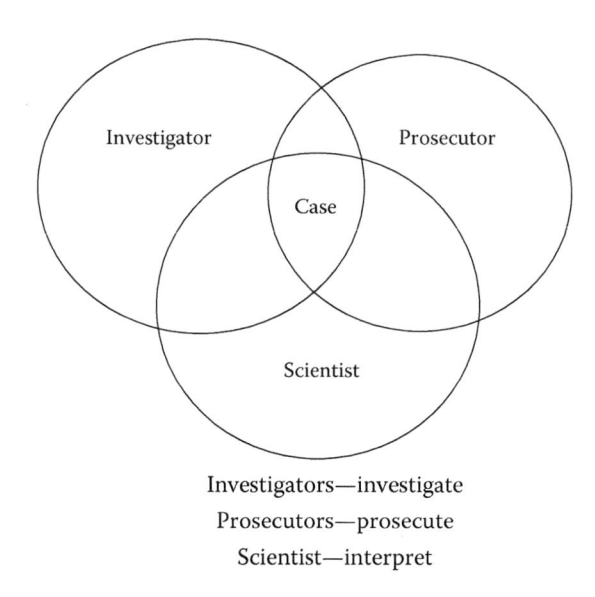

Investigators—investigate
Prosecutors—prosecute
Scientist—interpret

Figure 4.2 Spheres of responsibility.

It is difficult for even experienced investigators, and certainly for distraught families, to contain their excitement when a DNA hit is made. However, even a hit that does indicate an exact match or association between DNA from the candidate (unknown) sample and the target/reference (known) sample is presented in terms of probability opinions. These are supplied by subject matter experts who produce the DNA profile report, but can be subject to varying interpretations by other subject matter experts who use different assumptions, scenarios, equipment, protocols, and algorithms. Interpretations and assumptions or potential errors may not be disclosed in DNA associations and match reports or disclosed later when errors are discovered. In 2015, the FBI has notified crime labs across the country that it has discovered errors in software to calculate probabilities of a match, "Pop stats," used by 9 out of 10 laboratories, and may impact thousands of cases since 1999.* Unless we open the black box and critically challenge anomalies in cases and forensic science opinions, we may never know how many additional errors there may be. In my opinion, differences of interpretation, assumptions, opinions, and undisclosed known errors are more likely to occur more frequently when legacy DNA technology is being used due to the high level of human involvement.

In order to make DNA profiling more exact, and thereby to reduce the likelihood of widely varying interpretations of profile results, many laboratories

---

* Hsu, S. 2015. FBI notifies crime labs of errors used in DNA match calculations since 1999. *The Washington Post.* http://www.washingtonpost.com/local/crime/fbi-notifies-crime-labs-of-errors-used-in-dna-match-calculations-since-1999/2015/05/29/f04234fc-0591-11e5-8bda-c7b4e9a8f7ac_story.html (Accessed August 22, 2015).

are adding loci to their DNA profiles. In this way they can produce higher levels of discrimination between samples without having to resort to mtDNA (i.e., hair shafts that have been separated from their roots) or to the testing of baby teeth (from which legacy technology has difficulty extracting DNA). Laboratories outside the United States and domestic private laboratories have already added additional loci to their analyses and forensic reports. Although foreign laboratories may not use the same loci in their analysis or reporting, the same logic is used to calculate the STR frequencies within alleles and the positions of alleles at loci.

When UHR are especially degraded, the current legacy technology in use at most laboratories cannot extract DNA samples that contain enough intact loci to produce effective profiles to compare with MP, UD, and UHR profiles already in databases. The use of other loci in addition to the current 13 core CODIS loci should allow for more robust nuclear (STR) profiles to be produced without having to resort to the use of hair (mtDNA) samples.

In some cases, a DNA analysis contains enough matching alleles and loci for a viable DNA profile to be uploaded to the local level of CODIS, but not to the state or national levels. In such cases, laboratories are often willing to supplement their original STR (nuclear) DNA analysis with mtDNA analysis. However, this test is very labor intensive and also expensive because controlling for contamination is difficult.

In Table 4.3, hypothetical allele frequencies are shown for an UHR DNA profile and a known DNA profile to demonstrate the difference in the terms "high stringency" and "medium stringency" as well as to help explain the allele frequency presentations between a match and an association. The difference is critically important and quite confusing for anyone who is not a forensic DNA analyst, CODIS administrator, or geneticist. A "medium stringency" (association) is depicted by a single line underneath an allele frequency at the same locus of both profiles, for example, at loci FGA the frequency <u>12</u> is underlined for the UHR profile and also for the known profile. A "high stringency" (match) is depicted by both frequencies at the same locus in both profiles being underlined, for example, at loci TPOX the frequencies <u>8</u> and <u>11</u> are underlined for both the UHR and the known. Underlined alleles do not appear in DNA reports—the frequencies are only presented as underlined in Table 4.3 to draw one's attention to the single allele relationship at a particular locus between each profile. When both allele frequencies are the same at all loci the DNA profile comparison is referred to as a "match" or "high stringency match."

To help ameliorate deficiencies in investigative strategies with current legacy technologies, while well-meaning, they have not proven effective in my opinion. More cost effective, comprehensive, and newer technologies such as NGS (next-generation sequencing), SIA (stable isotope analysis), RDNA (rapid DNA technology), and NGI (next-generation identification)—to be discussed later in the book—are indispensable. Currently, mtDNA may be added to the association profiles of each for comparison (having medium stringency loci) to increase the probability numbers and in turn increase the comparison's rarity or to support an exclusion (no association); however, the effect for associations, in my opinion, is just the same as adding an additional locus in the probability calculations as some mtDNA profiles may match hundreds to thousands of maternal lines in a population. (Remember context—when we hear of the large CODIS database in the United States, it is really very insignificant in comparison to the world population and the cross border flows of masses of people seeking safety and a better life—more profiles in any type of database means more candidates have similar characteristics). When multiple medium stringency comparative associations occur there can be literally hundreds of possible candidates who should be dispositioned; however, that requires additional time, more people, and additional costs all around with legacy DNA technology. Also, the larger number of profiles in a laboratory's (LDIS) database, the more the possible candidates will need to be dispositioned (meaning to form an analyst's opinion as to the possible comparison). Another problem with associations is that relationships between the UHR and the known profiles may not be factual and multiple other known profiles of biological family members may be necessary to clear up indicated relationships for an analyst of form and opinion—more delay and additional costs. DNA analysts and CODIS administrators may rely on metadata (which has been found to be inaccurate in many cases as revealed through multiple cold hit identifications) to help pick a likely candidate among all possible candidates. The problem is that there is no probability threshold number for associations (medium stringency) to indicate the validity of an association as being the one and only relationship to the exclusion of all the others. Here is the real takeaway—can you imagine an association report being issued to a medical examiner/coroner or investigator in which the analysts' opinion relied on low probability numbers and circumstantial metadata that resulted in the statutory authority issuing a death certificate after calling a positive identification only to find out later that dental or fingerprint comparisons excluded the positive identification or the decedent is actually alive. Can you imagine the pain and anger of the family and the possible liability to all investigative parties for claims of conducting an incomplete or negligent investigation by multiple parties—especially if funds had been paid by insurance carriers or companies based on the death certificate? It should be patently clear at this point why deficient investigative identification strategies are becoming a major focus in criminal justice, scientific, social and commercial venues for not only resolving cold cases, but for combating fraud and identity theft.

When one looks at associations and legacy DNA technology from a holistic perspective, one may come to the conclusion I have. It is extremely expensive with the multiple samples needed to make a reasonable comparative, association together with a large number of candidates to disposition and becomes fraught with possible liability from families to investigators. While many problems (risks) are identified here, this reference book provides effective and easy, low-to-no cost strategies that may be implemented for overcoming such problems through utilizing multiple forensic resources (multi-modalities of identification) to support a valid resolution. The underlined alleles for the various loci in Table 4.3 is meant to give you a visual conception of an association versus a match, as well as a foundation for understanding why biological family member DNA associations have limited value as compared to DNA matches for the investigation of unidentified human remains.

Expense, time, and the possibility of contamination or other human factor errors are all increased when several rounds of DNA must be extracted from a UD or UHR in order to produce a DNA profile that is sufficient to upload to CODIS at any level. A DNA profile is useless if it cannot be readily searched against as many DNA bases as possible. The legacy technology known as capillary electrophoresis (CE) requires multiple analyses to be performed on DNA samples; in turn, each of these analyses requires its own consumables (chemicals) and procedures. However, obtaining a viable DNA profile from a UD or UHR and being able to search that DNA profile against as many databases and individual profiles as possible are two of the most crucial aspects of UHR investigations. Therefore, investigators and families alike must be prepared to weather delays and setbacks, as well as unexpected events.

When the comparison between a candidate DNA profile and a target/reference DNA profile produces a hit, whether that hit is an association or a match, it is used to generate leads in UHR investigations. Obviously, a DRS is the most advantageous type of target/reference sample to compare with an MP, a UD, or UHR. A DRS, which may come from items that contain an MP's cells, can be obtained from physical sources such as blood or tissue; personal items such as hats, shoes, or dentures; or from samples taken from arrestees or convicted felons. Other physical sources for MP cells include a blood type card filled out at birth, lab samples from medical tests, or stored tissue samples from medical procedures. Hair shafts (as previously mentioned) make poor samples for legacy technology analysis, as do baby teeth, although the mtDNA obtained from hair shafts may have limited use in particular situations. When NGS technology is available, however, hair shafts may become extremely valuable because the advanced techniques are able to recognize mtDNA variations that are outside the legacy range. Advanced technology is also more capable of extracting nuclear DNA from highly degraded remains.

In general, an additional confirming sample from a biological relative (i.e., an FRS) is required for the validation of a DRS when the latter has been lifted from an MP's personal items. However, depending on the testing laboratory's facilities, MP samples collected during previous medical procedures may be sufficient. Extracting DNA from tissue samples that have been stored in chemical fixatives is challenging but not necessarily impossible.

Collecting and testing a DRS is relatively straightforward compared to the production of viable DNA samples from a UD or UHR (i.e., samples that contain profiles that are sufficient for database entry). The success of this sort of work, which is demanding and may take months or longer to complete, depends upon the DNA lab itself and its analysts. Even if analysts possess the right equipment, they may not wish to put in extra effort or may not have the necessary skills. Some laboratories refuse to accept DNA samples that have been stored in fixatives other than saline solution or even discourage DNA submission altogether.

In any case, it is necessary to provide tissue, blood, or bone that contains enough DNA for profiling (0.5–2 ng; the optimal amount for most commercial testing kits is 1 ng).* Samples that do not contain enough DNA for legacy testing may be candidates for low copy number (LCN) DNA or low template DNA (LT-DNA) analysis. In this book, LCN refers to a series of techniques, strategies, and processes that are implemented to increase the amount of DNA available for analysis, such as increasing the amplification cycles (number of times DNA is doubled through amplification techniques). Usually, such approaches are not included in equipment manufacturers' recommendations or guidelines. LCN testing has been available since 1999 and has contributed not only to the resolution of cold cases but also to the conviction of felons who had previously been cleared by legacy DNA profile comparisons. However, LCN DNA is highly subject to contamination, and scientists who test it must have special training. LCN-developed profiles were originally allowed into CODIS, but were excluded in, shortly after I arrived at the University of North Texas in 2005. This meant that hundreds of LCN profiles of UD/UHR were no longer available for searching nationally through CODIS, and that hundreds of LCN UD/UHR profiles sent to national CODIS laboratories from around the country would never have an opportunity to be matched with corresponding MP profiles in other laboratories/states' DNA databases. I began to work on an alternate strategy to have those LCN profiles searched outside of CODIS but within the policies and practices of the human identification environment. More information about LCN appears later in this chapter.

> **Key point:** Investigators often have no choice about where samples for DNA analysis are sent for processing; agency policies may require samples to go a specific forensic laboratory.

---

* Butler, J.M. 2009. *Fundamentals of DNA Typing*, Chapter 6: DNA Quantitation. PowerPoint slide no. 3. https://www.google.com/?gws_rd=ssl#q=0.5%E2%80%932+ng%3B+the+optimal+amount+for+most+commercial+testing+kits+is+1+ng (Accessed August 2, 2015).

Once a valid candidate DNA profile has been obtained from a DRS, UD, UHR, or the personal items (also referred to as DRS) of an MP, it can be searched at all CODIS profiles at all CODIS levels if directed by the LDIS laboratory. However, a DNA analyst or CODIS administrator must still disposition (formulate a qualitative opinion of the data) the hit returned by CODIS. CODIS contains candidate DNA profiles from DRS, FRS and UD/UHR as well as profiles from state or federal convicted offenders (at SDIS and NDIS levels of CODIS).

DNA collection and profiling procedures differ from state to state according to statute and practice, especially when the reference donors are arrestees or convicted felons. Therefore, inconsistent and/or incorrect information may be provided to families and investigators—a situation that can be especially disappointing and frustrating for people who believe that clear DNA statutes, protocols, and policies are firmly in place everywhere and backed up with safeguards in every case. This danger makes it even more important for investigators to ascertain the differences among stated policies, protocols, and statutes, as well as the actual practices of all DNA laboratories—no matter where they are located, whether they are public or private, and how much they charge for their services.

In 2011, skeletal remains were found by a hunter in the Upper Midwest. Despite the efforts of several investigatory agencies, 3 years went by without resolution. Then, a private citizen notified police of a possible match to an MP. Two FRS samples were obtained but did not produce a match. However, a follow-up inquiry did confirm an association with an MP; moreover, it was revealed that the name of this MP had been stamped on clothing found with the UHR! The excuse given for the faulty results of the first test was simply that "a mistake" had been made.* According to the NIJ, such errors are common in sentinel event cold cases. In this case, it was an effective investigative strategy to critically challenge the results and obtain additional tests when unresolved anomalies were found that brought resolution.

The fact that a case has been sent to a CODIS laboratory, and its file includes samples of remains that contain DNA as well as sufficient reference samples, but no match or association has been made, does not necessarily mean that a match or association can never be obtained. Moreover, a match or association may not ever be made unless law enforcement agencies insist on getting confirmatory profile reviews. Insistence alone, though, does not guarantee that the results will be provided quickly or that they will be accurate. As previously stated, legacy DNA technology is very labor intensive and contains many opportunities for human error in analysis as well as evidence control and results reports. According to the *New York Times*, an FBI audit

---

* *The Daily Record.* 2015. Bones Found in Rittman 3 Years Ago Identified, December 15, 2014. http://www.the-daily-record.com/local%20news/2014/12/15/bones-found-in-3-years-ago-identified.

found errors in nearly half of the cases that were reviewed. Such errors may be definitive: "The report's findings, based on a review of more than 41,000 pieces of evidence in F.B.I. offices around the country, could have consequences for criminal investigations and prosecutions. Lawyers can use even minor record-keeping discrepancies..."*

If errors are occurring to this extent in FBI investigations, one must wonder about the error rates in other agencies. That information is not available, but even the possibility of comparable or higher error rates serves to remind us that debriefing and deconstruction of all cases by investigators is necessary if anomalies and errors are to be discovered and prevented from becoming systemic. Evidence handling and control procedures cannot be separated from forensic analysis and processing procedures, if for no other reason than that the quality of one may point to systemic failures involving others.

To summarize: DRS samples are the best source of target/reference DNA, and may be searched against all DNA profiles at all CODIS levels. The more nuclear DNA loci a candidate DNA profile contains, the more likely it is that a viable search for an association or match can be conducted. Complete MP (DRS from the actual missing person), UD, and UHR DNA profiles may be searched against all CODIS DNA indices. FRS (from biological family members) samples may be searched only against MP, UD, and UHR indices but cannot searched against other indices in CODIS. Thus, FRS DNA profiles have limited utility in terms of producing investigative leads.

Using DRS for DNA analysis is least likely to incur human error. For example, an article from *Promega Connections* (Promega is a leading authority in STR detection for human identification) about DNA analysis involving two living people describes a case of a wife who accused her husband's mistress of violence and intimidation against her. Target/reference DNA profiles of the mistress were obtained from saliva used to seal an envelope as well as lipstick used to write a threatening message, but analysis of these DRS profiles revealed a match to the wife—not the mistress.†

Table 4.3 shows alleles at all loci of a UHR sample profile and a reference sample profile with the same values, a condition referred to as high stringency. If both alleles of candidate DNA profile at a given locus match the same alleles at the same locus of the target DNA profile, the condition is referred to as high stringency; if only one of the two alleles are in congruency, the condition is referred to as moderate stringency. "Low stringency" (familial searches) refers to searches (usually not encountered in UHR investigations)

* Apuzzo, N., Schmidt, M. 2014. F.B.I. Evidence Is Often Mishandled, an Internal Inquiry Finds, *New York Times*, December 19, 2014. http://www.nytimes.com/2014/12/20/us/politics/fbi-evidence-keeping-criticized.html?_r=0.
† Sandquist, T. 2011. August 29, 2011. *Not My Shade of DNA*. Promega Connections. http://promega.wordpress.com/2011/08/29/not-my-shade-of-dna/.

premised upon matching only a subset of the available typed loci, usually, between crime scene (forensic) samples and convicted offenders. However, depending upon the state, the same logic could be utilized to search UHR DNA profiles against convicted offender DNA profiles—simply substitute the UHR profile for the crime scene profile in the software. As previously mentioned, a hit (either match or association) is achieved when two profiles in DNA comparative analysis exceed a certain level of resemblance. In this book, a match means that resemblance, indicated by two matching alleles at the every locus, has been found between a candidate DNA profile and a target DNA profile. An association refers to a statistically significant resemblance between the DNA profiles of two biologically related individuals (FRS and UD/UHR) with up to 50% of the alleles matching at all loci between the candidate and target DNA profile—excluding possible one or two mutations.

Some laboratories may use the term "inclusive" to indicate a possible match or association. An inclusive DNA profile, whether it is obtained from a DRS or an FRS, is of value because it may contribute to the identification of a UD or UHR, which of course is required so that authorities can issue a death certificate. However, as previously stated, additional information is required to determine if the possible match or association is correct because the first test has only indicated that there is a significant probability of biological linkage. For example, if two identical siblings are missing, an FRS association alone cannot be used to determine which of them is a UD or UHR; for certainty, a target/reference DNA profile must be provided for each of them. Legacy DNA technology cannot determine which of identical siblings is which. The simplest way to describe the difference between a match and an association is to say that a match is the result of the comparison of cell samples that have come from the same individual, whereas an association is the result of samples that have come from biologically related individuals.

Cases in which more than one family member is missing or presumed dead, particularly if they are identical, are of great concern to UHR investigators because in order to obtain FRS they must take into account factors such as dysfunctional family relationships, high numbers of runaways, dispersed families within the United States, and immigrants whose close family members live in other countries. Matches between DRS and UD/UHR do not evoke these concerns—although, as previously mentioned, a match made via legacy technology cannot be used to make a determination between identical multiple siblings. Investigators in such cases should also consider that the MP may have additional siblings or half-siblings whose existence is not widely known, but if contacted could provide viable FRS.

In some cases, the inability to identify which identical sibling is in question may ruin a case. One example occurred in 2009, when $6.8 million in losses resulted from a jewelry theft at a luxury department store in Berlin, Germany. DNA recovered at the scene was matched to identical twins, and both were arrested. However, using traditional legacy DNA technology, the German criminal justice system could not deduce which twin took part in the crime and was obliged to release both from custody.[*]

The birth rate of identical twins is estimated to be constant, at approximately four per thousand.[†] Birth rates for triplets, quadruplets, and so forth are more rare, but the point is that multiple births are not uncommon. For this reason, investigators must ensure that family structure has been fully disclosed and understood, and that the whereabouts of all living siblings are known. Such investigations are highly subject to error because most of the pedigree charts in MP submission packets do not mention the difficulties of determining DNA differences between identical siblings. This can be accomplished with NGS technology.[‡] The best possible FRS samples for DNA analysis are collected from first-order (consanguine) relatives: parents, siblings, or children. First-order relatives and MP will have up to 50% of their alleles at all loci in common. Siblings will most likely have 50% of their alleles at all loci in common with an MP who is also a sibling, but that percentage may be higher than 50% or may be nonexistent. These ranges may seem impossible, but investigators and families must keep in mind that DNA analysis deals with statistical probabilities, not factual absolutes.

The number of shared alleles declines according to consanguinuity (first-order relatives to second-order, third-order, etc.), which makes producing associations more challenging. Pedigree (familial) charts are supposed to be available from any lab, but the information they display may not be easy to understand. It is important for families searching for a missing loved one to know that second-order relatives are uncles and aunts, grandparents, and first cousins; third-order relatives are great-grandparents, great-uncles and -aunts, great-nieces and -nephews, and second cousins.[§] Samples from third-order relatives are acceptable sources of mtDNA and nuclear DNA from males (called Y-STR DNA after the Y chromosome that distinguishes males from females). Although second- and third-order relatives may not produce DNA profiles with enough statistical value to be of primary use, results may indicate that it is worth the expenditure of time and effort to locate other biometric identifiers such as fingerprints, medical records, dentals, or even to perform stable isotope analysis. All of the latter identifiers are discussed in later chapters.

[*] Himmelreich, C. 2009. *Despite DNA Evidence, Twins Charged in Heist Go Free.* http://www.Time.com.

[†] National Organization of Mothers of Twins Clubs, Inc. 2014. *Incident of Twins by Twin Type.*

[‡] Drake, N. 2014. *DNA Test That Distinguishes Identical Twins May Be Used in Court for First Time. Wired.* http://www.wired.com/2014/12/genetic-test-distinguishes-identical-twins-may-used-court-first-time/.

[§] Scientific Working Group on DNA Analysis Methods. 2014. Guidelines for missing persons casework. pp. 4–5.

> **Key point:** Any MP/UD inquiry could become a criminal investiga-
> tion; therefore, it should be treated as such from sample collection until
> resolution. Law enforcement personnel should handle all DNA samples
> with an unbroken chain of custody, from point of collection to delivery
> to the testing facility.

In general, the more FRS can be collected, the better. This can be done by
a simple buccal (cheek) swab or with a number of specifically designed collection devices. A blood draw is a viable alternative, but potential donors may not
respond well to invasive requests that involve needles. Acquiring a tissue, bone,
or blood sample from a deceased first-order relative may be difficult, but may
produce a viable DNA profile. As previously mentioned, any cells from an MP
may produce a viable DRS profile for a UP; this connection is analogous to how
DNA collected from a crime scene can link an offender to that location.

Cells from deceased family members, which may be collected from
personal items such as dentures, toothbrushes, or clothing, may be used to
obtain a viable nuclear DNA profile long after death. Another possible source
of viable DNA samples, as previously mentioned, are tissue blocks that have
been archived after medical procedures. It is necessary to obtain consent to
gather an FRS from a living family member. Some laboratories require that
express written consent accompany DNA analysis submissions; others may
only require verbal consent, along with an affidavit from the submitting law
enforcement personnel stating that the sample was voluntarily provided.

> **Key point:** In order to minimize possible liability, HIPAA health cover-
> age providers are more than likely to require a subpoena or other court
> order before they will give medical samples to police.

A viable nuclear DNA UHR profile can only be produced if there is enough
available cellular material from the deceased. As previously discussed, the
amount of effort required to obtain a UHR profile is totally dependent upon
the quality of the sample and the skill/resources of the laboratory conducting
the DNA analysis. The available cellular material may be blood, hair, one or
two bones, parts of the body, or even the full body in various stages of decomposition. Extraction methods differ, depending on the cellular material, but
the analysis processes are practically the same in both DRS and FRS cases.

Some laboratories may be more skilled at DNA analysis, as well as more
willing to perform it. Generally, their order of preference for UD/UHR samples
is blood, tissue, bones with high concentrations of calcium (often referred to
as long bones), and adult teeth. Many viable samples obtained from the psoas

muscle of bodies in advanced stages of decomposition have produced usable UHR profiles; this is because the psoas muscle is often among the last bodily tissues to break down. Even if an investigator is already familiar with a particular laboratory (for example, if he or she is required to send samples there because of agency policy), it should be contacted before submission of material for testing to ascertain its preferred samples and the preferred ways samples should be packaged/delivered, as well as the capabilities and readiness of the lab overall.

According to its policies, the testing lab should forward a complete report from the DNA analysis to appropriate agencies. To avoid later discrepancies, investigators should insist that any information about the results be documented in written form and should insist on receiving a printed copy of every report. All reports should be written in everyday language whenever possible, and contain some forms of certain key descriptors.* These are: excluded (the sample profiles are not a match or an association), not excluded or putative (the samples may be a match or an association), inconclusive or uninterpretable (no significant findings or the sample failed to produce a viable DNA profile), or consistent/not consistent with (respectively, excluded or not excluded). The disposition of waiting for more data, which may appear in certain circumstances, is explained later in this chapter.

A finding of association means that a biological relationship may exist between an MP/UD/UHR candidate sample and a DRS or FRS reference sample. It does not mean that UHR have been identified as belonging to an MP, or that a UD or UHR can be positively identified. It may be possible to prove these things, but how and when to engage in that additional research must be decided by the jurisdictional death investigator (usually an ME/C or JP, or another authority authorized to issue a death certificate). Such decisions lie outside the sphere of responsibility of testing laboratories, whose personnel do not have the training, expertise, or authority to make them. The reports can, however, be of significant influence on investigators, who should take a strong interest in them.

In part, because of the CSI effect, the reputation of DNA evidence has been somewhat inflated. It can happen, and does, that an association report based on DNA testing of distant relatives finds strong similarities between them and UD/UHR and MP profiles; the ME officially identifies the UD/UHR as a particular MP; and the family of the deceased and investigator on the case are satisfied with this outcome.

As the personnel of testing labs know, DNA testing produces evidence in the form of statistical inference. It establishes the probability or rarity that compared samples are similar. It does not inarguably prove that, even if two samples are exactly similar, they come from the same person. The probability

* Federal Bureau of Investigation. 2014. *SWGDAM Interpretation Guidelines for Autosomal STR Typing by Forensic DNA Typing Laboratories.* http://www.fbi.gov/about-us/lab/biometric-analysis/codis/swgdam-interpretation-guidelines.

may be astronomically high that a DNA match or association between two samples means that the samples have come from the same person. But without the ability to compare every gene and allele at every locus on every chromatid in every chromosome—an ability that science is not likely to ever provide—it cannot be 100%. It is important for families and the public to understand this last point, because the CSI effect has given the public inaccurate impressions of how easy it is to identify human remains.

In addition, a lab report may not be easy to understand. It may be written in simple, direct language or it may be full of scientific terms that are not put into context. Families should know that it is their right not only to receive a copy of their DNA profile report but also to have that report explained to them. If a report seems confusing, a request for clarification should be made in writing to the lab that issued it; verbal conversations should be documented. It is not unusual for lab scientists to be asked for additional explanations. However, they should not be expected to offer much reassurance or sympathy, because most of them have no experience with police investigations or the needs of families who are searching for a missing loved one.

A DNA profile issued by a testing laboratory should indicate whether unused DNA material has been retained. If an association is made, most lab's protocols require that the samples be reworked to confirm the initial results. It is also important for investigators to know about unused DNA so that it can be retested if/when the technology at a particular lab is upgraded. Federal funds are being spent for such upgrading. For example, in 2014, Battelle Inc. received a grant of more than $800,000 to encourage NGS at leading laboratories.[*]

When acquiring a DNA sample, whether it is an FRS or DRS or from UHR, investigators should know to collect and preserve more material than is required by the analyzing laboratory. They should also know to maintain an appropriate chain of custody in case it becomes necessary to send a sample later on to a laboratory that has more advanced technology. All samples should be stored as evidence: Nontissue (nondegradable samples) should be kept in porous containers and tissue (degradable) samples should be frozen. Blood should be stored on blood cards—not in glass vials, because blood stored this way tends to degrade over time and vials may crack or break. Human tissue should not be thawed once it has been frozen, because (as with edible food), it will start to decompose upon thawing. Frozen human tissue should not be kept in a frost-free unit and should be placed in the center of a shelf (away from the sides of the unit). As mentioned previously in this chapter, it is best to contact the laboratory about their preferred methods of sample maintenance and shipping.

[*] Battelle, Inc. 2014. *Battelle Awarded National Institute of Justice Grant to Study New Forensic DNA Tools: Partnership with Seven Leading Labs Will Help Spur Use of Next-Generation Sequencing in Law Enforcement.* http://www.battelle.org/media/press-releases/battelle-awarded-NIJ-grant-to-study-new-forensic-dna-tools.

Each laboratory has its own policies and procedures, some of which may not be compatible with state or jurisdictional statutes. As previously mentioned, there are approximately 190 CODIS laboratories in the United States, as well as thousands of private, commercial, academic/research, and health care laboratories that provide forensic DNA analysis but do not have access to CODIS databases. Several states require laboratories that test DNA to be accredited by the American Society of Crime Lab Directors (ASCLD) or the International Organization for Standardization (ISO). The International Electrochemical Commission (IEC) also publishes standards for laboratories.

Investigators and families alike should remember that the existence of rules, regulations, and statutes does not guarantee error-free testing, even in accredited laboratories. In part, this is because, unfortunately, laboratory personnel and accreditation authorities may inconsistently implement their own standards. Even audit standards may be so nonspecific that how to implement various methods or procedures is usually decided subjectively, rather than according to regulations. Subjectivity is increased because laboratories are allowed to write their own specific quality assurance (QA) standards, in terms of policy and protocol, to meet ASCLAD and ISO/IEC guidelines. In short, investigators should "trust, yet verify" by finding out how a lab really operates in addition to how it is supposed to operate.

Despite the best intentions and efforts of lab personnel, errors are not uncommon. A 2004 report by the Innocence Project detailed numerous errors at the DNA laboratory involved with the Earl Washington Jr. capital murder case.[*] As of January 2014, according to the *New York Times*, the FBI's "review of a national DNA database [had] identified nearly 170 profiles that probably contain errors, some the results of handwriting mistakes or interpretation errors by lab technicians."[†] Because accredited DNA lab personnel are aware of these problems, most QA protocols at such laboratories require two DNA analysts to review each case. These reviews include verification of results from source data to database input, technical review of the case information, and entry of the profile into CODIS only by a CODIS administrator who has reviewed the test results from source data.

For errors to occur in systems with so many built-in safeguards, there must be multiple failures. According to Eric H. Holder, Jr., at that time the U.S. Attorney General, "Criminal justice errors—whether they are wrongful convictions, premature prisoner releases, long-unsolved cold cases, or other

---

[*] Innocence Project. N/A. *Historic Audit of Virginia Crime Lab in Earl Washington Jr.'s Capital Case.* http://www.innocenceproject.org/Content/Historic_Audit_of_Virginia_Crime_Lab_Errors_in_Earl_Washington_Jrs_Capital_Case.php.

[†] Goldstein, J. 2014. F.B.I. *Audit of Database That Indexes DNA Finds Errors in Profiles.* New York Times. http://www.nytimes.com/2014/01/25/nyregion/fbi-audit-of-database-that-indexes-dna-finds-errors-in-profiles.html?_r=0.

serious oversights—are rarely the fault of a single actor."[*] The contribution to each case of multiple entities (investigators, other law enforcement personnel, ME/C, laboratory personnel, subject matter experts) thus raises the possibility of error despite the presence of safeguards.

> **Key point:** Selecting the right laboratory for nuclear DNA analysis may be the most important aspect of designing effective investigative strategies in UHR investigations.

The more technologically advanced laboratories tend to publish more research reports and case histories and to collaborate well with other laboratories and agencies. They also tend to collaborate with leaders in the human identification field. Those that cannot provide requested services in house should have outsourcing arrangements in place and proactively inform the investigator of these arrangements.

Progressive laboratories also tend to have multiple and/or dependable revenue streams. It's important to have some idea of how secure a lab's funding is, because those that depend exclusively on external funding may gear their management and direction toward qualifying for the next grant cycle or meeting key performance indicators. It's also important to find out whether the policies and protocols of a particular lab are available for public review. Ideally, investigators should be able to compare research policies and protocols of the labs they consider with state laws, and with the practices of other facilities.

Selecting the right lab does not mean that testing will proceed without problems or that test results will yield the information investigators and families are searching for. STR panels/kits used for DNA analysis may yield incomplete profiles;[†] in other words, a full scan (one that includes all 13 of the FBI core loci) may not be obtained. It is possible for a DNA profile to be eligible for searching with LDIS, SDIS, or NDIS even when it is not complete. However, hundreds of potential associations may be returned in such cases— if so, the tests may be marked "waiting for more data."[‡] This category is an intermediate disposition which indicates that additional genetic or other metadata is needed to confirm or refute an association or match.

Even when the right testing facility has been selected and sufficient materials have been properly delivered to them, other problems may arise.

[*] Holder, E. 2014. *Mending Justice: Sentinel Event Reviews—Message from the Attorney General*. U.S. Department of Justice, Office of Justice Programs, National Institute of Justice.

[†] Eisenberg, A., Planz, J. 2007. *Field Test of Current Technology Used in the Identification of Unidentified Remains*. NCJRS, Document 220297, 2004-DN-BX-K214.

[‡] The Arkansas State Crime Laboratory CODIS Section Quality Assurance Manual. 2014. Document ID: CODIS-DOC-01 Update 2/7/2014. p. 63.

The most serious are contamination (either of samples or in the lab setting), which can skew results, and delays, which are caused by numerous (and often unexpected) circumstances. Normal collection procedures are expected to be routine; for example, national missing person program laboratories that specialize in testing reference samples from biological family members usually provide agencies with buccal swabs in a collection kit. They may accept DRS from blood cards, or from personal possessions or objects that were in close contact with the missing person. An FRS profile (which takes time to produce) may be required to validate the DRS. Therefore, investigators may encounter delays concerning DRS (and, as previously mentioned, labs may refuse to accept or process them), even though a DRS profile is the most desirable. As stated earlier in this chapter, it is more difficult to confirm or refute associations between FRS profiles and UHR profiles than to confirm or refute matches between DRS profiles and UHR profiles.

Unfortunately, a CODIS search (i.e., a comparison of a UD/UHR DNA profile to DNA profiles from MP or convicted offenders/arrestees) is not guaranteed to produce a hit or even information that can be used as an investigative lead. CODIS also has restrictions that may cause tremendous setbacks in certain cases. For example, the NDIS level CODIS did not perform searches of LCN profiles prior to January 2015. It is unclear if a laboratory will be able to initiate LCN searches at SDIS or NDIS for LCN profiles developed before January 2015 (however, searching of LCN profiles developed prior to January 2015 may still be possible with manual searches that do not require the sample to be entered into the CODIS database). The UHR index of CODIS is the only index that provides the capability for victim profile entry and searching. This means that 50 or more SDIS and more than 100 LDIS laboratory indices may have to be individually searched. Or, if labs store LCN profiles in separate indices to ensure that they are not accidentally forwarded to SDIS or NDIS levels, these indices must be manually searched against indices in other CODIS laboratories.

As previously stated, agencies at every level (local, county, state, and federal) must obey numerous statutes, policies, and protocols about MP, UHR, and DNA profiles and processing. However, these rules may not be always followed by every lab in exactly the same way, due to subjective interpretation of them and discretion about their application. For example, a missing person report should be taken by any jurisdiction without any waiting period but this may not occur in practice. Or a sample for DNA analysis should be obtained from UHR prior to their disposal, but is not. Or family members in many jurisdictions are not advised of their statutory right to submit FRS samples within or after 30 days of filing an MP report. Or, despite clear instructions to do so, a laboratory does not share information about a DNA submission with another agency that is seeking to confirm or refute a potential match or association; in fact, a lab may even refuse to confirm that they have the DNA in question and have tested it.

Once a DNA analysis is complete, the submitting entity or agency should be notified; however, CODIS has no tracking feature to document such notifications. This lack of accountability means that many labs have evidence (letters and notes) that indicate notifications were sent, but no confirmation that the notices were ever received or acted on. According to one researcher, "There are truly two parts of the equation, the first being CODIS providing investigative leads and the second part being what happens after the hits are made."[*]

The above examples are not the only disconnects that can hinder an MP, UD, or UHR investigation. For investigators, value should be the driving consideration in the development of case-specific investigative strategies. By value, I do not mean financial cost. Instead, the concept has to do with outcomes. Investigators must realize that the communities in which they work define what is important to them, and that he or she delivers outcomes in support of those criteria. A criminal investigator is best suited to demonstrate appropriate leadership in a case, and to design effective strategies, by practicing critical thinking and collaboration in ways that demonstrate respect for his or her community by reducing cost and increasing value.

> **Key point:** Major costs are created not by DNA analysis, but instead by the expenditure of investigative resources.

An investigator's strategy should be directed toward allowing databases to link candidate MP, UD, or UHR profiles/biometrics and to target MP or FRS profiles/biometrics for national outliers. At its most effective, this strategy will proceed in clear steps that are based on facts, not assumptions. For example, the majority of identifications occur within a radius of approximately 150 miles around two locations: the place the UHR were found, and the last place the MP was last seen alive. Therefore, the first choice for processing a UHR sample is the LDIS laboratory nearest to where the remains were found; sending the samples to a national missing person program laboratory right away is not necessarily the best move. Above all, DNA profiles of the highest quality should be entered into databases that can be searched and compared automatically (by internal links) instead of by hand (by keyboard searches or manual comparisons). It cannot be overstated that the more human intervention that is involved in a UHR investigation, the more likely it is that errors will complicate it.

Making the transitions from local to state to national searches can be confusing as well as frustrating. Investigators as well as families should be aware that DNA profiles developed LDIS laboratories cannot be searched directly

[*] Brown, A. 2007. *A Study of the Efficiency of the Combined DNA Index System for the Orgeon State Police.* Fort Worth, TX: University of North Texas Health Science Center. p. 61.

against all local CODIS laboratories or local non-CODIS indices. The mechanism for searching local (LDIS) CODIS profiles against another laboratory's CODIS profiles takes place at state (SDIS) and national (NDIS) levels. Nearly all LDIS laboratories have profiles and indices that are ineligible for uploading to SDIS or NDIS levels. In addition, samples sent to a national program that operates at the LDIS level cannot always be searched against all indices maintained at the same program's local LDIS labs, or against SDIS indices from any source that do not qualify for uploading to NDIS. These situations are not always hopeless, however, because local investigators can still will need to facilitate (or insist) on manual comparisons of full or partial matches, or conduct familial searching at the state levels where permitted. Associations and matches may not be possible through traditional CODIS database searches for the following reasons: DNA profile has not been uploaded to SDIS/NDIS; insufficient STR results obtained from the UD/UHR; DNA data contains a common mtDNA or YSTR profile that is relatively common; and diminished allele sharing between relatives and remains when first-degree relatives (e.g., parents, offspring, and siblings) are not available to provide a sample.[*]

Again, once a valid DNA profile has been obtained from UD/UHR, an investigator's initial concern is to get that profile searched against as many indices as possible. Investigators should know of the existence and physical location of all DNA aliquots (i.e., partial samples) relative to their case in laboratories for use later on, when new or upgraded technology makes it possible to re-analyze the original sample and obtain more discriminating details from translation DNA technologies such as NGS. Profiles from reanalyzed samples may qualify for entry into NDIS, or if not they can be sent to national, state, or local laboratories to searched against samples that do not qualify for NDIS entry. Cost may be a drawback in such cases, because fees increase for repeated analyses. The point is that samples that were originally considered incomplete should be re-analyzed with advanced equipment to obtain an STR profile.

Proceeding from local through state to national searches is strongly recommended. The median radius for identification (Table 4.3) appears to be approximately 49 miles, with a mean of approximately 150 miles (Figure 4.3). Aside from data related to location, metadata related to potential exclusions may seem promising. However, these run a high risk of inaccuracy (13% for sexing, 56% for race), and so should not be initially considered. It is important to remember that metadata can be incorrect, particularly when date ranges, age estimates, and ethnicities are involved.[†] Sex assessment is also problematic because valid techniques are unavailable for fetuses, infants, and

---

[*] Federal Bureau of Investigation. n/d. *Laboratory Services: Missing Person Comparison Request*. www.fbi.gov/about-us/lab/biometric-analysis/codis/missing-person-comparison-request (Accessed August 5, 2015).
[†] Scientific Working Group DNA Analysis Methods. 2014. *Guidelines for Missing Persons Case Work Approved—01/09/14*. p. 8.

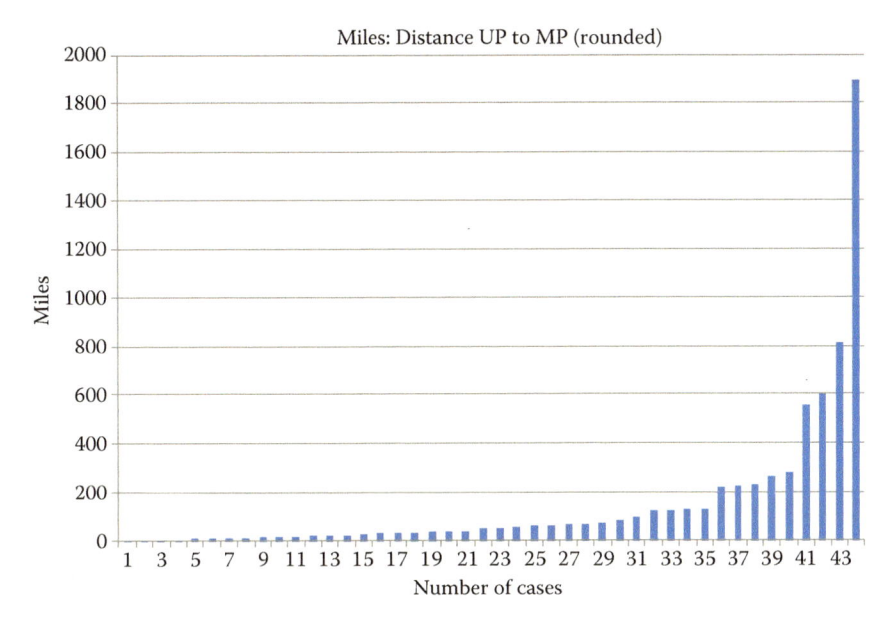

Mean: 150 miles
Median: 49 miles 22nd rank

Figure 4.3 Approximate MP ID distances.

children less than 12 years old.[*] In addition, adult skeletal remains exhibit both male and female characteristics, according to inter and intrapopulation differences, age, pathology, and degree of decay.[†]

Investigators and families should feel as if progress has been made when appropriate samples (tissue, blood, or bone) have been correctly collected and submitted to a qualified lab; sufficient DNA profiles have been generated from the samples; and the profiles have been uploaded to as many indices as possible. However, carrying a UD, MP, or UHR investigation to its conclusion involves designing strategies that go beyond gathering evidence. Some guidelines and initial strategies (Table 4.2) for working investigations are explored below (Figure 4.4).

As I conducted case reviews in preparation for writing this book, I discovered that it is not useful to consider associations between UD/UHR and convicted offenders when establishing working investigative guidelines unless an MP report is already on file. Without an MP report on file, it is too difficult to prove whether investigative or systemic error prevented the UD/UHR from being identified. I hope that, someday, a more comprehensive scientific study of

---

[*] Scientific Working Group for Forensic Anthropology. 2010. *Sex Assessment—Issue Date 06/01/2010.* p. 3.
[†] *Ibid.* p. 1.

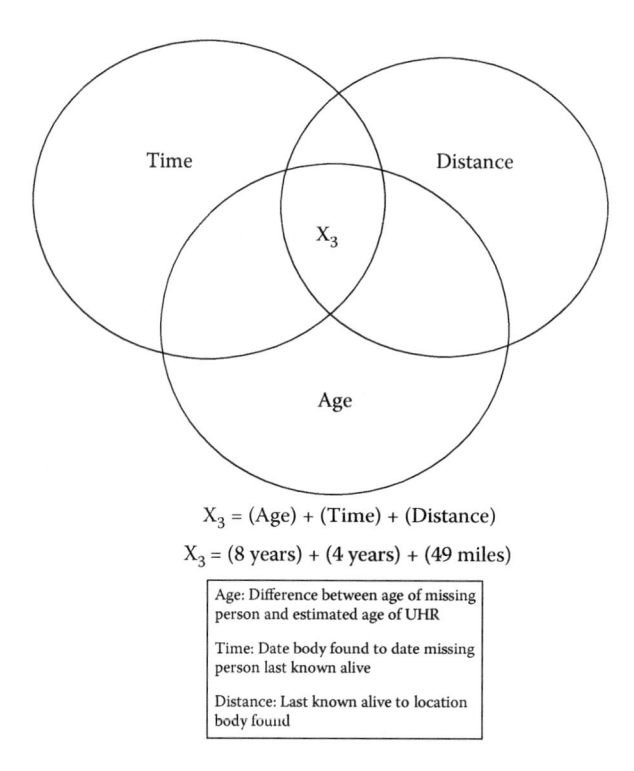

$$X_3 = (\text{Age}) + (\text{Time}) + (\text{Distance})$$
$$X_3 = (8 \text{ years}) + (4 \text{ years}) + (49 \text{ miles})$$

Age: Difference between age of missing person and estimated age of UHR
Time: Date body found to date missing person last known alive
Distance: Last known alive to location body found

Figure 4.4 Initial strategy development parameters.

cold hit identifications will provide more precise probabilities for establishing the accuracy of reported metadata than the anecdotal reviews used in this book.

I also found that most crime is local; that is, it is usually committed and resolved in a relatively narrow geographical area. Of course, it is already well known that many violent criminals have histories of minor offenses and that a small number of criminals commit more than 80% of the reported crimes in the United States. Accordingly, the police department of Palm Bay, Florida started its own local DNA database to address petty crime in its jurisdiction.

As previously stated, SDIS and NDIS labs (and databases) provide hierarchical coverage for large geographic areas. They do not have the resources (or bandwidth) to deal with DNA testing to resolve petty crimes.[*] State resources can help resolve local crimes, however, as when police in Lubbock, Texas searched the Texas Department of Public Safety's files of crime scene and familial DNA to link local aggravated kidnapping, assault, and homicide cases from 2008 to 2014 with an offender who was subsequently arrested and charged.[†]

---

[*] Berger, B., Chimera, J., Blackledge, J. 2008. LODIS, a new investigative tool: DNA is not just court evidence anymore. *The Chief of Police*, LXXV(4).
[†] Sanders, S. 2014. KCBD Investigates: DNA links Lubbock man to 2008 murder. KCBD. com (Accessed October 10, 2014).

The vast majority of DNA searches are done for forensic purposes. Proximity, another primary indicator, was crucial in the case of Maria Solias, who went missing in Houston in March 2003 and whose remains were found in Sugarland 5 months later by a work crew;* the distance between the two locations was approximately 26 miles. A preliminary mtDNA link was found by a local lab between the UHR and a biological family member, and additional nuclear testing was conducted to confirm the hit.† Outliers will always occur, such as the case of Tammy Vincent in 2007 (disappearance in Washington State, found in California, but the majority of disappearances and identifications are local.

Because nuclear DNA provides the most discriminating DNA power with current technology, the more loci are recovered from a DNA sample, the better chances there are for rapidly and efficiently finding a match or association. Therefore, investigators may find that the best initial strategy is to utilize a LDIS laboratory nearest the location where the body was found and to utilize national missing persons program laboratories to supplement the local lab's analysis. In fact, CODIS was designed with the premise that users would search LDIS profiles first (in other words, local CODIS DNA databases), SDIS second (in other words, state CODIS DNA databases) if no local hit turned up, and NDIS third (in other words, national CODIS DNA databases) when no SDIS hits turned up. This strategy has proven very effective. As of 2014, all 190+ public CODIS laboratories available to investigators had full access to all of the missing and unidentified databases within CODIS. Many of the laboratories with new access to MP and UP databases may be more skilled and willing to work with challenging samples.

When investigators are creating case strategies, some of the information previously explained in this chapter is particularly relevant. For example, if the LDIS or SDIS laboratory chosen by an investigator cannot extract DNA from UHR (e.g., skeletal remains), a sample should be sent to one of the national missing person program laboratories or to a private laboratory that has arrangements with LDIS and SDIS laboratories to conduct analyses in accordance with NDIS policies.‡ Another important step to remember is that an investigator should confirm with the DNA laboratory that a copy of the UHR profile will be provided to the investigating agency. Investigators must know that, depending upon the willingness of a particular laboratory, sufficient UHR profiles can be searched against all DNA databases in CODIS at any level and UHR profiles ineligible for CODIS upload can still be searched through the various CODIS databases at LDIS and SDIS levels via manual comparisons. In addition, an

---

* Center for Human Identification. 2011. *Success Stories: Maria Isabel Solis.* http://www.hsc.unt.edu/departments/pathology_anatomy/dna/Forensics/Initiative/Solis.cfm (Accessed 5, 2015).
† *Ibid.*
‡ DNA Labs International, 2009. *FDLE DNA Pilot Project.* DNA Labs International. http://www.dnalabsinternational.com/about.html.

LDIS or SDIS lab may request a one-time keyboard search at any CODIS level but such requests are difficult to fulfill and are not always granted.

All DRS, FRS, or UD/UHR samples should be sent to the investigators' local laboratory as an initial strategy for the following reasons: (1) Most crime is local in nature; in cases of foul play, it is both difficult and risky for an offender to transport a body to any considerable distance; (2) Using metadata to rank hits is a notoriously inaccurate and wasteful approach in UHR cold hit cases (bigger databases produce more false hits, each of which must be verified by a CODIS administrator); and (3) Grant-funded DNA programs may not be eager or even willing to reanalyze samples to produce more comprehensive profiles.

To summarize, an investigator should first submit all reference samples associated with an MP, UD, or UHR to a local laboratory. But whether the receiving/testing laboratory is local, state, or national, it must be confirmed that the investigating agency will be sent a copy of the UHR or DRS profile. An investigator should also attempt to confirm that the investigating agency will be notified of all hits, no matter when they occur or who authorized the search(es).

Furthermore, investigators should strive to obtain a DRS (direct reference sample) profile, because it is the most likely to produce a hit. A DRS profile can be obtained from items that contain cells of an MP, or from DNA samples taken from arrestees/convicted felons. Cells can also be extracted from a blood card, stored surgical sample, slide from a well-woman visit, or an object that was in close contact with the MP. FRS (biological family member reference samples) are the easiest to obtain and process for DNA; however, they are the least useful and the most costly because multiple samples must be obtained and tested. There are also possible issues with disclosure (e.g., previously unknown siblings), locating far-flung relatives, etc. Or a family member selected for testing may not be of the relationship that is reported by other family members. Women described as sisters have turned out to be mother and daughter; supposed mothers have turned out to be actual grandmothers.

Another reason that DRS are better choices for testing than FRS is that a DRS hit may match several partial (incomplete) UHR profiles, but FRS profiles often turn up partial UHR profile hits in unmanageable numbers. Labs should undertake the disposition of partial matches by disregarding all metadata other than location, distance, and time. For their part, investigators should work leads in order of distance. As previously explained, this means starting at the location closest to where the UD/UHR was found and moving outward in concentric patterns.

Notification is another major issue for investigators. As has been stated several times in this chapter, DRS samples may be searched against all databases within CODIS and local non-CODIS databases. However, investigators must confirm that those searches actually occur on a regular basis—it's not enough to know that the testing lab has a policy to conduct them. Most important, an investigator should be notified immediately when any investigative lead/hit is found between a DRS profile and a UHR profile, as well as the disposition of all such hits.

Upon notification, he or she can use the case file to confirm or refute that lead. Having documentation on file that a hit has been refuted supplies documentation for probable cause to end that line of investigation. Investigators should also consider gathering additional genetic data, if doing so would help to confirm a reported lead/hit. DNA profiles derived from translational technologies such as NGS for STR, mtDNA, SNP, or Y-STR may prove more discriminating than tradition legacy DNA technologies which includes LCN. Mitochondrial DNA may be of marginal utility, depending the statistical probabilities it reveals.

DRS profiles should be searched against convicted offender/arrestee profiles in case the MP has been incarcerated under an assumed name or transferred around the country at various prisons. For example, in July 2011, a man who had been thought missing for 30 years was found alive using the identity of another living person, which he had purchased for $800. The man, who had lived under aliases in Florida and California as well, had been arrested under different names in those states.[*] But any time a DRS profile or UD/UHR profile produces a hit to another database profile, the investigator can obtain additional verified metadata such as mug or booking shots, scars, birthmarks, tattoos, or fingerprints; all of these can assist with UD/UHR identifications. Not all fingerprints or other metadata are forwarded to national biometric databases. However, for every adult who has been incarcerated, a custodial file may exist that contains pictures, descriptors, and associations. Such information can be very useful in linking an individual to geographic locations, social groups, etc.

As previously mentioned, the databases at many LDIS and SDIS labs as well as private or agency labs contain DNA profiles that are ineligible for submission to SDIS or NDIS. One example is the high-risk potential victims DNA database of the Dallas County Sheriff's Office Prostitute Diversion Initiative (PDI). Other databases may include tests related to property crimes, or LCN samples. In fact, LDIS and SDIS laboratories may maintain multiple DNA indexes or databases and/or samples that cannot be entered at the NDIS level. This situation was acknowledged by the U.S. Supreme Court in 2012, in a stay order that mentioned the Commonwealth of Maryland had acquired 10,666 DNA samples but only 4327 were eligible for entry into the federal database.[†] Significant numbers of DNA profiles exist but may never

---

[*] Benka, C. 8 News NOW Staff. 2011. Man Missing for 30 Years Found Alive in Las Vegas. *KLAS-TV* Las Vegas.
[†] Chief Justice Roberts. July 30, 2012. Maryland *v.* Alonzo Jay King, Jr., On Application for Stay. 567 U.S._No. 12A48 Supreme Court of the United States. p. 3.

be searched if samples are sent initially to national MP laboratories operating at the LDIS level of CODIS. DNA profiles should be entered into CODIS at the local level (LDIS) and flagged by a CODIS administrator to go to the state level (SDIS) and then the national level (NDIS) if no hit (potential match or association) has been made. NDIS is just a computer program that informs both laboratories (the one that submitted the MP profile and the one that submitted UD/UHR profiles) of CODIS hits, so that the two laboratories can contact each other and arrive at a disposition for the hit.

As stated multiple times in this chapter, CODIS does not accept profiles of victims at any level, other than in its unidentified (deceased and alive) database. Therefore, investigators should establish close working relationships with their local LDIS labs; investigators and analysts should be able to collaborate in the development of additional strategies, or implement changes to strategies already in use. For its part, the National Missing and Unidentified Persons (NamUs) system should support all LDIS labs and use national MP laboratories as safeguards, not primary resources. Too often, samples are outsourced from national labs to hold down costs and reduce backlogs rather than to identify a UD/UHR. As has been mentioned in this chapter, LDIS and SDIS labs can flag DNA profiles for uploading to the SDIS and NDIS levels, but LDIS labs cannot search other labs' profiles unless a hit is returned to them through SDIS or NDIS for disposition of a specific association or match.

Also as previously stated, there are CODIS guidelines for entry of DNA profiles based on state and federal regulations but CODIS laboratories operate based upon their own interpretations. Confusion in DNA searches may result. For example, classifications of remains may differ. Some labs may enter blood or tissue from a crime scene, clothing, or in/on vehicles as UHR but others may designate them as ineligible for entry, even within the same state. Some labs may or may not maintain suspect databases, and the ones that do may have different entry criteria. Some may permit familial searching or partial match reporting but others may not.

Perhaps it is most important to remember that, because of the high levels of discretion and subjective judgement in the U.S. criminal justice system, investigators must confirm the actual practices of any laboratory that processes tissue samples and searches DNA profiles, and obtain confirmation after a CODIS hit is made at any level (local, state, or national). Actual practices, including posttest follow-up, must be verified and documented in writing throughout the investigation. Otherwise, the risk of liability to investigators, agencies, and local communities is high.

An association report from a DNA laboratory to an agency or investigator is nothing more than an opinion about statistical values (probability) relative to the likely relationship between an FRS DNA profile and a UD/UHR profile based on the assumptions, equipment, skill, and protocols of the analyzing laboratory. The statistical values may and probably will be different from laboratory to laboratory for the exact same testing. A "warm hit" association report usually functions in a confirming capacity to support a previously developed investigative lead or other modality (e.g., fingerprints, dental, and circumstances). It is the "cold hit" association that truly produces an original investigative lead for investigators. Regardless of the statistical values, an association report is nothing more than an opinion—it does not carry the same impact or relativity as a match report where all alleles and loci between a DRS profile and a UD/UHR profile are identical—the exception is a case involving the existence of identical twins or multiple births (i.e., triplets, etc.). An association report only documents that a possible biological relationship exists between the target and reference profiles. The DNA association cannot ascertain that the UD/UHR is the actual missing person in question based on DNA alone—additional information is required for identification.

Resolving cold hit associations is where investigators will need to have effective strategies in place as the case may at any time develop into a criminal case. Once the cold hit association report is received by the agency or investigator, there is now a probable cause to believe that the MP may be the UD. Now the investigator has an opportunity to locate suitable evidence for a DRS from the possible MP or items (e.g., undergarments, hairbrush, toothbrush, and shoes) that were in close contact with the possible MP. Once the DRS is acquired, it may be more appropriate to send the DRS to an alternate laboratory that did not develop the FRS or UD/UHR profile. An alternate laboratory that specializes in processing crime scene evidence for agencies has more experience and tested protocols for screening and analyzing physical items of DRS. Once the DRS profile is acquired, a quick manual comparison with the FRS laboratory may be used to validate the DRS or even confirm a match between the UD/UHR and DRS. The investigator then needs to confirm that there were not identical siblings if not previously confirmed. The confirmation that there were no multiple births should come from primary birth records of original custodians such as hospitals or county records clerk, not families or public databases. The death investigator may now present with two (FRS and DRS) separate and supporting evidentiary items for appropriate authorities to make the identification. This is another means of executing multimodality identification strategy though both are DNA based.

A serious concern for investigators is presented when the identification develops into a criminal case. That concern is a claim of negligent investigation, which hangs over the investigator like the "sword of Damocles."* The two separate evidentiary items, the association report with an FRS and the

---

* Pilger, L. 2015. Retrial Sought in Beatrice 6 Civil Rights Case. *Lincoln Journal Star On-line*, May 13, 2015. http://journalstar.com/news/local/911/retrial-sought-in-beatrice-civil-rights-case/article_e0c3848c-98fd-5a96-b191-f0f7197542b0.html (Accessed August 6, 2015).

match report with a DRS, provide an effective prophylactic strategy; however, all avenues need to be addressed. A complete copy of the laboratory's working DNA case file, bench notes, and LIMS (laboratory information management system) should be obtained and reviewed. Some laboratories may resist making the copies available to the investigator or may require a subpoena to provide the items. The files may contain information from other subject matter experts as odontologists, anthropologists or other subject matter experts or analysts of which the investigator was unaware. It may also reveal problems with internal COC (chain-of-custody) or contamination as the evidence moves throughout the lab and specimen number changes as the evidentiary items are altered for DNA analysis. Many laboratories' workflow centers on batch processing as the evidence moves through the laboratory. COC gaps in time from releasing an item from one party or place to another may give way to challenges that a third party was involved in moving the item but was not listed on the COC. Any unaccounted gaps in time movement present real problems with the case. It is best that the investigator discovers the problems at the onset of the investigation rather than later in evidentiary hearings or claims decades later in postconviction hearings. It is not uncommon for errors to develop involving DNA laboratories where results of many previously adjudicated case came into question.[*][†] Families need to understand that proper strategies are not only necessary for identification and prosecution in their missing loved one's case but for the protection of the investigator as well. The separate FRS and DRS processing strategies at separate labs provide the safety net necessary to cover many unanticipated problems.

UHR investigations, particularly when they become long-term cold cases, are complex. Therefore, they are often fraught with problems, errors, and unexpected events that delay resolution. "To manage the unexpected requires problem insight—becoming aware of small disturbances and vulnerabilities as they emerge, understanding the possible problematic consequences, and adjusting ongoing actions before they can turn into a tragic flaw."[‡] Understanding the basics of DNA testing, profile reporting, and profile searching, as well as maintaining good communication among all the parties involved, can go a long way toward preventing tragic errors and wasted years.

[*] Alexander, K., Zauzmer, J. 2015. Director of D.C.'s Embattled DNA Lab Resigns after Suspension of Testing. *Washington Post.* http://www.washingtonpost.com/local/director-of-dcs-embattled-dna-lab-resigns-following-suspension-of-testing/2015/04/30/1c619320-ef80-11e4-8666-a1d756d0218e_story.html (Accessed August 6, 2015).

[†] Jacobs, S. 2015. Judge Tosses Out Two Types of DNA Evidence Used Regularly in Criminal Cases. *New York Daily News*, January 5, 2015. http://www.nydailynews.com/new-york/nyc-crime/judge-tosses-types-dna-testing-article-1.2065795 (Accessed August 6, 2015).

[‡] Scutiff, K., Christianson, M. 2013. *Managing for the Unexpected.* Michigan Ross School of Business, Center for Positive Organization Scholarship. p. 2.

CODIS and NMPDD   5

As discussed in previous chapters, the Combined DNA Index System (CODIS) houses numerous DNA databases, which are also called indices (the plural of "index"); their primary purpose is to assist law enforcement agencies. The National Missing Persons DNA Database (NMPDD) is really the NDIS level of CODIS, but often used to indicate the combination of LDIS, SDIS, and NDIS databases. The FBI initially developed multiple CODIS indices for the purpose of generating investigative leads in criminal cases, but in 2004–2005 began to allow this information to be used in MP/UD and UHR investigations.

The official activation of CODIS in October 1998[*] allowed participating public DNA laboratories to upload qualified DNA profiles developed from case evidence so that they could be shared among laboratories at the NDIS level. The original goal was to allow DNA profile searches of all of the CODIS criminal indices. In 2004–2005, MP/UD DNA profiles, including mtDNA, began to be added to CODISmp (a separate version from CODIS criminal indices—the mp stood for missing persons) for use in UHR investigations. CODIS is now available in all 50 states and in some foreign countries, and is provided to some international agencies; however, as explained in the previous chapter, it does not have share or cross-search capability with the records of all laboratories that test DNA.

Each state in the United States must go through an application process to obtain CODIS access, and must execute a memorandum of understanding with the FBI that outlines how it will administrate CODIS. The state agency that is the signatory to this memorandum of understanding is the only agency in that state which may directly upload DNA profiles to the NDIS (national) level. However, every local CODIS-approved laboratory in such states is required to comply with the FBI administrative directions and policies in the memorandum of understanding. Thus, CODIS has three operational levels in each state: LDIS (Local DNA Index System), SDIS (State DNA Index System), and NDIS (National DNA Index System).

As has been explained earlier in this book, an LDIS lab is the lowest (most local) level of CODIS; it may be a one-room facility at a law enforcement agency or ME's office. LDIS laboratories can upload profiles to the state level (SDIS).

---

[*] Department of Justice, Office of the Inspector General 2001, September. *Audit Report: The Combined DNA Index System*, pp. 01–26.

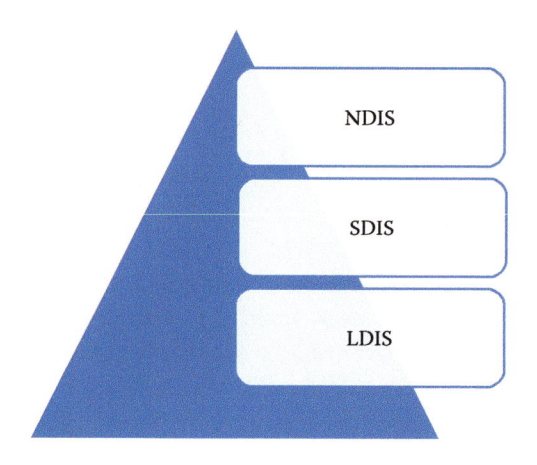

Figure 5.1 The three levels of CODIS.

When a DNA profile search at the local level is returned without a match or association, local DNA profiles may be uploaded to the state level (the second level of CODIS). When a profile that has been searched at the state level is returned without a match or association, it may be uploaded to the national level (NDIS). Decisions about whether or not to upload a profile to the next level are made at the lower level. Figure 5.1 illustrates the CODIS hierarchal structure.

As CODIS has developed, many changes have been made at all levels; these have mainly concerned policy interpretations and broad, subjective, discretionary interpretations of data. One lab may interpret a policy one way and another laboratory in another. This happens because, as I try to emphasize throughout this book, individuals often construe a sentence or circumstance quite differently—a human tendency that finds much expression in U.S. law enforcement, wherein varying levels of discretion and wide leeways of interpretation are allowed.

At the NDIS level, a UHR DNA profile can only be entered into the CODIS unidentified human index. Here is where the differences between human interpretations and human-invented procedures may become particularly relevant. For example, consider a large amount of blood found on bedding in an outdoor area. The policy of one laboratory may state that only bone or tissue qualify as human remains, and therefore may not conclude that this blood could belong to a UD; however, this same laboratory might designate a blood card from blood extracted from a body representative of human remains. Another lab may accept this blood as a UHR sample if it is accompanied by an ME report stating that a person could not survive after losing such a large amount of blood. Yet another lab, with no objections, may accept this blood as evidence submitted by a law enforcement agency.

In 2010, an older male in Texas attempted to kidnap a female who was able to get away and provide a description of his vehicle. A short time later, this same male attempted to kidnap another female at a truck stop; a relative who attempted to intervene was shot and killed. During his escape, the offender attempted to take two female juveniles with him; one was abducted and the other fled. A law enforcement officer happened to be passing the offender's vehicle when this juvenile jumped out. The offender, who turned out to be a truck driver licensed in several states, exited his vehicle and was shot and killed by the officer.[*]

The jurisdictional law enforcement agency wanted to enter the dead offender's DNA into CODIS, in hopes that it might clear sexual assault or homicide cases in other states. Here is where the confusion began. Even had the offender survived, his DNA could have been collected and entered into one of the DNA indices; however, that entry would most likely have been into a suspect index at the LDIS and/or SDIS level. As it turned out, one state accepted the offender's blood sample for DNA at both the LDIS and SDIS levels, because no policies prohibited them from doing so. But another state refused to accept the DNA sample for analysis and entry into CODIS at all because it had no policies that specifically allowed it to enter samples from a known deceased offender.

Investigators and families often know that such confusing and inconsistent circumstances exist, but not that such circumstances may directly affect their cases. Even lawyers hired by families may not know. It is the investigator who must understand that what may be true in one jurisdiction or state may not be true in another, and must take the most responsibility for creating an investigative strategy that effectively overcomes such differences.

The following profile records may be stored, uploaded, and searched at the NDIS level: biological father, sibling, or child; spouse; maternal or paternal relative; MP (deduced by DRS); and UP (living or deceased).[†] The following information is included in a DNA profile record: the profile itself; the ORI (agency identifier) number; specimen ID number; and the name of the DNA analyst.[‡] No information that can personally identify a DNA donor is included in a CODIS DNA record.

There are several indices related to MP (Table 5.1). Some examples are the Relatives of Missing Person Index (biological mother, father, sibling, child, or other maternal relative); the Spouse Index (spouse DNA only); the Unidentified Human Index (living or deceased UP); the Missing Person Index (deduced MP, actual MP); the Pedigree Tree Index (deduced MP, actual MP, biological parents and children).[§]

[*] Myers, S. 2010. *Man Killed after Killing Grandmother and Abducting Girl.* http://www.ConnectAmarillo.com 7abc.
[†] Federal Bureau of Investigation. 2103. *National DNA INDEX System (NDIS): Operations Procedures Manual: Version 1,* Effective January 31, Chapter 3.
[‡] *Ibid.*
[§] *Ibid.*

It is extremely easy even for professionals to become confused by all the different categories, rules, and indices in CODIS, not least because these frequently change without notice and because CODIS does not include the means to notify investigators of these changes. In addition, there are other indices to consider. These include the Forensic Index and its subindices of Forensic Mixture Index and Forensic Partial Index. The Offender Index includes Convicted Offender, Arrestee, Detainee, and Legal indices.[*] To make all of this even more complicated, LDIS and SDIS laboratories search indices at their pleasure or schedule. NDIS labs run searches of new or modified records in the indices shown in Table 5.1.[†]

> **Key point:** UHR profiles and MP profiles (DRS only) may be compared to any profile in any CODIS index. FRS may only be searched against unidentified human (living or dead) index profiles.

Keyboard searches, which can be done by special request through SDIS due to exigent circumstances, are exceptions to Table 5.2; they can be performed without having the profile officially entered into the database. However, keyboard search requests may meet with long delays or be refused outright. In Rivera v. Mueller (2009), the FBI refused requests for a keyboard search of a viable DNA profile at the NDIS level. Requests were met with long delays and refused out right. The court ruled in the petitioner's favor and order the search conducted.[‡]

Table 5.1   Missing Person Related Indices with Applicable Specimen Categories

Relatives of Missing Person Index	Spouse Index	Unidentified Human (Remains) Index	Missing Person Index	Pedigree Tree Index
Biological child	Spouse	Unidentified person	Deduced missing person	Deduced missing person
Biological father			Missing person	Missing person
Biological mother				Biological child
Biological sibling				Biological father
Maternal relative				Biological mother
Paternal relative				Biological sibling
				Maternal relative
				Paternal relative
				Spouse

[*] *Ibid.*
[†] *Ibid.*
[‡] Juan A. Rivera, Plaintiff, *v.* Robert S. Mueller, Director of the Federal Bureau of Investigation, Defendant. United States District Court, N.D. Illinois, Eastern Division. February 2, 2009. 596 F.Supp.2d 1163 (2009).

Table 5.2   STR Profile of Deceased (Fetal Tissue)

Locus	Deceased (Fetal Tissue)	CODIS Core Loci*
D8S1179	15	Yes
D21S11	29, 30	Yes
D7S820	10	Yes
CSF1PO	11	Yes
D3S1358	15	Yes
TH01	8	Yes
D13S317	12	Yes
D16S539	9, 14	Yes
D2S1338	17, 18	No
D19S433	14, 16.2	No
vWA	17	Yes
TPOX	8, 11	Yes
D18S51	10,15	Yes
AMEL	X, X	Yes
D5S818	13	Yes
FGA	20, 21	Yes

Source: Federal Bureau of Investigation. n/d. Laboratory Services: Planned Process and Timeline for Implementation of Additional CODIS Core Loci. www.fbi.gov/about-us/lab/biometric-analysis/codis/planned-process-and-timeline-for-implementation-of-additional-codis-core-loci (Accessed August 6, 2015).

* As of 2013, the addition of loci to boost discriminating power (for difficult samples) were under consideration.

In 2005 to early 2006, some laboratories were given the impression that cases required a NCIC (National Crime Information Center) number to be analyzed for DNA and entered into CODIS. In addition, contrary to protocol, DNA profiles from UHR were not searched against the convicted offender index. Agencies assumed the searches against the DNA offender and UHR indices were taking place because the searching matrix and bulletins indicated such search capabilities. However, it was quite obvious to experienced law enforcement officers that the convicted offender index and the unidentified human index were not actually being compared, because no cold hits were being returned via CODIS. Later, when the search mechanism between the unidentified human index and convicted offender index was corrected and the protocol was revised, CODIS produced multiple hits.

Cold hits between unidentified remains and convicted offender profiles are extremely common. Many families have lost contact with incarcerated individuals and remain unaware that anything suspicious has involved the person associated in the cold hit. The case below, which is typical, illustrates the difficulties (see Figures 5.2, 5.3, and 5.4) that unidentified decedent cases present to investigators and ME/C.

Unidentified Human Remains Case Study

Detective Mark Czworniak (Retired)
Chicago Police Department

The body of an unidentified female was discovered in an abandoned building in September of 2010. It was thought that she was an elderly female Black, and missing persons reports were examined for anyone fitting that particular demographic. There were no matches made.

At autopsy, the pathologist was unable to determine the race or age of the victim; however several hip replacement artifacts were discovered. An inquiry with the manufacturer, led only to a few hospitals where the implants may have been shipped to, but no particular patient was identified.

Metal braces surgically implanted in the victims jaw were also discovered at autopsy, but no identifying markings were present. The case was entered into NAMUS.

A DNA sample was sent to the University of North Texas, and a profile uploaded in to the National CODIS Database [NMPDD]. In September of 2013, a CODIS DNA association was made, via a DNA sample taken from a female inmate in the Wisconsin Department of Corrections, upon her incarceration there in 2009.

The identity of the victim was then determined and her parents were located and advised of the investigation. They had no idea their daughter was dead. The victim's remains were returned to her grateful parents.

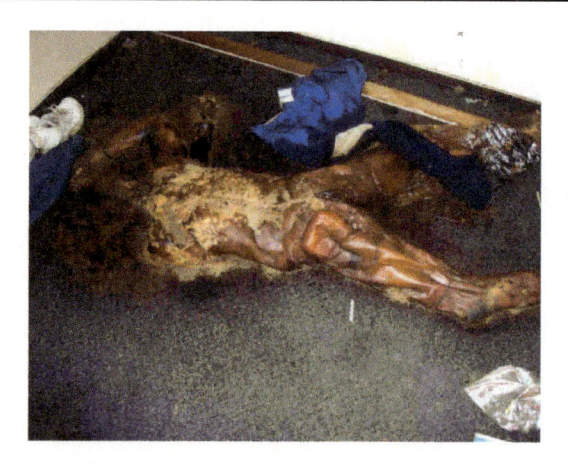

Figure 5.2 An example of an unidentified decedent in advanced stages of decomposition. (Courtesy of Detective Mark Czworniak (retired), Chicago Police Department.)

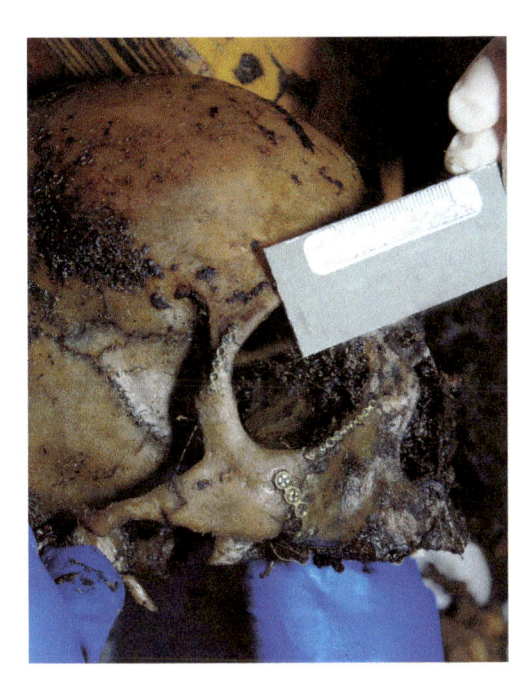

Figure 5.3 Skull showing dental artifacts. (Courtesy of Detective Mark Czworniak (retired), Chicago Police Department.)

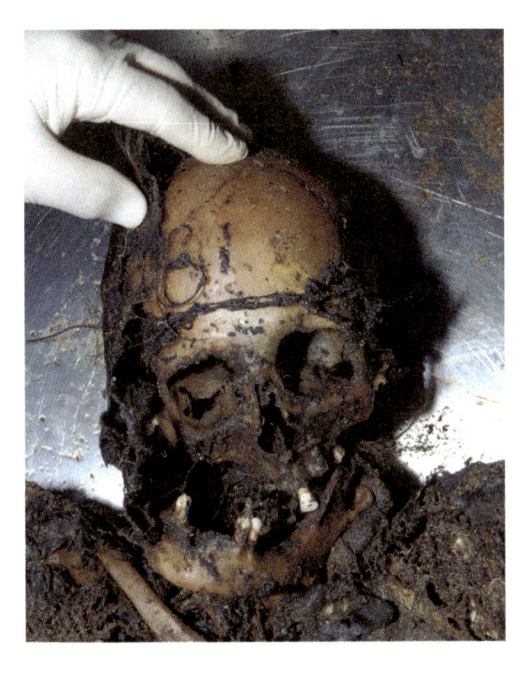

Figure 5.4 Frontal view of skull depicting challenging conditions of evidence facing investigators in their work. (Courtesy of Detective Mark Czworniak (retired), Chicago Police Department.)

The cold hit in this case speaks to the power of CODIS. It was a local laboratory that processed the sample and uploaded the case to SDIS and NDIS, where the match was made with an offender's profile.

Initially in 2005 as the UNTCHI program coordinator, I advised agencies that an NCIC number was necessary for submission of a DNA sample to laboratories on advice from the UNTHCI CODIS administrator as a requirement of the FBI. This requirement proved frustrating for some investigators. The NCIC number is important; however, when attempting to identify additional victims of convicted or deceased murderers, agencies may not desire to open another criminal case. The requirement for having an NCIC number was discontinued shortly afterwards, when I discovered that the FBI was sending cases to regional DNA laboratories without NCIC entries. Following the discoveries of these two anomalies, I was advised that I no longer allowed the agency to directly FBI CODIS management. Obfuscation of anomalies works to reduce the efficacy of all criminal investigations, not just investigations of unidentified human remains.

Key point: Although it is not required, all UHR cases should be entered into NCIC so that clearinghouse resources can be put to work finding associations through the Criminal Justice Information System (CJIS) as well as in the databases of facilities that use NGI technology.

As discussed in Chapter 4, UHR may be so severely degraded that enhanced DNA extraction techniques must be used to produce a viable profile. When the LCN (low copy number—enhanced extraction techniques) DNA is used, the resulting profile could be entered into CODIS at the NDIS level prior to 2015. In 2015, LCN profiles from single source (DRS, FRS, UHR) profiles may be entered into CODIS.* However, hundreds of LCN profiles are stored in separate indices at labs across the country and (with lab permission) can be searched at the LDIS and SDIS levels. Investigators may not know that previous LCN submissions could not be searched at the NDIS level—but this knowledge is essential. Agencies and investigators must now ascertain if the previous LCN developed may be entered and searched, or will the LCN samples have to be reanalyzed for entry.

DNA analysis results are explained using probability ratios that are calculated with various statistical software packages. In MP cases, the larger the ratio, the more likely it is that the UD/UHR may belong to the MP. The issue that investigators must struggle with has to do with what threshold level, or ratio size, is necessary to produce a good confidence level. Whenever an

---

* National DNA Index System (NDIS); *Operational Procedures Manual*; FBI Laboratory; Version 3; Effective January 1, 2015. Section 4.2.10.

investigator receives a report of a putative (possible) match or association, he or she should contact the person who has signed the report to confirm the rarity of the profile (in other words, to put the ratio into context). If contact is made by phone, the investigator should follow up with a confirmatory e-mail that restates the details of the conversation.

It cannot be overemphasized that investigators must obtain a copy of every DNA analysis report (i.e., a copy of every DRS, FRS, and UD/UHR profile). The number of STR (nuclear DNA) alleles that were examined is important: the more, the better. In addition, the investigator must know how each DNA profile was generated. When legacy technology is upgraded, the investigator will be responsible for making sure that UHR samples are reanalyzed.

Depending on the sample, the available equipment, and the analyst's skills, numerous procedures and technologies are available for developing DNA profiles. Investigators do not need to overly concern themselves with exactly which procedures are actually being used, however. This is because a direct hit between an MP profile and a UD/UHR profile is usually confirmed by reanalysis—whether the tests were done at the same lab or at different ones.

Nonetheless, investigators should keep an eye on the process by obtaining a copy of the complete case file after they have been notified of a match or association. It is possible that one or more labs will have confidence in their procedures and results but, all the same, for a sharp-eyed investigator to notice something in the case file that indicates the samples were incorrectly handled or that some other error may have impacted the test results. Of course, as with any investigation, it is preferable to correct any problems or repeat tests as soon as possible.

Investigators should keep two important factors about DNA tests in mind. One is the turnaround time of a test. This begins when the sample(s) is/are sent to the lab and ends when the DNA analysis report(s) is/are received by investigating agency. The second is how the disposition report is worded; it should be clear, concise, and simple.

No reliable estimates of turnaround times for MP/UD/UHD DNA test results are available; some samples have taken more than a year to process, and each case is unique. We do know, however, that the mean turnaround time for processing evidence in property crimes is 154 days and for violent crimes it is 106 days.* A reasonable estimate of how long it actually takes to process DNA samples is 60 h (between seven and eight full working days).† The rest of the time is consumed by waiting: for the analysis to be completed, for peer reviews to be turned in, for technical reviews to be completed, for

---

* Nelson, M., Chase, R., DePalma, L. 2013. *National Institute of Justice Special Report: Making Sense of Backlogs, 2012—Myths vs. Reality.* U.S. Department of Justice, Office of Justice Programs.

† Sargent, F. n.d. *DNA Testing Timeline.* Public Agency Training Council. http://www.patc.com/weeklyarticles/dna-timeline.shtml (Accessed August 6, 2005).

disposition reviews to be completed, and for the CODIS upload. Turnaround time in DNA sample processing appears to be related the number of staff available at the testing lab.

CODIS laboratories may accept sample profiles from to non-CODIS laboratories only if the CODIS laboratory accepts ownership of the profiles to be entered into CODIS. The CODIS laboratory may be required to send a representative to conduct an off-site visit to the non-CODIS laboratory, have a contract or memorandum of understanding in place, utilize the same technology as the non-CODIS laboratory, and conform to NDIS policies.

A CODIS laboratory usually has a template for final (disposition) reports. A typical template contains the match/association or nonmatch/nonassociation and little else other than case identifiers and possible circumstances. Although it is not uncommon for a UD to be a victim of a violent crime, indicators that the death was violent may not be included in the report. In general, the final report does not provide information other than (1) the statistical probabilities associated with an association or a match, (2) the type of analysis that was done, (3) the index or other source of the association or match, and (4) the names of the agencies that provided the samples from which the reference profiles were obtained. The organization and layout of disposition reports are specific to each laboratory.

CODIS does not have a tracking mechanism to document the receipt of a DNA report by a submitting agency. Most CODIS labs place notes or other documentation in case files to indicate that the disposition report was sent or communicated to the appropriate agencies, but do not require confirmation to be placed in the case file that the appropriate entities (the investigator, the family, other labs or agencies) each received their copy. As a result, reports can be lost or misplaced before agencies are aware of the results they contain—naturally, such cases are not resolved. In 2007, a study of CODIS in one state found that resolutions were unknown for slightly more than 27% of hits: "none of the software programs that were used provided information as to how cases were resolved."* Even cases that are eventually resolved may face needless delays.

It is not unusual for associations to be made between profiles that are stored at two different labs: one that has the MP (reference) profile and the other that has the unidentified (target) profile. In such cases, the lab that has developed the UHR profile usually makes the notifications. When CODIS finds a DNA match between an MP, UD, or UHR and a convicted offender profile the SDIS official is supposed to make the notifications. This does not always happen, however.

* Brown, A. 2007. *A Study of the Efficiency of the Combined DNA Index System for the Oregon State Police.* University of North Texas Health Science Center at Fort Worth. pp. 43–44.

When a CODIS laboratory faces a large number of backlogged cases, it may outsource testing to a private laboratory. It is also possible, when regulations permit, for investigators to choose a private laboratory. This alternative would be desirable if turnaround times can be shortened and if the condition of remains requires more advanced technology than nearby CODIS labs posses. Accredited private facilities with a history of successful operations also tend to invest more heavily in employee training than public labs do, and to acquire new technology routinely instead of basing their development on compliance with minimal standards that meet certification requirements. When investigators are evaluating which service provider(s) to use for DNA testing, they should consider labs' economic stability and sustainability, where labs direct their greatest investments of resources, the levels of education and training of lab employees, and the number and quality of research reports labs have published.

> **Key point:** After the testing lab has received the samples, the investigator should get a commitment to a deadline for the test to be completed and check in with the lab at regular intervals to make sure that the deadline can be met. Finding out about complications and delays as soon as possible allows the investigator to put alternate strategies into place.

Investigators who obtain DNA profiles from private labs should ask them to conduct manual searches, whether the profiles are full or partial, at the nearest LDIS laboratory and at the SDIS level. CODIS laboratories do not always like to work with private laboratories but do tend to support investigators.

As was mentioned in Chapter 4, a target DNA profile may be manually searched at against other laboratories' indices, at the LDIS and SDIS levels, without storing it in the CODIS database. Such searches are done at the discretion of LDIS and SDIS laboratories and many such labs handle LCN profiles and other noneligible NDIS profiles in this manner. LDIS laboratories associated with law enforcement agencies are the most likely to fully cooperate when investigators request them to collaborate with private labs.

If an MP is identified by a match or association before his or her case has developed into a criminal investigations, investigators can bring some resolution to the MP's family and friends though a criminal investigation may still be ongoing. Investigators and families alike should keep in mind that identification of remains, complicated and frustrating as that process may be, is possibly just the first step in a longer process of seeking justice. Patience is essential—not only between families and investigators, but also between investigators and forensic service providers/forensic support services. Most forensic service providers have difficulty in comprehending the needs of investigators, from my experience, as those same forensic service providers may have never made an arrest, interacted over extended periods of time (often years) with families in crisis, or been responsible for an investigation that incurs the level of liability (both criminally and civilly) with which law enforcement officers must deal with every day.

Investigators should first work to identify the UD/UHR, and then focus on conducting the criminal investigation if one is warranted. The initial goal for the investigator is to obtain a full nuclear DNA profile in the shortest amount of time. Each day of needless delay wastes investigative resources, makes prosecuting offenders more difficult, exposes the investigator to more liability, increases families' suffering, and may expose communities to additional risk.

DNA profiles can provide insightful information for developing investigative leads. For example, as noted in Chapter 4, it would be important for an investigator to know whether the deceased suffered incest or was a product of incest. A high number of loci that contain homozygous (identical) alleles may be an indication of incest; in a fetus, this number can be fewer than 10.[*] Higher numbers, of course, provide stronger indications. However, investigators cannot expect a lab report to place such information into context. In scientific terminology, all "homozygous loci" means is that both allele (marker) frequencies at two particular loci in a particular chromosome are the same. It is up to the investigator to understand the implications of such information.

In cases of unclear paternity or possible incest, an investigator should have all DRS, FRS, MP, and UD/UHR profiles reviewed by an independent, qualified geneticist. Because such an analysis would consist only of data review, a good investigator should be able to easily locate a suitable paternity laboratory or geneticist in any part of the United States. It is not necessary for such a person or facility to be local.

Once the final DNA analysis report of a UHR or DRS profile is delivered to the investigator, he or she should get confirmation from the testing lab that copies of the report have also been sent to other agencies that are involved in the case. Even more important, the investigator should request manual comparisons at cooperating labs (such as with convicted offender DNA profiles and indices, which are maintained at the SDIS level under the control of the state CODIS administrator) when an investigative lead links the UHR or MP to a specific geographic location.

Confirming a match or association does not indicate how the decedent died, or whether foul play was involved. To answer these questions, the case may morph from an MP or UD/UHR investigation to an investigation of homicide, sexual assault, kidnapping, or other crimes. In addition, new information may lead to other investigative leads that involve other crimes.

---

[*] Gunn, A. 2011. *Essential of Forensic Biology.* John Wiley & Sons (Table 3.4).

One published case report described the analysis of fetal tissue from a deceased female who, although pregnant, was so severely mentally and physically impaired that investigators doubted she could have consented to a sexual relationship. The analysis found homozygous loci in 8 of the 13 FBI core loci, which translates to 61.5% (a strong indication of incestuous parentage), and in 8 of the 15 female genetic paternity loci (53.3%).* This case report is important for two major reasons, of which investigators and families may not be aware, may not be able to infer from the kinds of information that CODIS lab reports contain, and may be prevented from finding out because of laboratory standards and procedures. First, high percentage of homozygous loci in a fetus, which may indicate incest, would allow prosecution of sexual assault against the mother even if no other charges could be filed. Second, this viable STR profile (meaning that it was eligible for uploading into any level of CODIS) was obtained from samples that had been fixed in formalin (a preservative) and embedded in paraffin; however, not all forensic labs accept such samples.

Additional NCIC offline searches should be considered if CODIS searches do not produce a match or association. Unfortunately, it is common for investigators to not follow up on cold cases with offline searches should CODIS not produce a match or association. In fact, NCIC searches should routinely include offline searches of purged records, which may contain information that has been gathered in situations not directly linked to criminal behavior (traffic stops, suspicious persons, etc.). Individuals who have had these types of interactions with law enforcement may have presented false names and addresses, or incorrect numerical identifiers such as birthdates, social security numbers, and so forth.

Although it may seem unbelievable that an offender could be jailed under a false identity, it is not uncommon; felons do so for numerous reasons, including attempting to hide previous involvements with the criminal justice system. The unfortunate fact that this sort of confusion occurs means that any information obtained from DNA databases should be validated by a DRS sample, if possible; if it turns out that the target was a felon, the investigator should obtain confirming images from facilities where he or she was incarcerated.

For many reasons, agencies may have difficulties maintaining control of case information and forensic services such as DNA analysis. One reason is high turnover of personnel, which is above normal in law enforcement. Another reason is that—contrary to the impression given by the CSI effect— the same investigator may not stay with a case until resolution, due to policies

---

* Robino, C. et al. 2006. Incestuous paternity detected by STR-typing of chronic villi isolated from archival formalin-fixed paraffin-embedded abortion material using laser microdissection. *Journal of Forensic Science*, January, 51(1), pp. 90–91.

about shift and duty assignments and rotations, as well as case assignments. Yet another reason has to do with difficulties and confusion around tracking when DNA samples are sent directly to national missing person programs rather than being routed in order through the nearest local LDIS laboratory.

These disconnects may seriously delay UHR investigations. This occurred in 2009, when the FBI's nuclear DNA program could not process bone evidence due to internal conflicts that reduced the ability of its National Missing Persons DNA Database (NMPDD) to support MP investigations. To address the problem, a cooperative agreement meant to take effect in 2011 was executed between the FBI and the Minnesota Department of Public Safety Laboratory. The agreement called for 720 cases to be analyzed in 12 months; however, the Minnesota DPS was able to analyze only 204 cases.[*]

A previous agreement in 2008, between the District of Columbia Metropolitan Police Department (MPD) and the FBI, had been made to address capacity restraints at the FBI Laboratory. The agreement provided for space at another facility to conduct FBI casework and for outsourcing nuclear DNA samples to a private laboratory. The logistics called for the FBI to create case files and send the evidence in each case to this private laboratory, in order to reduce the FBI's backlog of MPD (Missing Persons DNA) cases. However, 2 years later, 160 MPD cases (nearly 33% of the DNA unit's entire caseload) had not been sent.[†]

Numerous difficulties and sources of errors plague the tracking of DNA samples through laboratories. For example, the Office of the Inspector General's 2010 review of the FBI's DNA Laboratory found that it took an average of 635 days for submitters to receive results in MP cases.[‡] By contrast, a special report in 2013 by the National Institute of Justice found that the average lab turnaround time for property crimes and violent crimes had ranged from 106 to 156 days in 2011.[§] It is important to know that, along with other disconnects having to do with communication among agencies, clerical errors, and other problems, law enforcement calculates turnaround time differently than labs do. For scientists, the primary consideration is how long it takes to complete their testing. But law enforcement personnel calculate turnaround time from their submission of one or more samples until the disposition report is received back from the testing lab(s). When turnaround

[*] Office of the Inspector General. 2012. *Audit of the Federal Bureau of Investigation Laboratory's Forensic DNA Case Backlog.* U.S. Department of Justice, Office of the Inspector General Audit Division, Audit Report 10–39, August 2010, pp. 15–16.

[†] *Ibid.* p. 16.

[‡] Office of the Inspector General. 2010. *Review of the Federal Bureau of Investigation Laboratory's Forensic DNA Case Backlog.* U.S. Department of Justice, Office of the Inspector General Audit Division, Report 12–39, September 2012, p. 14.

[§] Nelson, M., Chase, R., DePalma, L. 2013. *National Institute of Justice Special Report: Making Sense of Backlogs, 2012–Myths vs. Reality.* U.S. Department of Justice, Office of Justice Programs.

times are based only on how long it may take a lab to do DNA analysis and prepare a report, underestimation is sure to result. The proper calculation of turnaround time includes multiple time frames: sample submission from agency to laboratory, comparisons of indices from lab to lab, report transmissions from lab to lab, and report transmission from labs back to not only the investigating agency of record but also every jurisdictional agency involved in the case.

In 2013, a *New York Times* reporter obtained an audit of FBI evidence-handling practices that found mishandling in almost 20,500 cases (50% of the 41,000 cases that were examined). Moreover, according to the audit, "A majority of the errors identified were due in large part to human error, attributable to a lack of training and program management oversight."[*] One cannot fail to understand, with numbers like these, why the FBI would want to outsource DNA testing. But one cannot also fail to understand, with such massive inefficaciousness at the nation's highest criminal justice institution, why investigators as well as family members become frustrated when DNA analysis takes exceedingly long amounts of time and/or evidence cannot be readily located. Here, the FBI's strategy of outsourcing was sound but could not succeed because the agency's own disconnects fatally undermined it.

As noted throughout this book, a great deal of the effort in MP, UD, and UHR investigations is undertaken by the investigator who is in charge of the logistical aspects. Without the support of transitional agencies such as state missing persons, clearinghouses, and nongovernment organizations, chances are high that an investigation will turn into a sentinel event (i.e., that a cold case will remain unresolved far longer than it should). Valuable assistance can be gained when an investigator notifies and coordinates state MP clearinghouses. These offices also provide resources for tracking samples, coordinating information, and resolving DNA hits; in addition, they usually have access to school records, juvenile justice records, and many individual law enforcement/department of corrections databases. If clearinghouse personnel have online access to NCIC, both NCIC and NamUs can be updated and changes to NamUs case entries can be reconciled and tracked.

The two most important events related to the associations and matches that are of greatest concern to law enforcement are when a CODIS laboratory provides a hit, which can be used as an investigative lead, and how that lead is followed up.[†] A 2007 audit of agency case files found that a high percentage were incomplete because they lacked information on lab work or how the

---

[*] RT. 2014. *FBI Mishandled Evidence Throughout United States.* RT.com http://rt.com/usa/216187-fbi-mishandled-evidence-storage/.
[†] Brown, A. 2007. *A Study of the Efficiency of the Combined DNA Index System for the Oregon State Police.* University of North Texas Health Science Center at Fort Worth. p. 61.

case was concluded.* Audits in several other states have uncovered similar problems. Clearinghouses' attempts to have laboratories furnish copies of their reports, or statuses of the reports when there delays, have often been unsuccessful. An excellent way for investigators to combat these disconnects is to routinely add their state missing persons clearinghouse to the list of agencies that must be provided with copies of each and every DNA disposition, and to confirm that list with each and every testing lab. This list is included in laboratory submission forms.

During their own internal audits of missing and unidentified case files, several state police departments have experienced findings similar to those above. Submitting jurisdictional agencies often end up trying to track down samples thought to have been sent to a particular CODIS laboratory on behalf of an investigator. Unfortunately, samples are frequently sent to one laboratory but are rerouted to another without notification. In addition, case numbers and specimen numbers are often changed from lab to lab; this disconnect becomes even more problematic when the submitting agency is not the same as the agency of record. In such cases, the first laboratory may not tell the next laboratory who the original agency was (and so on). Ultimately, the lab that finally does the actual DNA testing may not know where to send its disposition and the submitting jurisdictional agency may not be informed of sample transfers from lab to lab until it decides to commit resources to following the trail. In my personal experience, it has taken as much as a full week to locate samples by calling various laboratories and reconciling case numbers, evidence numbers, and shipping times.

Investigators who cannot do this kind of tracking may assume that samples have been lost and so advise the family. In reality, samples are always somewhere; labs have strict prohibitions against destroying material that has been submitted for testing. The problem is that nobody may know where a particular sample has been sent or where it is being stored. These factors all serve to emphasize why it is so important for investigators to call or contact any entity that has provided a DRS, FRS, or other sample as soon as he or she receives an association or match letter. The state missing person clearing house should also be notified. Above all, the investigator should make sure that all laboratories that handle DNA evidence and conduct any analysis or tests are fully identified in the case file.

It is impossible to understand how CODIS and NMPDD function without also understanding the basics of DNA analysis, evidence flow, and reporting. State statues reflect this necessity by addressing the importance of coordinating among agencies and sharing information with and through transitional

---

* Office of the City Auditor, Portland, Oregon. 2007. *Sexual Assault Response and Investigation: Portland Efforts Fall Short of a Victim-Centered Approach.* Portland, OR: City of Portland. p. 8.

agencies, particular state clearinghouses. Chapter 63 of the Texas Code of Criminal Procedure (CCP) contains an excellent example of such awareness.

Art. 63.003. Function of Clearinghouse

a. The clearinghouse is a central repository of information on missing children, missing persons, and attempted child abductions.
b. The clearinghouse shall
   1. Establish a system of intrastate communication of information relating to missing children and missing persons.
   2. Provide a centralized file for the exchange of information on missing children, missing persons, and unidentified dead bodies within the state.
   3. Communicate with the national crime information center for the exchange of information on missing children and missing persons suspected of interstate travel.
   4. Collect, process, maintain, and disseminate accurate and complete information on missing children and missing persons.
   5. Provide a statewide toll-free telephone line for the reporting of missing children and missing persons and for receiving information on missing children and missing persons.

Art. 63.015. Availability of Information through Other Agencies

a. On the request of any law enforcement agency, a city or state agency shall furnish the law enforcement agency with any information about a missing child or missing person that will assist in completing the investigation.
b. The information given under Subsection (a) of this article is confidential and may not be released to any other person outside of the law enforcement agency.*

---

* *Texas Code of Criminal Procedure*, Chapter 63. 2015. http://www.statutes.legis.state.tx.us/Docs/CR/htm/CR.63.htm (Accessed August 7, 2015).

SCJIS and NCIC

6

The National Crime Information Center (NCIC) and individual state criminal justice information systems (SCJIS) are key resources for an investigator. Their utilization also brings other powerful resources into the picture: terminal access coordinators (TAC) and state clearinghouses. These two entities provide MP and UD/UHC investigators with essential verification, coordination, and communication support that are absolutely necessary if case clearance rates are to be improved and resolutions for families are to be achieved quickly and efficiently. At the agency level, certain personnel function as contacts for systems and records validation; clearinghouses function as outside contacts for investigators and as liaisons between criminal justice agencies and families. In turn, both TAC and state clearinghouses depend upon CJIS and NCIC.

> **Key point:** In this book, all references to NCIC are based on NCIC 2000 policies and protocols.

NCIC, a division of the FBI, is a massive, rapid-response criminal justice database that was originally developed to enhance officer safety. The first version of NCIC was an information clearinghouse (i.e., a data bank whose participants communicated via teletype); it was established in January 1967 after extensive development in conjunction with the International Association of Chiefs of Police. NCIC operates on a 24/7/365 basis; it never closes or goes offline. As of December 2011, it contained 11.7 million records in 19 files and hosted an average of 7.9 million transactions per day.[*] The current record for entries in a single day, 12.2 million, was set on July 2, 2012.[†] CJIS, another FBI division, refers both to the department and the online system it oversees.

NCIC records, which are entered and owned by local agencies, bear unique originating agency identifier (ORI) numbers; any law enforcement agency and some individuals can obtain an ORI. The jurisdictional law agency of record, whether at the local, state, or national level, has control over

---

[*] Federal Bureau of Investigation. n/d. *National Crime Information Center.* U.S. Department of Justice. http://www.fbi.gov/about-us/cjis/ncic.
[†] Federal Bureau of Investigation. n/d. *National Crime Information Center.* http://www. fbi.gov/about-us/cjis/ncic. p. 1.

each case and owns all of the records pertaining to it. Both the agency and and the person/people who actually enter the information are responsible for record contents and may be subject to sanctions if NCIC or state policies/ statutes are violated. In the United States, more than 18,000 law enforcement agencies use NCIC* and are continually entering, modifying, and purg- ing (canceling or deleting) records. A little known but very important fact about purged NCIC records is that they can still be recovered. Therefore, the wealth of information contained in records that have been purged by mistake, or before a case is closed, are not lost forever. Purged and current (active) records may be requested and returned together in one search. NCIC contains several search algorithms, some of which that allow the entry of partial information in a specific field and the use of wildcard characters.† Investigators should be aware that all NCIC records are available, whether they are active or purged. For this reason, the problems that can result when records are removed prematurely or not reentered when appropriate (dis- cussed below) are not inevitable.

Records in databases that are part of NCIC can be searched nationally in accordance with memoranda of understanding between state departments of public safety and CJIS. Here again, the state serves as the coordinating link between local and national interests. Each state has its own version of NCIC that supplements it or, more often, serves as a conduit to NCIC as well as other databases and information systems and can be used for secure commu- nication among inter and intrastate agencies. These secure communications are transmitted through a secure independent law enforcement network known as NLETS (National Law Enforcement Telecommunications System).

An important difference between NCIC and CODIS has to do with access. Almost all NCIC records are viewable and searchable by authorized users. Although NCIC information exchange protocols and case entry poli- cies vary from state to state, all NCIC records are available to law enforce- ment agencies nationwide. Each state's department of public safety controls access to NCIC by auditing records and granting credentials to users, both individually and by agency, and the FBI provides one single Internet portal to each state and U.S. territory. This portal includes a host computer and connecting lines.‡ By contrast, CODIS users are usually laboratory person- nel and as such are not authorized to view or search records entered by other contributors.

---

* Federal Bureau of Investigation. 2010. *When Off-Line is Better: Another Way to Search Crime Records.* January 4, 2010. http://www.fbi.gov/news/stories/2010/january/ ncic_010410, p. 1. (Accessed November 1, 2014).
† U.S. Department of Justice. 2005. *The Off-Line Search.* Federal Bureau of Investigation, Criminal Justice Information Services Division. p. 1.
‡ *Ibid.*

Although NCIC was not originally designed for MP investigations, it has proven to be an investigator's most valuable tool for resolving such cases. This is particularly so in cases of adults who are voluntarily missing (i.e., hiding). Law enforcement personnel working on MP cases can find a wealth of information in the following NCIC files:

- Supervised Released
- National Sex Offender Registry
- Foreign Fugitive
- Immigration Violator
- Missing Person
- Protection Order
- Unidentified Person
- U.S. Secret Service Protection
- Gang
- Known or Appropriately Suspected Terrorist
- Wanted Person (including ascertaining welfare status—voluntarily missing)
- Identity Theft
- Violent Person
- National Instant Criminal Background Check System (NICS) Denied Transaction

Other data supplied by investigators to populate an NCIC record can be found with a special type of search called an offline search (these will be explained further in this chapter). Descriptors are included in NCIC/NGI records to help identify people[*] including UD/UHR.

State systems also provide access to numerous types of records, through various informational systems, for criminal justice purposes. This is because when NCIC was launched, it was recognized that no single system could be a one-stop information provider. Despite the enormous and rapid technological progress that has been made just in the past few decades, it is not possible to design one database that could function as a national clearinghouse. Therefore, each state system must operate in the diverse (and sometimes conflicting) political and legal environments. Accordingly, states have developed complementary systems of data entry, storage, and cross-checking. These measures have been taken not only to increase effective coordination, communication, and compliance in the pursuit of justice, but also to protect the rights and privacy of citizens. Although the CSI effect may give the opposite impression, the fact is that privacy and personal control of private,

[*] *Ibid.*

protected information is of primary importance within all law enforcement operations.

> **Key point:** States have increased the diversity of information within the NCIC structure by using it as the foundation for a powerful state-level network of criminal justice information systems.

The abbreviation NCIC, which is commonly used to refer to both federal and state systems, includes numerous databases such as Law Enforcement Data Systems (LEDS), Law Enforcement Agency Data Systems (LEADS), Texas Criminal Information Center (TCIC), and Wisconsin's Transaction Information for Management of Enforcement (TIME) System. Use of this abbreviation is appropriate, even though the 'N' stands for the word "national," because the state systems' software all contains the required core fields of NCIC; in addition, state systems must conform to NCIC policies. However, each state may have additional fields, records, systems, and administrative policies or protocols that NCIC does not use.

Lifestyles and habits of certain individuals tend to place them in high-risk situations in which they may die by violence. Two NCIC files house records related to such people: the Violent Person File (individuals with a propensity for violence against law enforcement officers) and the Detained Transaction File (individuals determined to be "prohibited persons" according to the Brady Handgun Violence Prevention Act).[*] Another index, known as III (Interstate Identification Index) contains criminal history record information that may have been added as the result of one or more investigations. Knowing criminal histories, court proceedings, and case dispositions may help investigators locate visual records (photographs, fingerprints, scars, tattoos, and other marks) that may be of tremendous assistance in UD identification (see Figures 6.1 through 6.4).

As explained in Chapter 5, investigators and families who are dealing with MP, UD, and UHR cases, as well as the jurisdictional agencies that are in charge of each case, cannot take full advantage of the wide variety of records and informational systems for criminal justice purposes available in each state without their state-specific transitional resources: state clearinghouses and criminal intelligence units. NCIC supplies valuable information for locating and identifying MP and UD/UHR. Its entries contain standard core demographic indicators that can be separately searched against MP and

---

[*] Federal Bureau of Investigation. n/d. *National Crime Information Center: NCIC Files.* http://www.fbi.gov/about-us/cjis/ncic/ncic_files. p. 1.

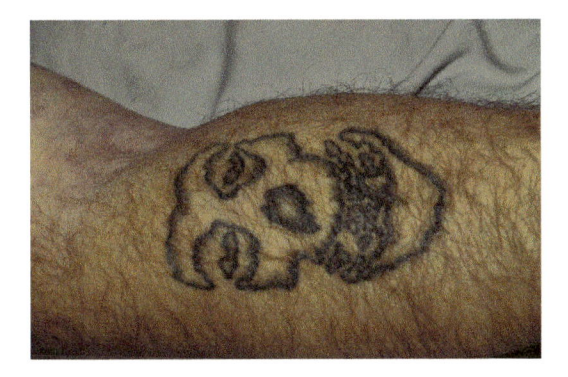

Figure 6.1 Tattoos unidentified decedent #1.

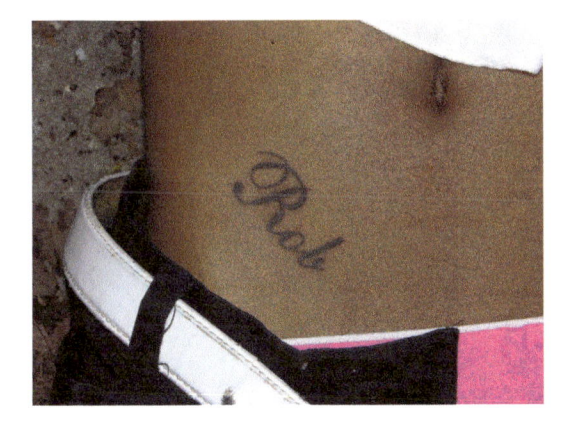

Figure 6.2 Tattoos unidentified decedent #2.

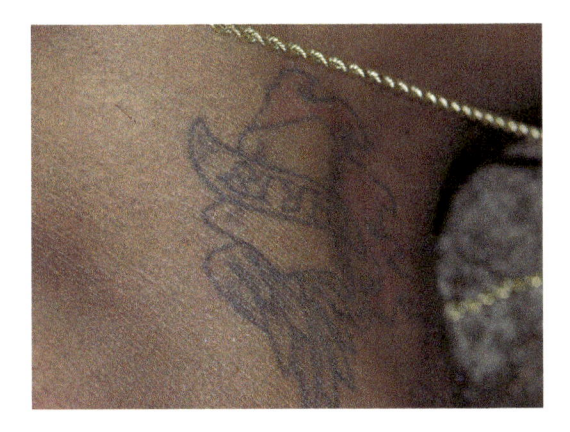

Figure 6.3 Tattoos unidentified decedent #3.

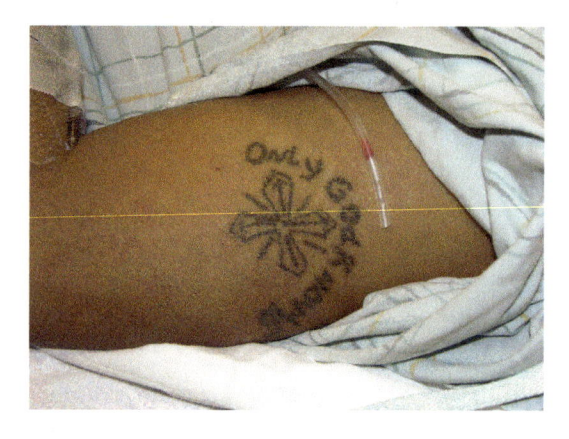

Figure 6.4 Tattoos unidentified decedent #4.

UHR entries. The core demographic indicators should be a focused search as indicated in Figure 6.5—local to national.

In 2007, some state agencies supplemented this information by adding DNA fields that indicate whether a DNA profile exists, and its location if it does.* The dispositions of retested samples and other new data should

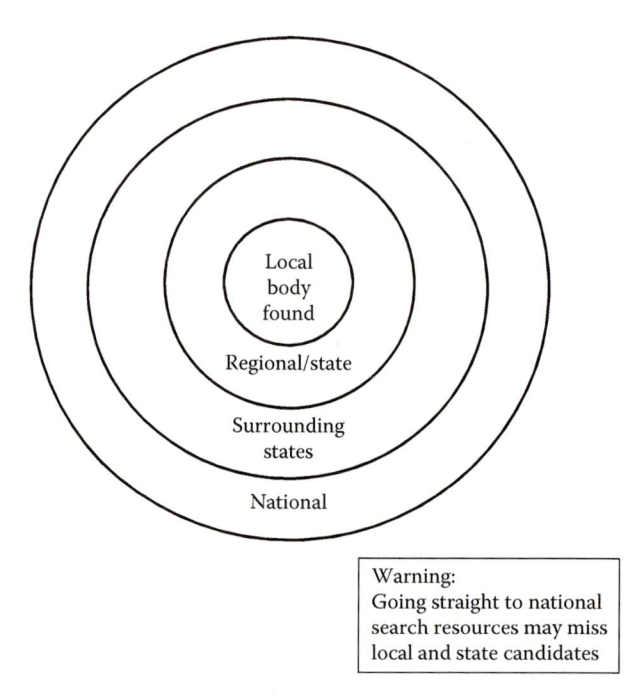

Figure 6.5 Focused searching order.

* Michigan Law Enforcement Network Field Notifications Index—2007–2010.

be entered into NCIC as soon as possible. Every time an MP or UD/UHR record is modified, it is automatically searched against all other missing, unidentified, and wanted records in the system; these $.M (potential match) reports are run and forwarded to the appropriate agencies if a hit occurs. Hits between physical or dental characteristics are ranked for probability according to an internal NCIC algorithm.

NCIC contains an administrative message feature which is a free text field. NCIC also includes a $.K missing information notification that is used to notify agencies of missing data fields in NCIC MP records. Additional administrative message (free text) fields are available in NCIC. This feature is used less frequently, however, because email has become prevalent. Many investigators prefer the privacy of email for messages that contain criminal history information, despite the possibility of hacking. The $.K report is still routinely used for interagency communications such as reminders that records submitted more than 30 days previously contain missing fields. For their part, submitting agencies are required to respond to such notices within 60 days.

NCIC is an irreplaceable tool for investigators in MP/UP cases because effectively working such cases revolves around three major activities: coordination, verification, and communication. All three are made vastly easier with use of the extensive resources that can be directly accessed through NCIC. Moreover, use of NCIC to access these resources is vastly more efficient than excessive reliance upon the Internet and mobile communications devices.

NCIC can be accessed only by authorized users. The vast majority of these are trained personnel in law enforcement/criminal justice agencies, which are held accountable for the security of its use. Access to NCIC records is strictly controlled, with severe penalties for security failures that put individual and community privacy at risk, impede criminal investigations, and threaten officer safety. Agencies have a terminal access coordinator (TAC) who oversees NCIC and IT communications among the agency and the state and national criminal justice information systems. This person also supervises an agency's other NCIC terminal operators (if there are any). Nearly all TAC attend national, state, and regional conferences to develop their networks and coordinate investigative relationships for the agencies they serve. They are very valuable resources for the investigator.

As previously mentioned, privacy is of paramount importance within the NCIC. Whereas the public may believe that the only people who live under assumed names are underage runaways or offenders—in other words, people who "should" be found for one reason or another—the truth is that many people who escape abusive environments may have no other alternative than to go missing and/or change their identity. In addition to this moral component, law enforcement agencies have fiduciary responsibility to treat all parties to a case impartially and are required by law not to undermine possible criminal prosecutions by maintaining confidentiality of NCIC.

Another excellent feature of NCIC, its administrative messaging function, allows texts to be sent through NLETS from one terminal to one or more other terminals and may be used for any official criminal justice purpose. Administrative messages are received by a TAC, who then initiates resolution activities. Messages are subject to audit.

The apparent complexity of NCIC and compliance requirements may cause an investigator to resist or stop entering NCIC records. Doing so, however, may result in disconnects that have devastating consequences for the case, investigator, medical examiner, ME/C, or family. Thus, an investigator's decision about whether or not to use NCIC is not necessarily a matter of personal preference. Regular, responsible utilization of NCIC inarguably helps investigators resolve cases—not only because the system can provide crucial information, but also through its automatic notification feature. The latter helps to resolve a problem that is systemic throughout law enforcement systems in the United States: the fact that one of the greatest problems in unidentified human remains investigations is insuring the investigating agency actually receives reports from forensic service providers and notifications of CODIS hits from DNA laboratories. This problem was introduced in the previous chapter, in which sources are quoted that highlight reductions in communication, verification, and coordination due to unlocatable lab results or CODIS dispositions of unknown. When an administrative message is sent to an agency, a state clearinghouse operated by state department of public safety may be added and notified at the same time that the case lab report has been sent to the agency on a specific date. In this manner, the clearinghouse provides an additional resource to ensure the reports are actually received by the agency, and the NCIC records are updated.

In 2006, the year before DNA fields were added to the NCIC entry template, ME were permitted direct access to NCIC for the first time;[*] their lack of ability to use its resources had greatly impaired investigators' ability to locate deceased MP whose deaths had been due to violent crime. Unfortunately, many ME/C still lack access to NCIC because of cost considerations and the time and effort involved in complying with its maintenance requirements and other regulations. Fear of assuming accountability or being sanctioned for noncompliance are other concerns. Involvement in NCIC on the local level is very important, however, because local law enforcement authorities may initiate and/or facilitate the entry of MP, UD, or UHR data into NCIC (which, as above, automatically initiates notifications to numerous other

---

[*] Hickman, M. et al. 2007. *Bureau of Justice Statistics Special Report: Medical Examiners and Coroners' Offices, 2004.* U.S. Department of Justice, Office of Justice Programs, NCJ 216756. p. 6.

agencies flagged on the record as having investigative interest) in their roles of assisting ME/C. In many jurisdictions, ME/C may acquire NCIC numbers (which enables them to conduct searches and utilize other forms of clearinghouse support) even if their offices do not contain an NCIC terminal. For local law enforcement agencies, use of NCIC provides the assistance and support of state missing person clearinghouses that coordinate and track the dispositions of MP cases.

The value of NCIC for local, state, and national agencies as a data resource is well illustrated by the state MP statistics published by the California Attorney General's Office. In 2013, approximately 35,019 adult missing reports were filed in California. Of these, approximately 33% of the MP were located by law enforcement and 49% returned on their own; these figures indicate that the cases overwhelmingly proceeded and were resolved at local and state levels. Only 1.16% were located deceased (Table 6.1).* The same conclusions can be drawn from the data about missing children (Table 6.2): approximately 86,652 missing children reports were filed. Of these, approximately 21% were located by law enforcement; 70% returned on their own; and 0.05% were located deceased.† As discussed in Chapter 1, because California has an unusually extensive system of tracking MP, UD, and UHD, reports from its department of justice are reliable indicators of disposition percentages nationwide.

Marvelous as it is, using NCIC can be complicated and confusing. For example, it has undergone changes over time, and the databases it contains are not identical from agency to agency or state to state. Investigators should be aware that some of these changes and differences involve MP and UD/UHR records. Coordinating with TACs and clearinghouse personnel may

Table 6.1   California Missing Adult Report

Status	2011	2012	2013	Average	Percent
Totals	32,711	35,975	36,372	35,019	100.00
Returned	16,694	17,583	17,104	17,127	48.91
Located	10,502	11,799	12,171	11,491	32.81
Voluntarily missing	1350	1642	1601	1531	4.37
Deceased	340	416	459	405	1.16
Removed/Canceled	2848	3380	3896	3374	19.70
Arrested	977	1155	1141	1091	6.37

* California Department of Justice. 2013. *Status of Missing Adult Reports in California.* State of California Department of Justice Office of the Attorney General. http://oag.ca.gov/sites/all/files/agweb/pdfs/missing/adults/adults_11-13_status.pdf? (Accessed October 26, 2014).
† California Department of Justice. 2013. *Status of Missing Children Reports in California.* State of California Department of Justice Office of the Attorney General. http://oag.ca.gov/sites/all/files/agweb/pdfs/missing/children/children_11-13_status.pdf?

Table 6.2   California Missing Children Report

Status	2011	2012	2013	Average	Percent
Totals	88,648	90,391	80,918	86,652	100.00
Returned	63,646	62,695	55,402	60,481	69.80
Located	17,840	19,407	17,513	18,253	21.07
Voluntarily missing	104	121	140	122	0.14
Deceased	36	46	47	43	0.05
Removed/Canceled	4855	4925	5194	4991	8.25
Arrested	2467	2837	2622	2642	14.47

prove to be one of the greatest case-management assets for investigators and for extracting the greatest value from NCIC/SCJIS.

Even though all NCIC records can be searched, whether they are current or purged, investigators may feel as if they are stymied when records are removed prematurely or remain active even after a case has been resolved. Records involving juvenile MP (runaways) are a good example. When a runaway is still below the age of his or her majority (which differs from state to state), he or she is entered as a missing juvenile. If this runaway is still missing when he or she reaches the age of majority, this record is supposed to be deleted and a new record is supposed to be uploaded that describes the MP as an emancipated juvenile. At this time, because the case is being reentered (even though the only different data are the age and category of the MP), it is assigned a new NCIC record number. However, this procedure results in dead ends when records are removed but not reentered. Sometimes this occurs because of human error, but in cases of juveniles who fled abusive environments, the record may not be reentered on purpose to protect the young adult's privacy and safety.

Clearinghouses work tirelessly to ensure that agencies do not delete records from NCIC without reentering them when appropriate. However, whether or not a young adult whose record has been removed has escaped into a safer life is not guaranteed. In 1984, the record of a 16-year-old runaway from Washington State named Marcella Bachmann was entered into NCIC, but later removed for an undisclosed reason. (Her case was mentioned in the preface to this book.) In 2006, her body was identified via a cold hit out of Missoula, MT; remains had been found 20 years earlier and tied to suspected serial killer Wayne Nance. Apparently she had traveled to Montana and began a relationship with him soon after.

Part of the reason it took two decades to identify these remains, which were skeletonized, was that the NCIC record had been purged. Ms. Bachmann's NCIC record was not re-entered after she reached her age of majority, and had left home voluntarily. In other words, Ms. Bachmann was off of everyone's list of possible candidates.

Ms. Bachmann's brother searched for her over the years without success. The case was resolved because law enforcement officers went out of their jurisdiction to follow up on reported missing persons around the period the Green River Killer (Gary Ridgway) was active. I coordinated the FRS submission with those officers working the case. Officers who worked outside of their geographic jurisdictions initially collected and submitted the FRS for analysis and entry into NMPDD. They were responsible for the first true interstate cold hit in CODIS.

Whether law enforcement agencies initiate the collection of dental records, DNA samples from biological family members, or other materials, resolution depends upon the particular strategies implement in each unique case as well as upon cooperation between investigators and families. When MP are young adults, open communication and the commitment to safeguard both their privacy and their security may be particularly important. But all MP deserve the same consideration if they are fleeing violent or otherwise dangerous situations.

Many other factors can influence how state systems handle MP records in NCIC. When a local entering agency locates an MP, missing person clearinghouses or TACs at local agencies may not be notified and therefore the record will remain active. Or the failure to delete an MP or UD/UHR record may simply be an oversight by an investigator who has authorization to enter his/her MP or UD/UHR cases into NCIC. If an agency other than the entering agency locates an MP, however, confirmation protocols are more likely to be followed; this means that the entering agency would be notified of the resolution and instructed to inform other agencies as well. In my experience with NamUs and the UNT Center for Human Identification, I have found multiple MP/UD/UHR active records in NamUs and NCIC for cases that were resolved years earlier as well as records containing multiple separate entries from separate agencies.

Numerous disconnects result when locate messages are not sent. MP records that mistakenly remain active continue to be searched against UHR; as a result, many $.M (potential hit) notices are needlessly sent to agencies and clearinghouses for disposition. So many $.M messages are sent to agencies that piles of them may remain unexamined for a year or more; in some cases, the $.M are simply ignored because they represent too much data and will produce limited results. In fact, only the first 100 $.M messages produced per day for a particular case will be sent on that day. This perpetual backlog and the overwhelming numbers of messages it represents make it even more important for records to be promptly removed from NCIC when cases are resolved. $.M messages should be prioritized for follow-up by location (proximity to the MP or UD/UHR to the investigator's case). The $.M messages will provide both ORI agencies of record, which can be used to pinpoint the agency's location by county and state—contact information is also available.

To ensure that unresolved MP case files remain active in NCIC, mandatory 60-day validation notices are sent out periodically to entering agencies. These are not always returned, however, and that failure may result in the deletion of records connected to cases that are, in fact, still open. Active records may also be deleted if a submitting agency fails to pass audits of its NCIC records, which are conducted periodically by state compliance officials.

As previously mentioned, every agency that can upload records to NCIC has a unique ID number, called ORI (originating agency identifier). As stated, agencies not only own the NCIC records that bear their ORI number, but also control the clearing, modifying, and updating of these records. The administrative workload that results from those responsibilities may cause an investigator to look for reasons to delete records other than resolution of cases. When NCIC records are purged, and the case is still unresolved, other agencies may need to view those records to resolve their own cases. The only means to find those records are by ordering offline searches from FBI's CJIS.

Of course, deleting active records also means that image files attached to them (which may be key to resolving cases) will be deleted—not lost forever, but much harder to find. Some law enforcement agencies have only had the ability to upload image files to NCIC/NGI records since 2013; such images are subject to the same rules as text entries.[*] To complicate their use even further, these image files may be accessible through NCIC only and are not viewable/searchable through all states' systems.[†]

Many states require agency files to include written documentation (i.e., an MP report) that contains the same information as an MP record in NCIC. In some states, the MP report must be initiated by an entity that operates independently of the agency that is handling the case; examples on the local level include close family members or guardians. Other suitable persons may include child protective services officers, correctional facility personnel, doctors, roommates, or clergy. Failure by the agency of record to maintain such documentation may cause NCIC entries to be canceled.

> **Key point:** Reporting parties may not know or may report incorrect dates of birth, dates or places of last contact, or even incorrect spelling of the MP name. Incorrect information is also entered into NCIC/NamUs when reporting parties use incorrect information that was deliberately given to them by the MP (because he or she may not have known the correct date or place of birth, or may have fabricated false information).

---

[*] State of Ohio *LEADS Manual,* Image File, July 2013.
[†] Missouri State Highway Patrol, *MULES: Missouri Uniform Law Enforcement System* 13-03.

Smaller law enforcement agencies and some ME/C may not have their own NCIC terminals. If they don't, they may link their ORI to a nearby agency, or access NCIC on less than a 24-h basis. As explained in Chapter 4, ME/C may not be the only legal authorities who are authorized to issue death certificates. Depending on state laws, auxiliary authorities who can issue death certificates may include JP, DA, or even funeral home directors or private physicians—one reason for this is because job turnover is higher for elected ME/C offices. Another reason, also mentioned in Chapter 3, is that it is not uncommon for coroners to take "their" files with them when they leave office. Some ME/C have even transferred UP remains and whole bodies to funeral homes for storage.

As is emphasized throughout this book, the first step designing an investigative strategy is to find the epicenter of the event (i.e., a death) and work outward. In UD investigations, the epicenter is the place where the body was found. The last known location of that person may not be known, or what is believed to be the last known location may be inaccurate. Investigators should consider geography in this order: local, regional/state, nearby states, and national.

Many agencies do not have a dedicated missing and unidentified persons unit due to limited resources and infrequent cases. Larger agencies may have such a unit but not enough personnel to staff it properly. In both scenarios, overworked investigators who are coping with inadequate resources often find themselves moving paper from one file to another or just placing a file on a shelf, where it is forgotten. High turnover rates among investigators, which is due in part to chronic job-related frustration, also contribute to these problems.

Investigations are impacted both by improper deletion of records from NCIC and by records that are still treated as active after cases are closed. In both cases, $.M hits continue to pile up but they may never be resolved because there are just too many; in addition, calls made to other agencies and investigators in order to hit or refute these $.M hits may never be returned. However, there are several strategies that may be implemented to build an efficient missing and unidentified persons unit with currently available resources. The first thing that an investigator must realize is that M/UP cases cannot be handled effectively without help. Collaboration and assistance are necessary in order to effectively deal with an M/UP investigation.

Whether an investigator is seeking MP records or UP records, most clearinghouses keep detailed case files in separate databases for easy of location and, in addition, can request offline NCIC searches (the latter is explained later in this chapter). Clearinghouses can also ask other law enforcement agencies to search their databases on behalf of an investigator, and may be able enlist the assistance of criminal intelligence units or fusion centers; these resources can access even more agency records and databases. Working through clearinghouses in this way can allow an investigator to find out whether a hit can be obtained in specialized public record databases that he or she does not have access to search directly. One such database is the TxGang database, which contains more than 30,000 entries.* Many cold hit identifications that state clearinghouses/fusion centers may help obtain come from metadata contained in probation/parole records, family/child protective services, and protective order registries, if available.

Clearinghouses are known to have reciprocal relationships with agencies in other states, as well as far-reaching interagency relationships that may reach into other countries. For example, I was contacted by a U.S. citizen who was living and working in Canada. She wanted to know how to enter an MP missing person case in NamUs because her boyfriend had left for work in the United States several weeks before and no contact had been possible since. I referred her to Canada's national MP/UP clearinghouse, the National Centre for Missing Persons and Unidentified Remains (NCMPUR) of the Royal Canadian Mounted Police. Within 24 h, her boyfriend was located in jail.

Another case concerned a woman in the United States who was having difficulty reporting her adult brother missing; she believed he was deceased. He had last been known to live in Florida, but last known to be alive in Louisiana. The Florida Department of Law Enforcement (FDLE) clearinghouse contacted an agency in Louisiana to initiate a missing person report. The Louisiana agency agreed to the request but declined to participate further on behalf of FDLE. In response, an investigator from FDLE located the MP's mother and another sister in Texas, and then contacted me (at that time, I was working for the University of North Texas Center for Human Identification) to have FRS collected from them for analysis and entry into CODIS. Unfortunately, this case has not yet been closed.

In short, state clearinghouses should be viewed as providers of analytical support; by contrast, TAC deal with agency-to-agency communications. When requesting assistance from or corresponding with another agency, rather than using email it is best to work through SCJIS or NCIC's administrative message function because it features a confirmed audit trail; in addition, it usually initiates tracking of responses, automatically sends out reminders, and so forth. In order to take advantage of their valuable networking relationships and superior capabilities, investigators should consult TAC and clearinghouses as an integral part of case strategy.

As previously explained, an ORI number is necessary if law enforcement and criminal justice agencies are to be able to share NCIC record information. Agencies that do not have their own terminals can ask local or county

---

* Texas Department of Public Safety. 2011. *CR News: Texas Gangs, Growth* 16(3), p. 1.

law enforcement to act on their behalf by managing their records and communications through NCIC, or by requesting offline searches from clearinghouses or directly from the FBI.

Of course, since 2006 ME/C have been permitted to use NCIC and to have NCIC terminals. However, some cannot afford to do so; some lack sufficient personnel; some may not have large enough jurisdictions to justify the expense; and some simply do not know that these resources exist. Those who are aware of them may gain the ability to enter old cases and have them searched, to take advantage of NCIC notification capabilities, and to use CJIS to enlist the help of law enforcement agencies all over the country. Having a terminal and a TAC to run it are not necessary.

ME/C and auxiliary criminal justice agencies that do not have their own NCIC terminals but do have an ORI assigned to them should contact a nearby law enforcement agency (sheriff's office) and request that agency to enter the MP/UD/UHR record into NCIC. NCIC records can only be shared with another law enforcement or criminal justice agency that has an assigned ORI. In some states, an ORI will not share certain NCIC records such as fingerprints and criminal histories with criminal justice agencies. Criminal justice agencies are usually support or service agencies that do not have statutory authority to arrest without a warrant. A criminal justice agency is identified by its ORI nine-digit number that ends with an alphabetic character (A through Z)—law enforcement agencies, nine-digit ORI number ends with a numeric character (0 through 9). If local help is not given or available, the state clearinghouse may help with "shopping the case"—a phrase that refers to seeking a nonjurisdictional agency to enter records into NCIC. In turn, it is very common for clearinghouses to shop cases—particularly older ones for which resolution opportunities appear limited. With the assistance of TAC and clearinghouses, and with collaborative efforts among medical examiners, coroners, and auxiliary criminal justice agencies, the ability to solve cold cases is amplified well beyond the capabilities of any single investigator.

Families can also benefit from the help of state clearinghouses if they feel as if they are being stonewalled. In some cases, local authorities may be more inclined to initiate a case if they feel that another agency is taking it seriously. For example, in late 2010 local police officers in Texas were in pursuit of a young man who eventually jumped off a bridge into a river to escape them. The officers, who witnessed the jump, saw the young man go under but did not see him surface. However, this local police department declined to enter an MP report into NCIC. After months of trying to persuade it to do so in response to family complaints, the state clearinghouse requested that another agency enter the MP report as a professional courtesy. Ultimately, when the declining local agency was informed that another agency had agreed to accept the case, it reversed its prior decision.

As previously mentioned, since September 2014 it has been possible to link NCIC record files to image files from other sources. This option is a great boon to investigators because even though state clearinghouses are wellsprings of information and assistance, not all state criminal justice systems have the ability or desire to maintain separate image files. Image inquiries can make or break a case; as we know, mistaken witness identification of individuals has led to numerous wrongful conviction inquiries and exonerations. In NCIC, candidates in image searches are ranked by their resemblance to the target data, a practice that provides a welcome visual baseline for criminal investigators serving law enforcement agents and death investigators serving ME/C.

In addition, state law enforcement agencies that control and oversee NCIC routinely use their respective SCJIS to acquire and enter information at the state level that is not accepted at the national level. In essence, state inquiries are conducted through SCJIS and national inquiries are conducted through NCIC. Still another major advantage to investigators who use these clearinghouses is that most TAC know which states have such fields that may be of especial use in a particular case. Here again, these personnel at law enforcement agencies may be able to provide the greatest assistance to an investigator. ME/C and criminal justice agencies that dismiss the ability of NCIC to provide valuable investigative leads are failing to utilize one of the most valuable tools available to them.

Perhaps the least-utilized feature of NCIC, the offline search option, is also one of its most valuable. (In one day in 2009, law enforcement officers in the United States ran almost six million online searches of NCIC records but approximately 22,000 offline searches were conducted in the entire year.*) This type of record comparison, which uses different and more flexible searching criteria than the online searches conducted through NCIC, may be able to return useful information in an active case from databases or state-level record fields that are not included in NCIC online inquires. Some states may not have full capabilities for both NCIC and SCJIC; however, every law enforcement agency in the United States that has an ORI can request offline searches. As previously discussed, the pressure to clear or cancel cases can make it difficult for investigators to keep cases active; it is human nature to want to show good results. Offline searches offer a safety net to the investigator, but he or she must know why and when to initiate them as well as how to do so.

State clearinghouses are valuable sources of current information on offline search applications. Through them, investigators may request transaction

* Federal Bureau of Investigation. 2010. *When Off-Line Is Better: Another Way to Search Crime Records.* January 4, 2010. http://www.fbi.gov/news/stories/2010/january/ ncic_010410, p. 1. (Accessed November 1, 2014).

logs for various data fields (e.g., missing person, deceased person, age, and vehicle) of an NCIC record for specific time periods.* The transaction logs from offline searches can tie a specific field to a particular time and geographical location by pinpointing the NCIC terminal of record and relevant ORI (which will be attached to any records related to the inquiry). An investigator can use this information, along with the original time stamp that appears on every transaction record, to identify the ORI (agency location) to better focus the search.

Offline searches can also point an investigator toward sources of useful information if a CAD (computer-aided dispatch) system was used by the agency of record. For example, a CAD system operator who entered records for the ORI of record may be able to provide additional details about interactions between a law enforcement officer and a person or about key items (e.g., auto registration or driver's license numbers) that can help to place an individual in a particular place at a particular time. Some agencies' CAD systems can be programmed to automatically run searches of many different databases both within (online) and outside of NCIC.

So much information can be produced by offline searches—stemming from law enforcement, medico-legal death investigators who work in ME/C offices, and other auxiliary agency personnel—that it may be very difficult for an investigator to manage. Such problems, however, are minimized when MP/UD/UHR investigators are prepared to design flexible strategies in which each activity has a purpose. Online searches are conducted first because results are returned immediately. Offline searches, if appropriate, may conducted later to supplement the investigation. But however key investigative factors are obtained, it is best to keep them to a manageable number. Basic key investigative factors include the name/aliases of an MP, numerical identifiers (date of birth, driver's license, etc.) or the name/description on evidence found with UP, the location where an MP was found (living or dead), the estimated ages of an MP candidate and at UD, the date on which the UD was found, and the last date an MP was known to be alive. MP and UD/UHR intake forms and releases for medical/dental records may be obtained from state MP clearinghouses or from state bureaus of public safety, as per the SCJIS/NCIC protocols and statutes of each state.

Metadata such as sex, estimated time of death, estimated weight, estimated height, race, eye color, and ethnicity should not be highly ranked. This is because as an investigator widens the geographic parameters of an MP search, the number of associated hits may increase by leaps and bounds. After the online search options have been exhausted, the initial offline search may return a large number of records that are tied to the last place an MP

† U.S. Department of Justice. 2005. *The Off-line Search*. Federal Bureau of Investigation, Criminal Justice Information Services Division. p. 1.

was seen alive or to the location where UD was found. This situation need not frustrate investigators, however, because even high numbers of records can be sorted and ranked automatically with spreadsheet programs such as Excel. In addition, many law enforcement jurisdictions use volunteers and interns for data manipulation if crime analysts are unavailable at an agency or from clearinghouses.

Along with realizing that the most effective investigative strategies are flexible, that assistance is both possible and abundant, and that efficient data management is necessary, investigators must keep in mind that no one person can do everything that is required to pursue and resolve an MP/UP case. Instead, he or she should maximize time and effort by obtaining help in finding information; when information has been obtained, he or she should focus not on manipulating it but on managing it and extracting the most meaning from it.

In general, law enforcement investigations are moving from an incident-based approach to a victim-centered approach. This transition is particularly helpful in MP/UD investigations. The growing acceptance of volunteers to assist investigators in these types of cases also indicates that law enforcement is recognizing not only that such people can function as victim advocates and advocates for families of MP/UD but also that they provide necessary technical data manipulation assistance that saves time and energy for professional crime analysts. One very successful volunteer program is the Volunteer In Police Service (VIPS) program sponsored by International Association Chiefs of Police; its goal is to "enhance the capacity of state, local, tribal, and campus law enforcement agencies to utilize volunteers through the provision of no-cost resources and assistance."* As of April 2008 139,138 VIPS volunteers were supporting 1700 law enforcement agencies[†] in activities that included resolving cold cases.

After they have been vetted, volunteers at law enforcement agencies usually function in noncommissioned positions (unlike reserve officers and deputies, who are commissioned). Volunteers who work in supporting roles at law enforcement agencies are considered to be force multipliers, even though they are not commissioned.

---

* International Association of Chiefs of Police. n/d. *Volunteers in Police Service Add Value While Budgets Decrease.* http://www.theiacp.org/Portals/0/documents/pdfs/VIPS_police_service_add_value_while_budgets_decrease.pdf. p. 3.
† National Criminal Justice Research Service. 2008. *Volunteers in Police Service Program Exceeds Milestone,* May 1, 2008, 14(9). U.S. Department of Justice, Office of Justice Programs.

NamUs 7

As described in Chapter 1, three phases of relationship develop between investigators and victims' families during MP/UD investigations. First is the mutual trust and support phase. Second is the caution and concern phase in which families begin to have doubts about the investigator. Third is the phase of criticism and accusations of incompetence in which families' frustrations take their toll on investigators. It is common during the third phase for an investigator to taper off communicating with the family or purposely fail to return calls from them.

These phases manifest in nearly every case that is not resolved immediately. They also may be inevitable because families view the investigator as the only person who can provide the information that will end their uncertainty, fear, and suffering. The National Missing and Unidentified Persons System (NamUs), which attempts to introduce a victim-centered approach to MP/UD investigations, bridges the abyss between investigators and families by allowing families to act on their own behalf in terms of entering information into databases, searching it, publicizing it, and enlisting the help of other members of the public. NamUs was designed as a force multiplier for investigators and ME/C by facilitating the involvement of the public, (nongovernment organizations) NGOs, ME/C, and law enforcement, which includes clearinghouses. NGO support is critical as they can provide victim social services support that agencies, law enforcement, and ME/C cannot provide due to the lack of resources and skills. The four foundational key performance indicators of NamUs that drive its ability to function as a force multiplier to resolve MP/UD/UHR cases are (1) number of registered public users, (2) number of registered law enforcement personnel, (3) number of ME/C personnel, and (4) number of registered clearinghouse users. According to one account:

> [NamUs] was developed as a result of the 2005 National Institute of Justice "Identifying the Missing Summit" … A major component of this initiative was to develop a system that would improve information access for all the people who might be able to help solve these cases.[*]

---

[*] Community Oriented Policing Service. 2013. NamUs: Partnering law enforcement, medical professionals, and the community to solve missing and unidentified persons cases. *COPS Office*, January, 6(1), p. 1.

I first became involved with NamUs by joining its missing persons advisory group, which convened shortly after the summit in 2005.

The technological resources development contract for NamUs was awarded to the National Forensic Science Technology Center (NFSTC) in Largo, FL. During the development phase, meetings were often contentious; in fact, at least three NIJ program managers came and went before NamUs became fully operational in 2012. Nonetheless, in order to argue every aspect of the project from every conceivable perspective, NFSTC brought together state and national criminal justice professionals, victim advocates, families of the missing, medical examiners, forensic experts, and members of the public to participate in advisory groups. The National Center for Missing and Exploited Children (NCMEC) joined forces with NamUs during this phase to advise on the management of missing children cases.

The first NamUs database to be launched, in 2008, was the unidentified deceased database. Its design allowed anyone to search its records although data could be entered only by ME/C.[*] (This policy has been revised, however, because conflicts arose in jurisdictions where law enforcement by statute were responsible for investigating UD cases.) A press release in 2007 described the forthcoming system as "a new national database for matching unidentified human remains with records of missing persons. [It will serve] as a repository for information […] all of which, like DNA, can be vital to the identification of remains."[†]

In May 2008, it was my pleasure to be among the first to introduce NamUs publicly, in Albany at the Seventh Annual New York State Missing Persons Day—just ahead of the UD database launch.[‡]

In January 2009, the NamUs missing persons database was launched.[§] Because it was set up to function as a quasi-ME/C electronic case file, it includes fields for physical attributes such as hair and eye color, as well as for forensic identification descriptors. Unlike MP records in CODIS and NCIC, these can be searched by anyone and "Missing Person" fliers can be printed from them.

In July 2009, the third phase of NamUS was released. It allows cross-searching of the MP and UD databases. In 2012, the unclaimed persons database became fully functional; entry and editing rights for its records of bodies that have been identified but not claimed are restricted to ME/C.

---

[*] Department of Justice. 2010. Statement of Kristina Rose, Acting Director, National Institute of Justice, Office of Justice Programs Before the Committee on the Judiciary Subcommittee on Crime, Terrorism, and Homeland Security, United States House of Representatives. January 21.

[†] U.S. Department of Justice, Office of Justice Programs. n.d. Bringing Hope to the Families of Missing and Unidentified Persons Program. *News Center.* http://ojp.gov/newsroom/events/missingpers_photos.htm.

[‡] Murray, J. 2008. Hope For The Missing: New National Program Launched To Help Solve Missing Person Cases. *The Waterbury Observer,* May, p. 21.

[§] *Ibid.*

NamUs was the first national database designed for members of the public to initiate entry of MP cases. If cases are successfully vetted by law enforcement agencies (which is desirable but not required), they can be published and disseminated.* Cases can be entered into NamUs without being entered into NCIC. The first two NamUs databases contain both publicly viewable sections and restricted sections for law enforcement, ME/C, and other qualified criminal justice users; the third, as mentioned, is entirely restricted to ME/C.

A 2004 survey funded by NIJ found that many ME/C did not maintain case files on UD in their jurisdictions; this means that many ME/C have numerous cold cases in their possession. Because of the UP database in NamUs, ME/C and other death investigators are able to publicize cold cases. Part of the purpose of NamUs is to bridge communications gaps between law enforcement and ME/C; however, it has not been able to eliminate dissonance between these two criminal justice communities.

NamUs began as a facilitator between families and investigative entities such as law enforcement and ME/C. Along with its database capabilities, it offered referrals to forensic services such as DNA testing, odontology (forensic dentistry), physical anthropological analysis, and fingerprint analysis. The UNT Center for Human Identification provided DNA analytical services with grant funds and a few other agencies have also obtained such grants. Eventually, NamUs began to offer such services directly. However, accessing such services directly from NamUs is meant to be a last resort because offering them risks generating conflicts with other forensic service providers. These conflicts may include

- Competition for scarce/dwindling funds. Fewer available funds means that it may not be possible to offer forensic services to agencies or individuals free of charge.
- Preference for using free testing and other services from NamUs rather than paying local providers for them. If this preference becomes widespread enough, NamUs would be forced to spend funds intended to facilitate support for families on other needs such as chemicals, specialized training, continuing education, and a host of other expenses that do not directly support the agency's original purpose.
- Duplication of efforts with primary sources of forensic services, and marketplace competition with them. These situations would make NamUs into a rival of law enforcement rather than a collaborator

---

* Department of Justice. 2010. Statement of Kristina Rose, Acting Director, National Institute of Justice, Office of Justice Programs Before the Committee on the Judiciary Subcommittee on Crime, Terrorism, and Homeland Security, United States House of Representatives. January 21.

and complementary partner. Furthermore, NamUs would in effect be creating more information silos for families and agencies that are already struggling with information overload.

- Increased costs to grantee forensic investigation agencies and the federally funded NIJ for the provision of expert testimony and additional paperwork related to fiscal control. These costs, which could be considerable, would possibly be borne by other agencies for years at a time.
- NamUs is scheduled for competitive solicitation every 3–5 years. Having sole-source control of the forensic services supporting NamUs would be duplicative and have an anti-competitive effect on future solicitations, which could result in higher costs than necessary.

For a time, NamUs interfaced with the FBI's Violent Criminal Apprehension Program (ViCAP), which maintains the largest investigative repository of major violent crime cases in the United States,* to populate both agencies' records. While NamUs interfaced with ViCAP, it did not interface with NCIC, the FBI's Integrated Automated Fingerprint Identification System (IAFIS), or DHS's IDENT. This is because NamUs is considered a criminal justice entity, not a law enforcement agency. Agencies can enter cases one at a time, or groups of cases can be "cross walked" into NCIC by a NamUs IT contractor.

As stated earlier in this chapter, NamUs data fields are divided between publicly viewable fields and law enforcement-sensitive (LES) fields. All users are required to be registered with NamUs before they can enter cases into the system or update records in the system; searching the system, however, does not require registration. Unlike law enforcement user registrations, which must be vetted by a regional system administrator, the registrations of public users are not vetted. In addition, a regional system administrator or case manager must review a case before records pertaining to it can be accepted by NamUs, no matter who is entering the information, and must also review new information every time a case is modified.

It is truly unfortunate that only larger and more affluent ME/C offices are able to afford NCIC terminals and qualified staff to operate them. However, NamUs can be used when expense or other obstacles make it difficult to access NCIC. NamUs is more easily accessible for a number of reasons. First of all, the NCIC validation process requires agreements with individual law enforcement agencies and the state as well as mandatory certification for NCIC users. Because approximately 18,000 law enforcement agencies—along with countless other agencies—use NCIC on a daily basis, NCIC is administered through the states under MOU (memoranda of understanding)

---

* Federal Bureau of Investigation. n.d. *Wanted by the FBI.* U.S. Department of Justice. http://www.fbi.gov/wanted/vicap.

between each state and the FBI. The states control the training and validation of NCIC users through the established resources of various state agencies and authorities, which are also responsible for monitoring their users for compliance with NCIC regulations. Similarly, state authorities are responsible for auditing agency performance and compliance with NLETS and their own state criminal justice systems. Points of identification used for auditing and evaluation include NCIC record content and status, and ORI numbers (which are unique to each agency or subdivision thereof) for accurate contact information and agency status. By contrast, it is not possible to monitor each individual user of NamUs or each computer from which it is accessed. This is why information that is uploaded to NamUs or changed after uploading, no matter who is doing the entering or changing, must be approved by an RSA, a NamUs administrator, or a case manager.

Between October 2011 (when the MP database was launched operationally) and January 2012 (when the UP database was launched operationally), NamUs added salaried personnel. NCMEC continued to manage the child and adolescent MP cases and supplied field resources to assist some ME/C. In addition, regional NamUs training academies were established for volunteers and used to create a national network of leadership resources for education and victim support; however, these were discontinued when the operational phase of NamUs began. Academy participants were "nominated by the appropriate leadership of various stakeholder organizations to develop a five-person team in each state."[*] Participants in the training academies included

- Sworn law enforcement officers
- State clearinghouse employees
- Forensic experts in good standing with the American Academy of Forensic Science
- ME/C
- Victim advocates (paid or volunteer representatives of a recognized state or national nonprofit missing person organization in good standing)[†]

Some organizational spokespersons and family members with national recognition who had helped propel NamUs' initial rapid growth were dropped from training and outreach when its operational stage began.

The victim-centered approach of NamUs rests on the premises that families suffer greatly when a loved one goes missing, and that this suffering impacts communities by extension. This is the core reason for the NamUs

---

[*] International Association of Chiefs of Police. 2010. March 2010 IACP News: National Crime Victims Week. *The Police Chief*, March, LXXVII (3).
[†] *Ibid.*

policy of allowing the public to enter cases. In turn, information contributed by the public may help the investigative efforts of victim advocates, law enforcement officers, and ME/C. NamUs was the first national missing and unidentified database to fulfill the public's desire to help identify UD and support families of MP.

NamUs's public access policy means that non governmental organizations (NGO) with victim-centered advocacy programs can contribute to its databases. Unlike information that is entered into NCIC, which is owned by the jurisdictional agency of record, the information entered into NamUs is in public domain. This is because NamUs operates under the auspices of the Department of Justice, a federal agency; therefore, its records are in the public domain "may be reproduced, published, or otherwise used without the Department's permission."[*] But these public data fields, which give families ways to contribute and share information, also make it easier for law enforcement and other agencies to shield sensitive investigative information. Many agencies have strict general orders that forbid sharing information about cases under investigation; for families, these rules may save much heartache by protecting them from knowing about false or unreliable leads. However, not knowing what's going on in an investigation that impacts every facet of their lives can be unbearable for families. On January 21, 2010, Stephen L. Morris, deputy assistant director, Criminal Justice Information Services Division, Federal Bureau of Investigation, and Kristina Rose, acting director, National Institute of Justice, Office of Justice Programs, U.S. Department of Justice acknowledged, "CJIS acknowledges the need for a capability to allow some level of access to missing and unidentified person information for the general public" when both spoke in support of NamUs as articulated in the "Help Find the Missing Act."[†]

When a case is entered into NamUs, a family's anguish can begin to heal and their hope for resolution may be rekindled. They may not know everything about their case, but they are able to know some things and can participate in publicizing their situation. Feeling as if they are participating in the process of finding a loved one also increases a family's sense of security. In the normal progress of an MP investigation, not only are families generally unaware of what an investigator is doing, investigators themselves may be unwilling or too overworked to share even routine investigative details.

These communication disconnects may leave families with an inadequate sense of resolution when their cases are resolved—even though after

[*] The United States Department of Justice. 2014. *Copyright Status and Citation.* http://www.justice.gov/legalpolicies#copyright.

[†] Federal Bureau of Investigation. 2010. Congressional Testimony of Stephen L. Morris, January 21, 2010. http://www2.fbi.gov/congress/congress10/morris012110.htm (Accessed August 8, 2015).

resolution they are technically free to go on with their lives. When a case that has been investigated with a victim-centered approach is resolved, that family has been empowered throughout the process. Therefore, they are less likely to blame the investigator for "taking so long" and are more likely to view him or her as a partner or even a hero who never gave up.

The NamUs MP database contains 13 navigation tabs and its UP database contains 12 navigation tabs. Each of the tabs links to multiple screens for viewing or entering data. Although the screens in these databases may look similar, not all of their data fields appear or function the same. Readers should know that the NamUs policy manual can be viewed online at www. namus.gov; the "resources" tab on the menu bar links to explanations of the functions of NamUs tabs and data fields. Another operational resource, *A Guide for Users of the National Missing and Unidentified Persons System: Draft 2.0*, may be found online by typing the title into any browser. Because NamUs is constantly being improved and upgraded, these resources may be slightly out of date. However, the information and screen shots they contain are of great value.

Under most state MOU and policies, information within the NCIC system may only be shared among law enforcement users who are attached to an agency with an active ORI. By contrast, information in all but one database of NamUs has information that has already been approved for public disclosure and restricted law enforcement-sensitive information that is not approved for public disclosure. However, the nonpublic database causes compliance difficulties for some law enforcement agencies. This is because NamUs regional administrators vet the identity of individual law enforcement officers, via phone calls or emails, rather than agencies as a whole.

A major difference between NCIC and NamUs, which everyone who uses these resources should keep in mind, is that an agency is not responsible for NamUS uploading activities or the content of uploads generated by its employees. Instead, such users (law enforcement personnel, ME/C, et al.) are responsible for the content of what they upload and how well they follow NamUs policies and procedures. Agencies have no monitoring or auditing responsibilities in NamUs and are normally not provided with feedback about their NamUs users. In addition, parties other than those from the agency of record can modify case records in NamUs. It is the records themselves that are vetted, by regional administrators or case managers to control the accidental or improper release of publically identifiable information of the MP/UD/UHR and to link to comments or figures in image backgrounds. Also, in contrast to NCIC, NamUs has no independent audits and reports that ensure compliance or enforce security.

Law enforcement users and other users may view records related to the access and status approved by the NamUs analyst on a state-by-state and/or county-by-county basis, depending upon whether access has been authorized to NamUs three databases (MP/UP/UCR). Such law enforcement officers may be willing to validate MP cases for NamUs RSAs but not to assume management responsibility for the NamUs data about those cases. Whether cases or information about them have been obtained law enforcement, ME/C, families of missing persons, or from other sources, NamUs RSA are responsible for contacting law enforcement investigators for case validation and subsequent publication based upon certain information (agency name, last place an MP was known to be alive, or the location where a UD was found), according to when a case is submitted and its place in the pending queue for NamUs acceptance. Clearinghouse personnel with NCIC access are a great resource to identify multiple nearby law enforcement agencies or agencies that have concurrent jurisdictions. NCIC has an ORI lookup function for location information; in addition, state and county codes are part of each unique nine-digit ORI number.

Unlike NCIC, once a case has been entered into NamUs there are no mechanisms to systematically revalidate the case or to ensure its status as active or resolved. Like NCIC, NamUs contains duplicate cases, improperly purged cases, and resolved cases. For the fewer than eight NamUs RSA who provide user and case validation for 18,000 law enforcement agencies and 698,000 law enforcement officers in 50 states, as well as uncounted ME/C and auxiliary entities (judges and DA, for example), the workload is tremendously challenging and labor intensive. Once an MP case is entered into NamUs and is validated by a NamUs regional administrator with a law enforcement agency, or the ME/C of record, it will remain active until it is marked "found" by the agency, it is discovered to be resolved or to be a duplicate case. The latter are often discovered through alternative sources such as a newspaper article or information from an NGO, family member, other agency, or the actual MP. There are no internal cross-check procedures between NCIC and NamUs, which means that cases that may have been removed from one source because they have been resolved may still appear as active in the other. Case managers who have both NCIC and NamUs access can and should make sure that case designations match in both resources.

Agencies may think that NamUs is an acceptable primary source for forensic services (DNA or fingerprint analysis, odontology, physical anthropological analysis) in MP/UP cases. However, NamUs forensic services are limited in application and utility when compared to mainstream criminal justice resources for law enforcement. Fingerprints sent to NamUs by investigating agencies cannot be searched through NGI (which replaced IAFIS or IDENT in September 2014) as the NamUs' managing grantee of NamUs is identified as a criminal justice agency with an ORI of TX220035Y (the last digit of an ORI that is alphabetic is considered a criminal justice service or support agency). In addition, NamUs (Version 1.0–Version 2.0 is understudy as of January 2015) does not support uncompressed image files such as NEF or RAW, or the higher-resolution DIP images involved with NGI searches. Instead, many fingerprint records that are attached to NamUs cases are stored as compressed image files in JPG/JPEG formats unless resubmitted by the agency. Compressed image files have a tendency to alter the minutia of a fingerprint that is crucial for fingerprint analysis.

Because NamUs cannot accommodate the most advanced kinds of digital images or access NGI records, fewer fingerprint records are available in NamUs for comparison. When a fingerprint hit is found between two records (MP and UP databases) in NamUs, investigators should treat the result as an investigative anomaly, and attempt to confirm the reason why the hit was not made through the normal investigative channels associated with NGI. Fingerprints of both MP and UD/UHR should be entered/registered with the state for access to the NGI and reconfirmed every six months (at minimum) to ensure that the prints are still available in NGI (note different states and agencies may have different processes).

NamUs has tremendous potential to help with one of the most important challenges in MP/UP cases: getting the word out about an MP or UD as widely as possible to law enforcement, the media, and the public. Agencies, investigators, and families alike should utilize the power of NamUs to generate public exposure and rely upon NCIC to securely disseminate LES information. As a law enforcement agency resource, NCIC cannot generate public exposure; as a criminal justice entity, NamUs complements that mission. Therefore, NamUs should make as many key forensic demographics as possible (e.g., location timelines and physical descriptors, most of which are flagged as minimum required fields in NamUs during the case entry process) available in its publicly viewable fields, while keeping LES information separate and limiting access to it.

Many NGO cannibalize NamUs cases from the public portal for their own missions to locate and identify MP which may be children or adults, people in specific geographical areas, or people specific at-risk groups (such as Alzheimer's patients). In doing so, NGO work to amplify the power of NamUs (a fairly extensive list of NGO may be found at http://www.media-forthemissing.org/missing-persons-organizations/). This is a practice that families and investigators should promote; a great number of identifications are made when family members see an image of their loved one or an image that they can associate with their loved one. In the mission to identify the deceased, I believe that territoriality (competition rather than cooperation among agencies, institutions, and other parties) has no place in MP/UP investigations.

Case managers, who have an investigative interest in case outcomes, should be selected by the law enforcement agency of record. Case managers should have direct online access to NCIC; good candidates include state clearinghouse personnel and personnel of jurisdictional agencies with NCIC access. The case manager who is listed on a NamUs contact screen may act as a conduit between NCIC and NamUs to verify, update, or reconcile records. NCMEC RSA, who have privileges at both databases ensure that entries are correct and also manage child and adolescent MP cases. (By contrast, NamUs RSA for adult cases only have NCIC offline capabilities.) Progressive agencies that utilize victim-centered approaches may use trained volunteers as case managers, in order to free up commissioned investigators. The Volunteers in Police Service (VIPS) program, which is sponsored by the International Association of Chiefs Police, recommends that volunteers be trained, vetted, and supervised to support MP programs.[*]

The value of utilizing both NCIC and NamUs is demonstrated by the following story. In 1992, the remains of a homicide victim were discovered in an Oregon river. Data, including dental information, were entered into NCIC and searched without success. A few months later, the mother of an MP filed a report; several years later, however, it was deleted from NCIC for an unknown reason. Both of these cases languished until 2013, when a cold case unit from a local Oregon PD verified that the MP case was still open, reentered it into NCIC, and also uploaded its records into NamUs.

Upon the reentry of this case, NCIC automatically generated a cross-match report ($.M) and sent it to the Washington State Police's Missing and Unidentified Persons Unit (the state clearinghouse). Typically, $.M reports are generated the day after an NCIC record is modified and copies are sent to the agency that owns the MP records, the agency that owns the UP records, and the clearinghouses of states that contain locations tied to the case. This report ranked candidates in order of match likelihood; as it happened, the UD found in the river was ranked as number one.

A forensic odontologist with the Washington clearinghouse located the NamUs MP file and the dental information it contained, including x-rays. On April 13, 2013, a forensic odontologist with Washington State Police called the local police agency and notified it of the match between the UD records in NCIC and the MP records in NamUs.[†] In this instance, NamUs functioned as the repository for the forensic demographic information, which was dental information; the previously purged NCIC record was restored (that is, updated and given a new case number); an automatically generated NCIC returned an association; and local forensic resources confirmed the match.

Furthermore, this case exemplifies exactly how NamUs was designed to work: as a complement to NCIC, with a state clearinghouse functioning as a

[*] International Association of Chiefs of Police. n.d. *Missing Persons: Volunteers Supporting Law Enforcement.* Alexandria, VA: Volunteers in Police Service Program, International Association of Chiefs of Police. http://www.theiacp.org/Portals/0/documents/pdfs/missing-persons.pdf.

[†] Federal Bureau of Investigation. 2009. NCIC's Dental Matching Program Plays Key Role in Solving Cold Case. *CJIS Link*, April, 16(1), p. 7.

conduit and safety net for all. There was no duplication of forensic resources. The development of NamUs 1.0 under the guidance of the initial NamUs advisory groups sponsored by NFSTC (National Forensic Science Technology Center) did not design NamUs as a primary source of forensic services for achieving the common goals within the Department of Justice as to avoid the unnecessary duplication of competing resources and efforts.* NamUs was used in a victim-centered manner by local agencies, which sought to give the family of the MP tangible involvement by entering the MP records into a database (NamUs) for the first time—which did not exist in 1991, when the original MP report was filed.

It bears repeating that NamUs was not designed as an investigative case management system, although some agencies attempt to use NamUs as such. NamUs should be conceptualized as a forensic demographic warehouse and public information repository, or as a locator service for such information. However, perceiving NamUs in this way may dissuade investigators from placing case-sensitive information, even though they are placing it in restricted-access LES files. Investigators who have such concerns should consult an RSA or a state clearinghouse. Each state has its own restrictions, customs, and practices to ensure as much cooperation as possible while also ensuring the security of personal information and conformity with federal and state privacy statues.

Another concern about NamUs is related to its status as a database with public access portions hosted by a federal government media platform; these portions are considered public domain and as such are subject to Freedom of Information Act (FOIA) requests. However, FOIA requests may include investigative information from the LES sections of NamUs, which are intended to be secure from public disclosure. If data from the LES sections is released without the knowledge of the agency or investigator of record, the ability to solve cases may be compromised. As it happens, NamUs as an NIJ database is under the control of the DOJ. The DOJ is composed of administrators who work for the current administration in Washington, DC—which means that in 1 year permission is granted to release certain information, but in 4 years, if the administration changes, that decision may be altered or even reversed.

Investigators and others who enter information into NamUs should keep in mind that if highly sensitive investigative case information is not in NamUs, it cannot be publicized from NamUs. Security concerns have risen since September 2014, when NGI replaced IAFIS (the Integrated Automated

---

* Department of Justice. 2013. *Smart on Crime: Reforming The Criminal Justice System for the 21st Century.* http://www.justice.gov/sites/default/files/ag/legacy/2013/08/12/smart-on-crime.pdf (Accessed August 8, 2015).

Fingerprint Identification System).* NGI maintains access to "over 100 million individual records that link a person's fingerprints, palm prints, iris scans, and facial-recognition data with personal information like their home address, age, legal status, and other potentially compromising details."† Many agencies and other sources have thousands of old and new fingerprint records that are being continuously added or linked to NGI. Many agencies and states have policies that prohibit or control the sharing and searching of fingerprint records with outside law enforcement agencies or with any criminal justice agencies. The latter can usually be identified by the nine-digit ORI, which has either an alphabetical character for its last digit (representing a criminal justice agency) or a numeric character as its last one or two digits (representing an investigative law enforcement agency).

Perhaps, the least risky way for NamUs to be used is as an information location resource or informational warehouse so to speak. Publicly viewable NamUs records, which should be completely populated, should also be continuously reconciled with their sister records that have been entered into NCIC. If privacy of information is of concern to an investigator, he or she should make sure that critical investigative information is maintained only in NCIC. It would be foolish, however, for investigators to forego the greatly enhanced fingerprint searches now available through NGI and to rely exclusively on NamUs. Case managers should maintain a list of all the NamUs cases for which they are responsible, and ensure that fingerprints are resubmitted for searching against new NGI records on at least a semi-annual basis.

As previously stated, it is critical to investigators and families that records that have been entered both in NCIC and NamUs remain reconciled and updated as needed throughout the life of a case. Updating may be necessary more often than investigators expect; when the original reports are taken, families rarely have all the information necessary to complete the input fields in NamUs or NCIC. Often, they must gather additional information from friends and other family members, or they discover that information they originally supplied was incorrect.

Moreover, without continuous monitoring and reconciliation of every case between NamUs and NCIC, cases that have been resolved may stay open. As a result, multiple agencies and NGO may expend investigative resources that are needed elsewhere, and unresolved cases are deprived of the attention they deserve. When agencies cross walk cases in bulk, some may be included that should in fact be closed. I have found more than one UD case in NamUs

---

* Federal Bureau of Investigation. 2014. *CJIS Link: NGI Officially Replaces IAFIS—Yields More Search Options and Investigative Leads, and Increased Identification Accuracy.* http://www.fbi.gov/about-us/cjis/cjis-link/october/ngi-officially-replaces-iafisyields-more-search-options-and-investigative-leads-and-increased-identification-accuracy.
† RT.com. 2014. *FBI's Facial Recognition Program Hits Full Operational Capability.* http://rt.com/usa/187968-fbi-facial-recognition-biometrics/.

listed as active that had in fact been resolved many years before NamUs was even built. When discrepancies do occur between records in NamUs and NCIC, the NamUs case manager is the best person to contact about reconciling them. As previously recommended, the case manager should a member of the state clearinghouse or personnel (employee or vetted volunteer) of the agency of record, or a cooperating agency that has direct access to NCIC.

NamUs' ability to publicly disseminate images of UP is one of its greatest assets for families and investigators, because the availability of such images often results in investigative leads. (Unfortunately, however, NamUs cannot automatically search images within the system as NCIC/NGI can.) Numerous studies indicate that people in close contact may be able to mentally associate images (pictures) to people they know; however, strangers have very marginal success in associationg images (pictures) of people when there is not a close relationship. Witness identification based on photo lineups is less accurate than perusal of cases online in the National Registry of Exoneration. In my experience, most of the NamUs investigative leads that have ended in a confirmed identification originated when someone saw an image of a UD and associated that image with a missing family member. However, some limited positive investigative leads have developed when a stranger to an MP/UP was able to associate an image of a UD/UHR to an MP. NamUs personnel (RSA) should not assume the position of a case manager on a NamUs case. NamUs personnel were to be facilitators and relationship managers, not investigators. NamUs personnel do not have online access to NCIC. Often investigators see case managers of NamUs as assuming an investigative position attempting to take over their cases. In 2011, when I was appointed a NamUs director, I resigned my Texas Peace Officer's commission (still retaining my Advanced Peace Officer's License) as a demonstration of the role what NamUs personnel were to play—facilitators, not investigators. The case manager is critical to ensure NamUs and NCIC contain exactly the same information. Congress made their desire that both systems were to be reconciled in the text of HB 5519 Section 3:

Sec. 3. GAO report on information sharing between NCIC and NamUs. (a) Study—The Comptroller General of the United States shall conduct a study on—(1) how to better integrate the national missing persons databases, including the NamUs databases and the NCIC database; (2) any technical challenges that may exist in integrating the databases described in paragraph (1); and (3) practices, procedures, or technologies that would assist States, local law enforcement agencies, medical examiners, and coroners in reporting missing persons and unidentified remains to the NamUs databases and the NCIC database.*

---

* 113th Congress 2nd Session. 2014. *H.R. 5519: In The House of Representatives: September 17, 2014.* http://www.congress.gov/113/bills/hr5519/bills-113hr5519ih.xml (Accessed August 8, 2015).

To summarize, NamUs forensic service supports were originally developed for backup when local forensic services were not available. NamUs does not have access to most mainstream law enforcement databases or to many forensic resources that are available through clearinghouses and law enforcement agencies. Relying on NamUs forensic services as a single source for forensic support, rather than additional support, may increase the likelihood of a case staying unresolved.

NamUs analytic services are also limited in that only offline searches can be conducted; online searches must be conducted by a case manager who has access to both NCIC and NamUs. However, NamUs can search several public and some privately maintained LES databases for case-detail analysis.

For a family or investigator to get the most value out of submitting a case to NamUs, the role of the case manager is pivotal. He or she should and have the appropriate skills to deal with all parties connected with a case. In addition, because a sustainable and effective investigation requires specialized and current knowledge of complex resources, clearinghouse and agency personnel with NCIC access are the best candidates for case manager positions. Such people have deep knowledge of NCIC as well as of anomalies that have developed in similar investigations. Sharing such with investigators knowledge may be just as important, or even more important, as any other investigative activity.

Because NamUs does not have any systematic case audit capabilities, the case manager must be able to simultaneously access NCIC and NamUs to the keep records in both systems reconciled and active, or purged. (NamUs does maintain LES activity logs and chronology logs, however, so that law enforcement can monitor case activity.) When hits occur, validation and audit activities are automatically handled by NCIC; a TAC who receives a validation request can easily check the records in NamUs to see if the case is still active. Case managers should periodically review and update the cases and document the NamUs case files (activity logs) to allow TACs and investigators to know that cases are still being actively worked. The idea is to involve others in the maintenance of a case so that the investigator is free to manage the actual investigation.

NamUs was developed as an integrated collaborative model for all facets of missing persons and unidentified human remains investigations through publicly viewable case details. It is the publically viewable case details that bring value to investigative efforts through adding highly motivated public persons and NGOs to assist without interfering with the investigation. The relationship between NCIC and NamUs can be compared to icing on a cake: NCIC/NGI/forensic services at the local and state levels are the cake; NamUs is the icing. A cake composed only of icing would be as pointless as an investigative strategy that relies exclusively on national resources.

Metadata

8

Metadata, which may also be called secondary (qualitative) data, simply means data about other, primary (quantitative) data. In MP and UP investigations, primary data includes objective measurements in autopsies, objective measurements anthropological studies, allele reports, weight and height measurements (not qualitative opinions of their meaning), and sex (primarily determined by amelogenin results or visible genitalia). The verb "sexing" refers to the final determination of sex. For UHR, this is usually scientifically characterized by DNA; as explained in Chapter 4, males will have XY amelogenin markers and females will have XX amelogenin markers. The process of sexing a UD does not include evaluating gender appearance.

Some of the most important metadata in MP/UP investigations are race and ethnicity. These terms refer to standards promulgated by the National Center for Education Statistics (NCES); a designation of unknown/unsure is also possible. Although the terms "race" and "ethnicity" in fact refer to different human qualities, they are often used interchangeably in law enforcement to indicate specific populations or geographic origins. Investigators who treat both race and ethnicity as functions of biology in the context of UHR investigations are able to design strategies that may resolve larger number of cases more expediently. In this book, race is used to indicate self-reported descriptors (such as White , Black, or Asian) and ethnicity is used to indicate ancestry (such as Oceanian, Eastern European, or Middle Eastern).

Although race is usually assumed to be a scientific finding, it is actually a social construct (this was discussed in Chapter 2). My experience of debriefing hundreds of cases has shown me that forensic subject matter expert opinions often have difficulty determining the ethnicity of skeletal remains, let alone their racial designation. NGS, which is replacing legacy DNA analysis methods, can usually identify the ancestry (ethnicity) of UHR with much greater specificity than direct examination by physical anthropologists or with CE technology. When physical anthropologists are able to depend on the higher sensitivity provided by NGS, the accuracy of their opinions—and thus the amount of metadata they can provide—may greatly improve.

Metadata traits such as age, height, and weight are often assumed to be linked with or even indicative of race/ethnicity. These traits, however, are not given such power in UD investigations. Instead, genetic markers are used to calculate race. The focus for the purposes of this book is upon the accuracy of metadata determinations by means of cold hit identifications, which depend upon comparisons with preidentification descriptors of MP. The questions of whether race classifications help or hinder in UD/UHR investigations, and which correlates may raise or lower estimates of date of death or age at time of death, remain unresolved (see Figure 8.1 for MP–UP age comparison).

This chapter contains reviews of cold hit cases in order to evaluate the accuracy of metadata in databases, particularly metadata that seem to match MP descriptors and UD/UHR descriptors. Criminal justice agencies rely upon reports and entries in databases to guide their investigations. If these metadata are inaccurate and investigators rely on them, UHR cases could be doomed from inception and become sentinel event cold cases. (For more detailed discussions of sentinel events, please refer to Chapters 3 and 11). Of the 48 MP and UHR cases I reviewed that produced cold hits (i.e., searches of various databases produced no associations that could be used as investigative leads), hits to convicted offender databases were not considered unless an MP report had been filed about that offender.

Interpretation of the meaning of metadata, and its significance in a case, are highly subject to bias. As was noted in Chapter 2, which considered bias, objectively verifiable facts are the best remedy. In terms of cold hit

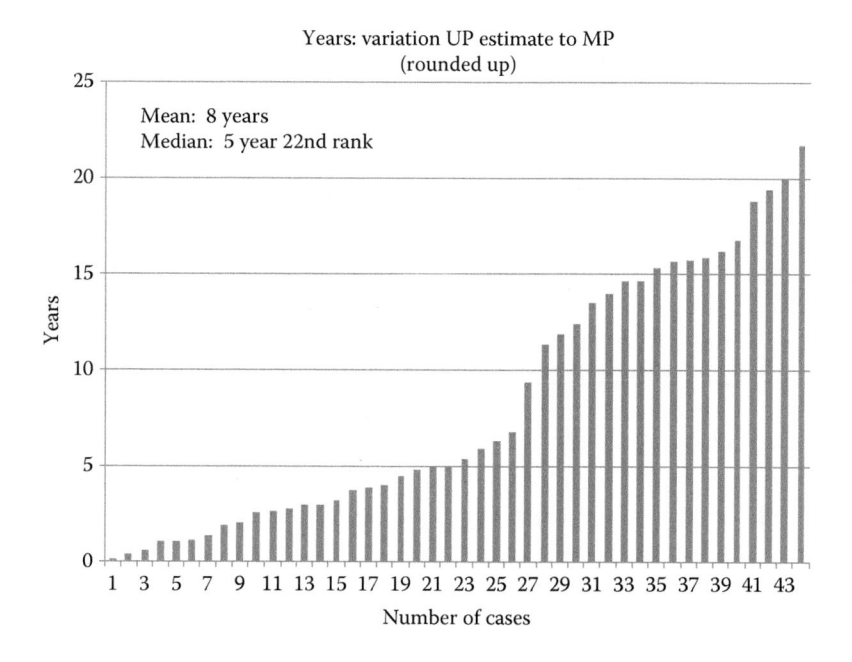

Figure 8.1 Age difference between MP and mean estimate of the unidentified deceased.

associations, the thresholds in CODIS for nuclear DNA samples (for example, that small samples from the same source cannot be combined in order to produce more DNA) eliminate the possibility of conflicting interpretations. The vast amounts of data included in NamUs, which are consulted by researchers, activists, law enforcement agents, ME/C, and others, similarly help such people to reduce bias and speculation in their work.

As was discussed in Chapter 2, research is showing that bias is harder to eliminate than has been recognized in the context of flawed human reasoning.[*] Often, the piece of information that is weighted disproportionately is one of the very first ones encountered. One tends to seek closure and to view the initial part of an investigation as a "sunk cost" that would be wasted if not used.[†] As stated in Chapter 2, forensic examiners' potential to develop bias after visiting a crime scene or viewing crime scene photos and reports may be reduced by reviewing cold hit associations, followed immediately by debriefing and dissemination of the results. Bias-controlled cold hit associations (a phrase of my own invention) may allow researchers to examine and evaluate cost–benefit models of various empirical investigative strategies in light of possibly flawed forensic analyses of UD/UHR. In other words, until we encounter an anomaly and investigate, we may never become aware of flawed processes or pervasive biases.

Law enforcement agencies have long wished for more-efficient systems to assist UP investigations, particularly in the initial stages. Unless information with a high degree of accuracy is made available to investigators, any conclusion may be considered suspect and a case may not stay unresolved for an unacceptably long period. However, metadata in UD/UHR cases— particularly metadata related to race and ethnicity—are notoriously subject to inaccuracy.

Despite the general belief that race indicates permanent, fundamental differences in the cellular makeup of human beings, "Human genetic variation is the consequence of a long history of migration, of cross-mating, of piracy, of slave taking … messing things up, leaving behind some variation."[‡] As the migration of various population increases, ethnic diversity will continue change all over the world, which in turn will make the work of UD/ UHR investigators more difficult. One hopes that public perceptions of race will cease to be based in concepts that are decidedly nonscientific. A good example would be the term "White" in reference to race, which was not

---

[*] Whitman, G., Koppl, R. 2010. Rational bias in forensic science. *Law Probability and Risk*, 9, pp. 69–90.

[†] National Academy of Sciences. 2009. *Strengthening Forensic Science in the United States: A Path Forward* (1st ed.). Washington, DC: The National Academies Press. pp. 123–124.

[‡] Goodman, A.H., Moses, Y.T., Jones, J.L. 2012. *Race Why Are We So Different* (1st ed.). Malden, MA: American Anthropological Association. p. 134.

codified by law in North America until 1661.* The concept of a "White race" was not considered scientific until 1795, when a German scientist named John Blumenbach used the skull of a female from the Caucasus Mountains to illustrate it (this is where the conflation of "Causasian" with "White" originated).†

Most scientific "research" on race is the result of celebrity case fallacies— in other words, conclusions about the ethnicity or race of a group have been based on very few cases or circumstances that display discrete characteristics of a single race/ethnicity. In Europe, which provided the basis for American civil and criminal law, scientists and scholars for centuries viewed the world as unchanging. But the conviction that both ethnicity and race are fixed enti- ties, which was challenged in the nineteenth century by evolutionary theo- rists such as Charles Darwin, eventually gave way to the realization that there is no clear demarcation point at which one race/ethnicity ends and another begins.

Skin color, which is the basis of biological race descriptors, changes from place to place, individual to individual, and is described differently by observers—who may themselves be more or less subject to bias. What may be considered White in the United States may be considered an admixture in Northern Europe. Variation among individuals and populations involve many traits that typically lack consistency from one part of the world to another.‡ Thomas Merton helped to explain why such events became so deeply engrained in American culture when he wrote that "The self-fulfilling prophecy is, in the beginning, a *false* definition of the situation evoking a new behavior which makes the original false come *true*. The validity of the self- fulfilling prophecy perpetuated a reign of error."§

In the 1700s or 1800s, in my opinion, a person's ideas about human bio- logical variation would probably have been shaped by what he or she observed on the street. (Readers may reach the same conclusion after reading the 2002 book *Race and Membership in American History: The Eugenics Movement*).¶ Therefore, personal experience and travel would have been highly influen- tial. Because terms that referred to race/ethnicity were often the only means to describe observed differences in biological variation, such terminology

---

* NPR Staff. 2011. *Black Scholar of the Civil War Asks: Who's with Me?* http://www.npr .org/2011/12/08/143291199/black-scholar-of-the-civil-war-asks-whos-with-me.
† Goodman, A.H., Moses, Y.T., Jones, J.L. 2012. *Race Why Are We So Different* (1st ed.). Malden, MA: American Anthropological Association. p. 48.
‡ *Ibid.* p. 96–97.
§ Merton, R.K. 1948. The self-fulfilling prophecy. *The Antioch Review*, 8(2), 193–210.
¶ Facing History and Ourselves Foundation. 2002. *Race and Membership in American History: The Eugenics Movement*. Havard Facing History Project & Facing History and Ourselves National Foundation, Inc., Brookline, Massachusetts. http://www.facinghistory. org/sites/default/files/publications/Race_Membership.pdf (Accessed August 8, 2015).

became accepted as "scientific" and is still accepted as such today by many scientists, investigators, subject matter experts, and families.

In 1979, William Bass published a review of observations that had been used over the previous decade to establish the race of unidentified skeletal remains. He noted the need for "basic research on some of the fundamental topics of age and race."[*] Historically, the qualitative and quantitative analyses of human skeletal morphology (changes) have been handled by physical anthropologists. In 1948, one such scientist credited racial assumptions for the accuracy (75%–90%) of sexing skeletal remains.[†] In other words, even what people think of as male or female skeletons depends on what race they think the person belonged to in life. However, there are no definitive scientific boundaries between races; existing race classifications do not reflect many populations around the world; and difficulties in identifying or conveying degrees of certainty and uncertainty[‡] in the physiology of one race that may be identified with one trait are not in accordance with those identified traits in other races. The truth is that all people are different in some respects but the same in others. It is biased opinions about what the differences mean that have caused spurious results in forensic science.

As with race, opinionated estimations of the sex of UHR often turn out to be inaccurate. One must not be unduly influenced when reading or hearing of "showcase" examples, which are probably exceptions to the norm rather than illustrations of it. It is particularly risky to design investigative strategies based upon a small number of cases whose outcomes assumed to reflect or generalize reality. In the United States, whatever relevance previous studies may have had, the growing racial and ethnic diversity is quickly making them less relevant to UD/UHR investigations.

The report titled *Guidelines for Missing Persons Casework*, produced by the Scientific Working Group on DNA Analysis (SWGDAM, a group of scientists representing federal, state, and local forensic DNA laboratories in the United States and Canada) was released in January 2014. Among other observations, the group noted that "It is important to remember that metadata can be incorrect, particularly when date ranges, age estimates and ethnicities are involved." A similar doubt was raised in 2010 by the Scientific Working Group for Forensic Anthropology, which stated in its *Sex Assessment Report* that "It is generally unadvisable to assess sex for fetal/infant/child [under 12 years] remains because valid sex assessment techniques are unavailable." The latter statement was supported by a search I did in NamUs, in December 2014,

---

[*] Bass, W.M. 1979. Developments in the identification of human skeletal material (1969–1978). *American Journal of Physical Anthropology*, 51, pp. 555–562.
[†] Brues, A.M. 1948. Identification of skeletal remains. *The Journal of Criminal Law, Criminology, and Police Science*, 48(5), pp. 551–563.
[‡] *Ibid.* p. 552.

of active cases based on "not recognizable body condition" with an age range of 0–11 years of age: 116 "unable to estimate" cases were returned for males, and 91 cases for females. These cases appeared to cover the entire United States.

To date, cold hits between MP and UHR database entries are only valid resource or methodology upon which to base definitive comments about metadata results for adults. Therefore, investigators are advised to be cautious about relying on subject matter experts' determinations of sex and age in UHR cases. In the Donna Lisa Williamson case (date of last contact or DLC: August 1982; cold hit: June 2004), inaccurate charting of dental records led to an early elimination of Ms. Williamson as a likely candidate. In the Maria Isabel Solis case (DLC: March 2003; cold hit: February 2005), the anthropology report indicated her race as Black when she was in fact of Hispanic origin. In the Cory White case (DLC: October 2002; cold hit: November 2006), the anthropology report incorrectly sexed the remains as female. In the Terri Troublefield Reyes case (DLC: May 2006; cold hit: June 2007), the anthropology report incorrectly identified the remains as Anglo/Black admixture; Ms. Reyes was White. In the April Repka case (DLC: June 1991; cold hit: October 2007), the anthropology report indicated the remains were Mestizo (Spanish/South American Indian) or Amerindian admixture; Ms. Repka was White. In the Donna Snowden case (DLC: April 1988; cold hit: March 2008), the autopsy report stated that the body had been dumped 3 to 4 years before it was found. (The Snowden case highlights opinionated errors related to estimated date of death—another form of metadata errors investigators much must contend.)* These six cold hit cases, which document inaccuracies in the first 15 UHR cases managed by the Texas Department of Safety Clearinghouse, strongly indicate that metadata inaccuracies are systemic.

The Scientific Working Group on DNA Analysis report of January 9, 2014 identifies metadata as non-DNA data used in conjunction with DNA analysis. Whether metadata is a help or a hindrance in UHR investigations depends upon the type of metadata and how it is used. The question becomes how an investigator to know what is accurate and what is not? Accurate metadata can be of great benefit; inaccurate metadata can cause a case to go cold. Dental records, a type of metadata more thoroughly discussed in Chapter 9, provide a good example.

Dental records can be the only way to identify victims of disasters, which are labeled as closed or open events depending on how much information about the victims is readily available. In an airplane crash, a closed event,

* Texas Department of Public Safety. n.d. *Unidentified Persons & DNA Unit. Criminal Law Enforcement Bureau of Information Analysis.* file://C:/Users/Owner/Downloads/FischerUtilizationofDNAAnalysisbyLawEnforcement%20(1).pdf.

the number of victims as well as their names, addresses, and sex are already known from records such as flight manifests. For full identification, ME/C or mortuary personnel can retrieve dental records (usually this involves contacting families of the UD). In an open event, such as a multivehicle highway crash or a nightclub fire, the victims are located at the scene; families and friends contact authorities after hearing about the disaster. In both types of situations, a limited number of dental records must be gathered from dentists and compared to a limited number of known victims; these records are usually fairly current if the individuals regularly practiced good dental hygiene. In other words, dental records can be quite effective in identifying UHR when there are a limited number of investigative leads.

In UHR cases, the analogy to mass disasters (open or closed) is invalid for dental records because the context is different. If dental records are available from a UD, they must be compared to records from an indeterminate number of candidates who were involved in one or more incidents that could have occurred years or even decades previously. If dental records are available for a possible MP, they must be compared to an indeterminate number of UHR—some of which may have already been disposed, cremated, or buried.

In the 10 years that I have been working in the area of human identification, I have found fewer than five cold hits via dentals but have seen numerous inaccurate dental records in databases. The main reason for this difference is that very few candidate (target) MP dental records are available. In addition, HIPAA compliance must be considered by healthcare providers (medical and dental) and law enforcement officers when they are searching for an MP but have no reference profiles for comparison.

The risk of liability may be too high for a dentist to release dental records related to a possible voluntarily missing person, particularly because many of the missing may be hiding on purpose. For the same reason, officers may be reluctant subpoena dentists for records from a dentist as well as to post the records in a database; eventually, an angry patient could end up filing a HIPAA complaint against the dentist. In fact, dentists may be averse to releasing any records to law enforcement. When this happens, ME/C may be able to obtain dental records according to statutes in most states. The best time to do this is during the autopsy; in addition, investigators should keep in mind that acquiring dental records without an investigative lead may require an entirely separate line of inquiry.

Strategic acquisition of dental metadata by law enforcement investigators (as opposed to ME/C at autopsy) should be undergo cost–benefit analysis. If the effort and time associated with the collection of dental data will distract from other activities that may produce better results, collecting dental data may not take an initial high investigative priority since dental data is historically a postmortem mode of identification. If the collection and use of other metadata are considered in the same light as dental metadata, and there are concerns about the accuracy of opinionated metadata such as age estimation, weight, height, sex, and race, the best strategic approach is to rank the various types of metadata in terms of their relevance.

Metadata such as scars, marks, tattoos, and physical anomalies are probably going to be more relevant than metadata derived from a subject matter expert's opinion. Other highly relevant metadata include

- Distance between the location where the body was found and the location where the missing person was last known alive
- Time between the date of last contact and the date the body was found
- Age estimations between the remains and the MP

Investigators and families may find it more useful to consider metadata in order, from nonopinionated to more opinionated. As previously stated, searching efforts should always be undertaken in the following order: local, regional/state, surrounding states, and national. When an inconsistency (anomaly) develops with metadata, the investigation should focus on resolving the inconsistency as the investigation continues.

Dental Resources

9

Forensic odontology (dentistry) was brought to the forefront of forensic investigation in the 1960s with a formal instructional program provided by the United States Armed Forces Institute of Pathology.[*] Dental analysis and reporting are of primary importance in forensic science because teeth are the most durable human tissue and are usually the last body parts to deteriorate after death. Forensic odontology is particularly useful when fingerprint comparisons are not possible (due to the condition of the body or because fingerprints cannot be located for comparison) or when only the skull has survived scavenging by animals or degraded by exposure to environmental factors (see Figures 9.1 through 9.4).

ME/C may augment their autopsy personnel with a forensic odontologist or use a contracted or volunteer forensic odontologist or dentist. Without board certification, the minimum qualifiers to practice forensic odontology are the completion of an accredited dental education, a DDS or DMD degree, or state licensure (requirements vary).[†] The main role of a forensic odontologist in MP/UP cases is to provide an opinion about comparisons of charts, records, and radiographs from a UD and the dental information of an MP. An investigative lead is usually necessary to establish a presumed identity for the UD. When an opinion is rendered, it should indicate one of four classifications: positive identification, possible identification, insufficient evidence, and exclusion.[‡]

The purpose of this chapter is to provide information about the functions of dentistry in UD/UHR investigations, including

- Role of the forensic odontologist
- Environment in which the profession functions
- Resources that support the forensic dentist or odontologist
- Sufficient understanding of odontology to make strategy development choices
- Common pitfalls and how to avoid them

[*] Avon, S. 2004. Forensic odontology: The roles and responsibilities of the dentist. Dental Issues, 2004, *Journal of the Canadian Dental Association*, 70(7), pp. 453–458.

[†] International Association for Identification. n/d. *Forensic Odontology: Frequently Asked Questions Forensic Odontology in the IAI.* http://www.theiai.org/disciplines/odontology/faq.php.

[‡] American Board of Forensic Odontology Guidelines and Standards Draft 5-2014-6.Doc.

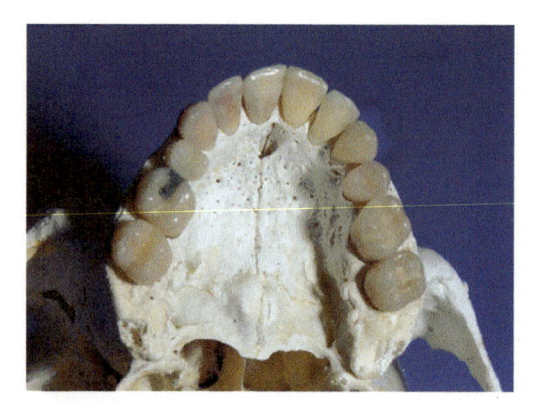

Figure 9.1 Lake Michigan Jane Doe, Dental view #1. Courtesy of Detective Mark Czworniak (ret.), Chicago Police Department.

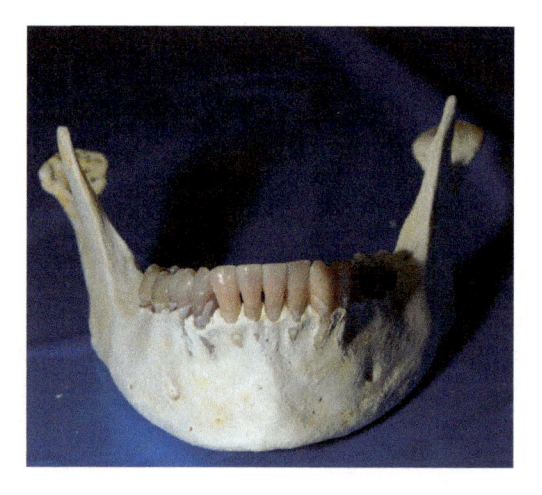

Figure 9.2 Lake Michigan Jane Doe, Dental view #2. Courtesy of Detective Mark Czworniak (ret.), Chicago Police Department.

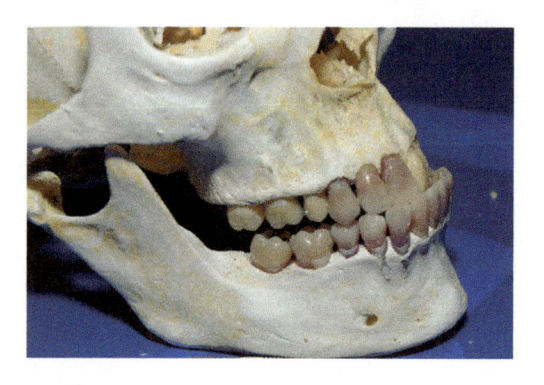

Figure 9.3 Lake Michigan Jane Doe, Dental view #3. Courtesy of Detective Mark Czworniak (ret.), Chicago Police Department.

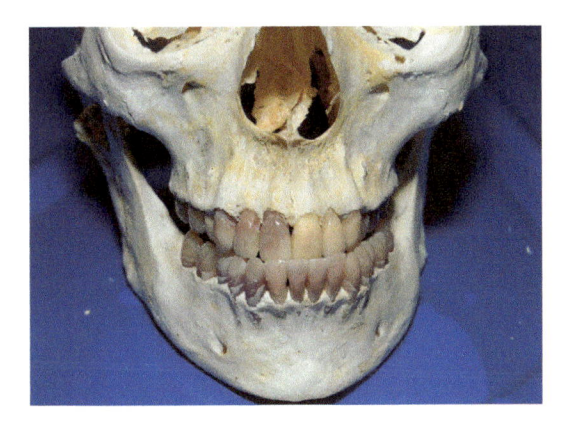

Figure 9.4 Lake Michigan Jane Doe, Dental view #4. Courtesy of Detective Mark Czworniak (ret.), Chicago Police Department.

The CJIS initiated the National Dental Image/Information Repository (NDIR) in 2005.* NDIR may be accessed through Law Enforcement Online for agencies to upload dental information and images related to missing, wanted, and unidentified persons. The files are maintained to assist agencies with completing NCIC MP and UP reports; the NDIR files are stored and retrieved in folders that are assigned NCIC case numbers. An experienced odontologist reviews newly submitted records and compares them with extant NCIC records for accuracy and consistency.[†] All 18,000-plus law enforcement agencies can use NDIR and NCIC for automated searching.

By the end of 2009, the FBI was using 200 volunteer dentists who had completed a 16-h NCIC dental coding workshop.[‡] The FBI still conducts free workshops across the United States in groups of up to 50 participants for the purpose of assisting law enforcement and ME/C. Although dental records have been variously coded in the past, NCIC dental coding is rapidly becoming the international standard format for dental record comparisons. NCIC searches the dental coding fields in an MP record whenever a new record is entered or an extant record is modified, and sends a $.M report within 24 h to the agencies that have investigative interest in the case. The report includes the top possible hits[§] and is copied to state clearinghouses.

---

* Missouri State Highway Patrol. n/d. The CJIS Newsletter: National Crime Information Center (NCIC), Dental Image/Information Repository (NDIR) 10-03.

† *Ibid.* p. 5.

‡ U.S. Department of Justice, Federal Bureau of Investigation, Criminal Justice Information Services (CJIS) Division. 2009. The NDIR helps law enforcement agencies exchange dental record information. *The CJIS Link*, 11(3), 3. December 2008/January 2009.

§ *Ibid.* p. 4.

NamUs, which can store dental images with its own dental coding format and search algorithms, also provides translations into the NCIC coding format. As of 2014, NamUs employed two part-time forensic odontologists to respond to agency requests for help with coding. Dental support for MP and UHR investigations by agencies without staff odontologists may choose between local volunteer dentists and odontologists who are trained and certified by the FBI (using NCIC and NDIR), and NamUs odontologists (who should be consulted as backup to FBI-certified personnel).

Dentists and odontologists who are covered under HIPAA (the Health Income Portability and Accountability Act of 1996) should know that when they receive law enforcement requests for information, under Title 45 CFR 164.512 (f) they may not disclose for the purposes of identification or location any protected information related to an individual's DNA or DNA analysis; dental records; or typing, samples or analysis of body fluids or tissue.* Entities who are covered by HIPAA regulations should obtain legal advice before releasing any medical or dental records, and/or should insist that requests for information be submitted in the form of a subpoena or statutory release from law enforcement.

Dental records related to MP are primarily used to identify UD when fingerprints are not available from the remains, through NGI (see Chapter 10), or in locally archived fingerprint databases. Dental records that contribute to identification efforts may include any or all of the following:

- Charts
- X-rays (radiographs)
- Photographs
- Records of casts and/or dental appliance providers
- Treatment procedures
- Recommendations and referrals

Dental records are also used to identify people who are mentally/cognitively impaired, amnesiac, or comatose. If the person in question is not suffering from mental retardation or dementia, cognitive impairment may be the result of injury, long-term drug use, or a recent overdose. In addition, people who have suffered severe deprivation or trauma (from an accident, a catastrophic event, or prolonged abuse) may not be able to identify themselves or answer questions because they are experiencing catatonia; this condition is

---

* U.S. Government Printing Office. 2014. §164.512 Uses and disclosures for which an authorization or opportunity to agree or object is not required. *GPO Electronic Code of Federal Regulations.* http://www.ecfr.gov/cgi-bin/text-idx?SID=6b861100aa0e3f7543f27 8b9635c144b&node=se45.1.164_1512&rgn=div8.

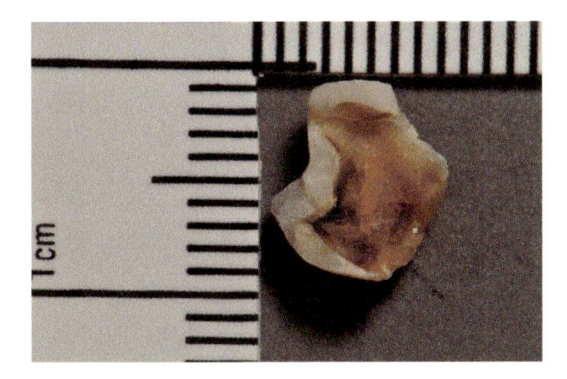

Figure 9.5 Scale of perspective for dental images. Courtesy of Detective Mark Czworniak (ret.), Chicago Police Department.

more common in children and adolescents than in adults.[*] Catatonia, which is a state of unresponsiveness to external stimuli in a person who is apparently awake, is categorized as (1) catatonia associated with another mental disorder (catatonia specified); (2) catatonic disorder due to another medical condition; and (3) unspecified catatonia.[†] Descriptions of children exhibiting fear during the crisis on September 11, 2001 include panicked, crying behaviors, or withdrawn/catatonic reactions. Often, such reactions are due to fear of being separated from a loved one or to the terror and chaos of events they have witnessed.

Fingerprints from juveniles may be difficult to acquire in normal times, but during outbreaks of violence or following a major disaster it may be impossible. In such situations, volunteer dentists who were trained by the FBI exemplify the proactive aspects of the NDIR program. Many of the same volunteer dentists will be present at mass disasters as members of DMORT (disaster mortuary operational response teams). Even though circumstances during a mass disaster are chaotic, care should be taken when recording evidence for future use. Figures 9.5 and 9.6 are typical of the evidentiary documentation of dental images. In Figure 9.5, a scale can be utilized; in Figure 9.6, a scale cannot be utilized. Notice that Figure 9.6 includes a medical device that can later be used as a point of reference for scale. It is in these situations that coordination with state clearinghouses and local law enforcement agencies becomes critical.

Disconnects in odontology are often connected with dental charting errors, which are a constant concern for investigators. When charting is done by a person with less skill and training than the patient's actual dentist or

[*] Dhosssache, D., Ross, C., Stoppelbein, L. 2011. The role of deprivation, abuse, and trauma in pediatric catatonia without a clear medical cause. *Acta Psychiatrida Scandinavica*, 125(1), pp. 25–32.

[†] Medscape. 2014. http://emedicine.medscape.com/article/1154851-overview.

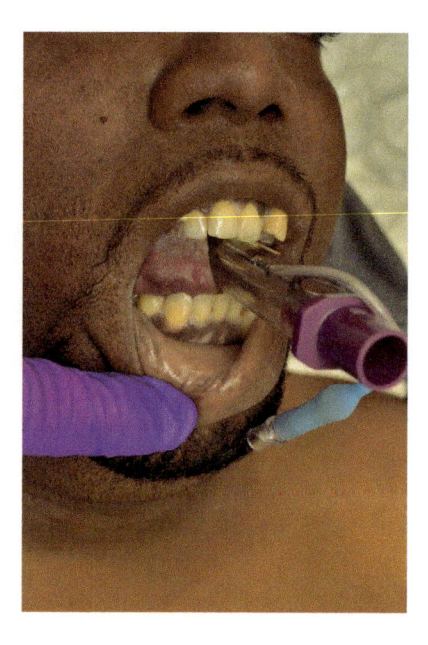

Figure 9.6 Initial UD dental image. Courtesy of Detective Mark Czworniak (ret.), Chicago Police Department.

odontologist, an incorrect tooth may be coded as having undergone a particular procedure or an incorrect procedure may be indicated for a particular tooth. Or when law enforcement requests or subpoenas copies of dental records that should include x-rays, the x-rays may not have been placed in the patient file.

A small fraction of all MP records contain dental records; UP files are more likely to include them. In Missouri, for example, only 2% of MP records contain dental information but 32% of UP records in NCIC do.* Without a mechanism that gives HIPAA-covered dentists and odontologists more leeway to share dental records, the number of dental records in NDIR may not improve significantly.

UP files that contain dental records are mostly generated by ME/C who have access to a forensic dentist and are exempted from HIPAA statutes. Practicing dentists or odontologists may have much greater concerns about liability associated with releasing patient records in an MP case, such as

- Lack of a valid release form.
- Unclear disposition of dental records after an MP is located or returns.

---

* Missouri State Highway Patrol. n/d. The CJIS Newsletter: National Crime Information Center (NCIC), Dental Image/Information Repository (NDIR) 10-03.

- Contribution to the location of an MP who is in hiding for valid reasons.
- Particular complexities around the release of juvenile records and the purging of such records when the juvenile returns and/or reaches legal age.

As previously explained, inaccuracies in dental charting are another major concern. Dental records are transcribed and coded into patients' files by humans who may be poorly trained, poorly motivated, or who are working under pressure to conform to appointment schedules. Such circumstances may contribute to basic human errors in coding.

The 2004 identification of Donna Williamson, who went missing in 1982, was the first cold hit for the Texas Missing Persons DNA Database and among the first national cold DNA hits between an MP and UHR. Although NCIC records in both the MP and UP files associated with her case contained dental information, as mentioned in Chapter 8, Ms. Williamson was eliminated as a potential match to the remains because the dental report charts were entered backwards (the right side of her mouth was identified as the left side, and vice versa).* A similar case involved a UD in the Southwest who was thought to be a homicide victim and was later identified after a cold hit; dental records were available for both the MP and UP but, again, they had been reversed.

In a study of the discrepancies between the antemortem and postmortem data used to identify 100 randomly selected subjects, the mean percentage of positive (accurate) identification was 74.49%. Most of the discrepancies were attributed to dynamic changes in the dental status during the time lapse between initial charting and postmortem examination (such as a restored or missing tooth in a postmortem examination that was clearly visible and/or healthy in an antemortem examination) and human error during the initial charting.† Clearly, accurately charted and entered dental records can be of tremendous value in UD/UHR investigations.

Malpractice is of a major concern to practicing dentists, especially in states where Medicare/Medicaid use is extremely high. When medical records related to an individual have been released to outside parties and an error is discovered, the inaccuracies, deficiencies, or omissions may be used against the issuing party. Still another concern is comments that dentists may have entered into the records, or diagnoses that might mention or imply illicit drug use as a possible causative factor. The latter, in particular,

---

* Austin, D. n/d. *Who Are You? Case Studies in Human Identification.* Tarrant County Medical Examiner's District. http://www.slideserve.com/kinsey/who-are-you-case-studies-in-human-identification.
† Zahrani, A. 2005. Identification of unidentified human remains—Validity of dental records. *Forensic Dentistry Oral Surgery: Pakistan Oral and Dental Journal,* 25(1), pp. 3–6.

could cause devastating labeling of a patient or subject him or her to criminal investigation.

In a list of common mistakes in dentists' records, number seven is "Inaccurate charting of restorations, bridges, missing or extracted teeth, root canal filings and planned restorations, bridges, extractions, root canal filings, etc."* State laws differ widely, and may change over time; therefore, subjective reviews cannot be interpreted as factual. Medical practitioners are well aware of their liabilities and patient concerns about the release of HIPAA-protected records. For dentists and odontologists, these concerns may include fiduciary duty to their patients, loss of control of records after release, and unanticipated liability due to complex and changing laws.

Fraudulent practices may also impact a UHR investigation. For example, a dentist may be indicted for false billing (i.e., charging for work that was never performed).† Just in the state of Oklahoma, in 2014 dental clinics agreed to pay $5,050,000 for billing Medicare for claims that "were false because they were either (1) upcoded by billing for more restored surfaces than were actually performed or (2) not performed at all."‡ Dental fraud is far more common than the public knows, and much more serious as well because dental records are key pieces of evidence that many investigators and ME/C regularly use to quickly eliminate candidates when secondary modalities of identification are unavailable.

No modality is available for UHR investigations that can produce a positive identification with 100% accuracy. To help families understand the relationships between each modality and the necessity of using multiple modalities to support UHR investigations, I recommend a combined custom/practice and logical relationship approach that contains three levels. The primary and most widely used modality is visual identification because it is the least time-consuming and costly; unfortunately, it does not work well with identical twins§. Secondary modalities of identification consider natural attributes of the UHR that are derived from the actual body, such as

---

* Morse, D. 2004. *Dealing with Dental Malpractice, Part 2: Malpractice Prevention.* Dentistry Today, Sunday, February 29, 2004. http://www.dentistrytoday.com/practice-management-articles/risk-management/1898-dealing-with-dental-malpractice-part-2-malpractice-prevention.

† The United States Attorney's Office: Eastern District of California. 2014. *Sacramento Dentist Indicted For Fraudulent Billing Scheme Involving Unnecessary Dental Work.* United States Department of Justice, February 20, 2014. http://www.justice.gov/usao/cae/news/docs/2014/2014_02/02-20-14Lewis.html (Accessed November 14, 2014).

‡ The United States Attorney's Office: Western District of California. 2014. *Oklahoma Dental Clinics Pay Over $5 Million to Settle Allegations of False Medicaid Claims for Dental Restoration Procedure* United States Department of Justice, February 20, 2014. http://www.justice.gov/usao/okw/news/2014/2014_10_31.html.

§ Hammer, R.M., Moynihan, B., Pagliaqro, E.M. 2006. *Forensic Nursing: A Handbook for Practice;* McDonough, E. *Chapter 15: Death Investigation: Identification of Human Remains.* p. 429.

DNA, fingerprints, and teeth). Tertiary modalities are attributes observed in or with the UHR that concern alterations, such as tattoos and scars; identification papers; and lot numbers or serial numbers of medical artifacts. The advantage of using multiple modalities is that they complement each other. Any dissonance between one or more modalities should be viewed as an anomaly that requires immediate dissection and resolution. It is a very real possibility that one modality of identification may not be permitted as evidence; examples include improperly handled evidence (as described in Chapter 4) or a broken chain of custody (COC).

If an MP/UD investigation becomes a criminal case, investigators may not become aware of such anomalies until trial. I have personally seen two different lower mandibles (jawbones) submitted for the same UHR; agencies attempting to locate a forensic sample at a lab to which the investigator's case notes indicate the sample has been submitted, without the lab ever having received the sample; and evidentiary samples that have been damaged simply because evidentiary packages have been piled upon top of one another. Investigators are admonished to keep an eye on the process by obtaining a copy of the complete case file after they have been notified of a match or association. Doing so will help them avoid spending investigative hours and resources on a pointless criminal (because the single critical identification modality was compromised and could not be used).

Because UD cases that are active for years or decades may become homicide investigations (e.g., the April Repka case), the records associated with the entire investigation from the beginning must be completely reliable. When they are not, sanctions to and damaged reputations of practicing healthcare providers may also last for years or decades. Families and investigators should understand the importance of ensuring that protected healthcare information is collected properly and that information that is improperly collected, or unreliable, may have consequences that extend far beyond the case at hand.

Forensic dentists and odontologists should compare dental evidence from an MP (antemortem) and a UHR (postmortem) to formulate the most reliable opinions. Any discrepancies between the dental opinion and other metadata should be resolved as part of the investigation before an identification of the deceased is announced. When discrepancies exist between antemortem records and postmortem records, both the identification process and holding an offender accountable may be delayed or derailed.

In 2007, after a juvenile was reported missing in Oklahoma, an unidentified body was located not far from where the juvenile was last known to be alive. From the various pieces of evidence, investigators had reasonable suspicion that the UHR were from the MP. However, the dental records of the MP were not in agreement with the dentals of the UHR and no fingerprints of the MP were available. The case was resolved only after a reference DNA sample confirmed an association with a target sample taken from the UHR.

In developing strategies to manage the collection and analysis of dental records, investigators and families must communicate clearly about why these records are necessary and must consider whether or not to use them based on the elements of the case, available resources, and current privacy statutes. The latter differ from state to state. In addition, the security of personally identifiable information and the privacy of healthcare records may change within a single state. A single line of reasoning cannot be used for all cases in all states; "one size" does not fit all situations.

Interpretations of HIPAA requirements may be particularly subjective when they are related to MP and UHR cases, or investigators may simply not be aware of them. As a result, families and investigators may become frustrated during the process of obtaining dental records. According to national law (Title 45 CFR 164.512 (f))

A covered entity may disclose protected health information

1. As required by law, including laws that require the reporting of certain types of wounds or other physical injuries [...]
2. In compliance with and as limited by the relevant requirements of
   a. A court order or court-ordered warrant, or a subpoena or summons issued by a judicial officer
   b. A grand jury subpoena
   c. An administrative request, including an administrative subpoena or summons, a civil or an authorized investigative demand, or similar process authorized under law, provided that
      i. The information sought is relevant and material to a legitimate law enforcement inquiry
      ii. The request is specific and limited in scope to the extent that is reasonably practicable in light of the purpose for which the information is sought
      iii. Deidentified information could not reasonably be used

Permitted disclosures include: Limited information for identification and location purposes. Except for disclosures required by law as permitted by paragraph (f)(1) of this section, a covered entity may disclose protected health information in response to a law enforcement official's request for such information for the purpose of identifying or locating a suspect, fugitive, material witness, or missing person, provided that

1. The covered entity may disclose only the following information:
   a. Name and address
   b. Date and place of birth

c. Social security number
d. ABO blood type and rh factor
e. Type of injury
f. Date and time of treatment
g. Date and time of death, if applicable
h. A description of distinguishing physical characteristics, including height, weight, gender, race, hair and eye color, presence or absence of facial hair (beard or moustache), scars, and tattoos

2. Except as permitted by paragraph (f)(2)(i) of this section, the covered entity may not disclose for the purposes of identification or location under paragraph (f)(2) of this section any protected health information related to the individual's DNA or DNA analysis, dental records, or typing, samples or analysis of body fluids or tissue.[*]

Under federal statutes related to HIPAA, law enforcement (also called "a covered entity") is also defined:

The Privacy Rule at 45 CFR 164.512(f) permits a covered entity to disclose protected health information to a law enforcement official for law enforcement purposes in compliance with court orders, grand jury subpoenas, or certain written administrative requests. 45 CFR 164.512(f)(1)(ii). As defined in 45 CFR 164.501, a law enforcement official means an officer or employee of any agency or authority of the United States, a State, a territory, a political subdivision of a State or territory, or an Indian tribe, who is empowered by law to investigate or conduct an official inquiry into a potential violation of law or to prosecute or otherwise conduct a criminal, civil, or administrative proceeding arising from an alleged violation of law.[†]

The ORI number of an investigative law enforcement agency will either end in "00" or the last number will be a numeric character. If the last character is numerical, it represents a law enforcement agency. If the last character is alphabetic, it designates the agency as a criminal justice agency (usually without enforcement/arrest powers). When the ORI number ends in an alphabetic character, the dentist or odontologist should check with his/her legal advisor before releasing any information.

---

[*] U.S. Government Printing Office. 2014. §164.512 Uses and disclosures for which an authorization or opportunity to agree or object is not required. *GPO Electronic Code of Federal Regulations.* http://www.ecfr.gov/cgi-bin/text-idx?SID=6b861100aa0e3f7543f27 8b9635c144b&node=se45.1.164_1512&rgn=div8.

[†] U.S. Department of Health and Human Services. n/d. *May a Health Plan Disclose Protected Health Information to a State Child Support Enforcement (IV-D) Agency in Response to a National Medical Support Notice?* http://www.hhs.gov/ocr/privacy/hipaa/faq/disclosures_for_law_enforcement_purposes/759.html.

Under HIPAA regulations, ME/C do not have the level of liability that dentists and odontologists have. For example:

(g) Standard: Uses and disclosures about decedents—(1) Coroners and medical examiners. A covered entity may disclose protected health information to a coroner or medical examiner for the purpose of identifying a deceased person, determining a cause of death, or other duties as authorized by law. A covered entity that also performs the duties of a coroner or medical examiner may use protected health information for the purposes described in this paragraph.

(2) Funeral directors. A covered entity may disclose protected health information to funeral directors, consistent with applicable law, as necessary to carry out their duties with respect to the decedent. If necessary for funeral directors to carry out their duties, the covered entity may disclose the protected health information prior to, and in reasonable anticipation of, the individual's death.*

Most states have statutes that outline a process for providing statutory immunity to dentists and odontologists, if certain procedures are followed. A representative example, the Chapter 63 of the Texas Code of Criminal Procedure articulates how dentists and odontologists may assist law enforcement officials under HIPAA and provides immunity for the release of dental information and records:

Release of Dental Records

1. At the time a report is made for a missing child, the person to whom the report is given shall give or mail to the reporter a dental record release form. The officer receiving the report shall endorse the form with the notation that a missing child report has been made in compliance with this chapter. When the form is properly completed by the reporter, and contains the endorsement, the form is sufficient to permit any dentist or physician in this state to release dental records relating to the child reported missing.

2. At any time a report is made for a missing person the law enforcement officer taking the report shall complete a dental release form that states that the person is missing and that there is reason to believe that the person has not voluntarily relocated or removed himself from communications with others and that authorizes the bearer of the release to obtain dental information records from any dentist or physician in this state.

3. Any person who obtains dental records through the use of the form authorized by this article shall send the records to the clearinghouse.

---

* U.S. Government Printing Office. 2014. §164.512 Uses and disclosures for which an authorization or opportunity to agree or object is not required. GPO Electronic Code of Federal Regulations. http://www.ecfr.gov/cgi-bin/text-idx?SID=6b861100aa0e3f7543f27 8b9635c144b&node=se45.1.164_1512&rgn=div8.

4. The judge of any court of record of this state may for good cause shown authorize the release of dental records of a missing child or missing person.
5. A dentist or physician who releases dental records to a person presenting a proper release executed or ordered under this article is immune from civil liability or criminal prosecution for the release of those records.[*]

Most states have similar procedures. A dentist or odontologist may receive a request to assist in a forensic investigation by law enforcement authorities that identify themselves and present a valid warrant, court order, subpoena, or administrative request; various state laws articulate the conditions under which dentists and odontologists may choose to release records.[†] The majority of dentists and odontologists desire to assist law enforcement in UD cases as well as MP, and have a good understanding of how they may protect themselves from liability risks while safeguarding the privacy of their patients.

States' MP clearinghouses are good sources for obtaining the needed information for all aspects of an MP/UD investigation, including dental records as well as the URLs of secure nonpublic databases. The collection process for dental records usually begins 30–60 days after an MP report is filed with a law enforcement agency. The delay is meant to allow MP to return or for law enforcement to locate them through normal channels. Children are likely to return or be found within this time frame, as indicated by an Office of the Inspector General audit in 2009 that indicated only 0.0068% of missing children were kidnapped by a stranger and that 99.8% returned on their own or were located by law enforcement.[‡]

Collection of dental records should be done in a way that protects the privacy of the MP and manages liability risks for investigators, dentists, and odontologists.

A state- or agency-approved standard release form that provides liability protection for dentists and odontologists should be the first choice for obtaining records. Investigators and families should not be surprised, however, when a dentist or odontologist declines to release dental information to minimize liability exposure and protect patient privacy. In such cases, a subpoena *duces tecum* [production of evidence] can be obtained.

---

[*] State of Texas. 1999. *Release of Dental Records*. Code of Criminal Procedure, Title 1, Chapter 63, Missing Children and Missing Persons Subchapter A. General Provisions. Art. 63.006.
[†] Council on Dental Practice: Division of Legal Affairs. 2007. *Dental Records*. American Dental Association. p. 21.
[‡] Office of the Inspector General. 2009. *The Federal Bureau of Investigation's Efforts to Combat Crimes against Children, Chapter 3: Child Abductions*. Audit Report, 09-08.

The protocols in the following timeline should be implemented in an organized manner.

1. A credible person of standing makes an MP report to an appropriate investigative law enforcement agency. This establishes probable cause for the agency to begin an MP investigation.
2. The 30–60 days recommended waiting period begins. After this time, dental records can be requested if there is reasonable suspicion that the MP may be at high risk, incapacitated, or deceased. When obtaining the dental information, investigators may find it wise to explain to all parties how the dental information will be used, stored, redisclosed, and returned. Dentist and odontologists are concerned with HIPAA compliance, patient protection, and possible liability; investigators are concerned with state statutes.

For records in an external or accessible public database, it may be beneficial to use clearinghouse representatives as the primary contacts and to have them assist with ensuring only permissible and accurate dental and medical information are entered. An effective protocol may involve these steps, which should be taken by investigators

- Waiting 30–60 days after an MP report is filed with a qualified investigative law enforcement authority before seeking dental records.
- Presenting a properly completed release or subpoena *duces tecum* to the dentist or odontologist to obtain the dental records.
- Obtaining dental records, with copies retained by the dentist, under normal evidentiary protocols with a solid chain of custody. The latter does not include family members and individuals not associated with law enforcement.
- Delivery of dental records to the state clearinghouse or the investigating agency, according to state statute.
- Coding and entering the dental records into NCIC.
- Digitizing and entering dental records into NDIR files.
- Meeting with the dentist or odontologist and making sure that the records as entered into various databases match copies that have been retained by the dentist or odontologist; this step helps control the COC and prevents redisclosure accusation claims against the law enforcement agency.

Key point: Dentists and odontologists may be more likely to cooperate if they are presented with a release that is statutorily approved (usually available through state clearinghouses) or with a subpoena.

Although dental records have not proven to be very effective for searching and locating MP, dental records and fingerprints are the most commonly used evidence to make initial or confirming secondary identification of UD. Dental records are very rarely used in the identification of living MP who are not cognitively impaired.

Because MP may be escaping abusive domestic environments, investigators may never be certain about all of the circumstances related to an MP or to the complainant who initially requests the filing of an MP report. Therefore, it is best to proceed with caution and consideration as an MP case is investigated and personal information is released outside of NCIC.

Translational Technologies

Translational technologies go beyond the legacy technologies currently in use to improve the efficacy of UHR investigations. Section III includes discussions of mtDNA, Y-STR, SNP, and familial searching in relation to NGS. Stable isotope analysis (SIA) is also discussed as a complement for NGS that establishes a trajectory for the UP before death and may establish a place of birth or adolescence. These technologies are on the cusp of dominating UHR investigations, as the NIJ has recognized with an $88,000 award to the nonprofit Battelle Corporation to develop NGS for law enforcement use. Battelle, founded in 1929, serves the national security, health and life sciences, energy, and environmental industries by designing and manufacturing products and delivering critical services.

Next-Generation Identification

10

An era in biometric identification and investigation came to a close and a new one began on September 7, 2014, when the FBI's Criminal Justice Information Services (CJIS) Division officially decommissioned the 15-year-old Integrated Automated Fingerprint Identification System (IAFIS) and, in turn, deployed the Next Generation Identification (NGI) system.

Kristi Mayo[*]

Next-generation identification (NGI) may be one of the most valuable tools in law enforcement's investigative toolkit for human identification. As we have already seen in previous chapters, reasons for people going missing, as well as the dangers that may drive them into making this decision, can be very complicated. But there are additional complications that must also be considered. NGI offers many ways to protect the identity, and thus the safety, of missing individuals. It can also be used to reveal identity theft and associated fraud.

In law enforcement, the protection of victims—including their identities—is a central concern. But protection can be an issue for officers as well. Domestic violence provides useful statistics and examples. An estimated 1.3 million women in the United States are annual victims of physical assault by intimate partners, but most intimate partner violence (IPV) events are never reported to police.[†] When police respond to the calls that are made, they do so at the risk of their own lives: an estimated 14% of law enforcement officers who are murdered die as they respond to domestic violence calls.[‡] In addition, IPV is deadly to women: almost 33% of female homicide victims are murdered by their partners.[§]

---

[*] Mayo, K. n/d. Leveraging the next generation IDE notification system. *Evidence Technology Magazine.* http://www.evidencemagazine.com/index.php?option=com_content&task=view&id=1845 (Accessed August 10, 2015).

[†] Gerberding, J., Binder, S., Hammond, W., Arias, I. 2003. *Costs of Intimate Partner Violence against Women in the United States.* Department of Health and Human Services Centers for Disease Control and Prevention National Center for Injury Prevention and Control. Atlanta, Georgia. March 2003. p. 14.

[‡] Meyer, S., Carroll, R. 2011. When officers die: Understanding deadly domestic violence calls for Service. *The Police Chief,* 78. May 24–27.

[§] Rennison, C. 2003. *Intimate Partner Violence, 1993–2001.* U.S. Department of Justice, Office of Justice Programs. February 2003, NCJ 197838. p. 1.

Although women are most vulnerable to being killed when they try to escape abusive situations, many IPV victims are able to flee successfully. They must build new lives after escaping their abusers, however, and this can be very difficult. For example, obtaining new social security numbers is usually not a viable alternative because all of a woman's credentials (including credit information) will simply be reattached to her new social security number. This makes her easy to trace. However, the biometrics associated with NGI allow law enforcement officers to rapidly confirm the identity of someone who is missing voluntarily (i.e., in hiding), to advise the originating law enforcement agency that this person is alive and well, and to cancel the NCIC MP record—all without letting the abuser know the location of his victim.

NGI works from fingerprints as well as other linked biometric components. Dictionary.com defines biometrics as "the process by which a person's unique physical and other traits are detected and recorded by an electronic device or system as a means of confirming identity," and adds that "Scanning of the human iris is a reliable form of biometrics."

Under the assumptions that people can be viewed as biometric sets, and an individual is one such set that can be identified by fingerprints linked to multiple aliases, NGI functions to identify a person through multiple linked biometrics, rather than relying upon a name and numeric identifiers of someone who has interacted with law enforcement at some point in time, as with an NCIC records and wanted inquiry, or eyewitness identification of the decreased. This way of looking at people demonstrates a paradigm shift that began in 2013 with *King v. Maryland*, in which it was stated that "[because] a name alone cannot address this interest in identity, the Court has approved, for example, a visual inspection for certain tattoos and other signs of gang affiliation as part of the intake process."[*] Such inspections reduce the numbers of false arrests due to misidentification, which are a major problem in U.S. law enforcement. An arrest involving mistaken identity occurs almost every day, according to experts at the National Association of Criminal Defense Lawyers. In Colorado alone, the ACLU found at least 237 cases where police arrested the wrong person.[†] Many misidentifications stem from the initial arrest, during which the accused offender may give false information.

Quite often, abusers report fleeing victims as MP in order to obtain assistance in finding her or to instill fear in her through posting information about her in public MP databases. Because so much domestic violence is kept secret even from victims' families, friends, and coworkers, it may be difficult for families to understand why their loved one has disappeared. The problem is very common, however: "Nearly 3 in 10 women in the United States

---

[*] Maryland *v.* King. No. 12-207, Decided June 3, 2013.
[†] Chen, S. 2010. Officer, You've Got the Wrong Person. CNN Justice. http://www.cnn.com/2010/CRIME/02/15/colorado.mistaken.identity.arrest/index.html.

(28.8% or approximately 34.3 million) have experienced rape, physical violence, and/or stalking by an intimate partner."* The prevalence of such violence across the United States makes it even more crucial for investigators to take all precautions in releasing any information, including images and records on databases and public forums, that might place an abuse victim in harm's way or unfairly damage her reputation (for example, an IPV victims self-medicate as a coping mechanism and enter the criminal justice system as a result). The biometrics associated with NGI can identify such individuals, whose MP data can then be removed from NCIC and NamUs.

Identity theft, which is a growing concern worldwide, also contributes to misidentification because people (whether they are abuse victims trying to build new lives or criminals hiding from past crimes) can simply purchase new identities and use them, sometimes for decades. On October 25, 2014 it was reported that "Investigators were poring over the conflicting backgrounds [...] of a Utah couple accused in a crime spree that killed two deputies, with federal authorities saying the 34-year-old man charged in the slayings has used at least two identities and has been deported from the United States twice in the past."† Court records revealed this offender's history of about 10 tickets, misdemeanor traffic offenses between 2003 and 2009, a speeding ticket in 2009 and several small claims filings attempting to recover outstanding debts.‡

An Alaskan police officer, using a false identity of another individual from Mexico reportedly known to the officer, was arrested in 2011. He was thus able to commit passport fraud over a 20-year period; obtain a driver's license and mortgages; file for bankruptcy filings; commit voter fraud; and falsify documents to obtain a position as a peace officer.§ In 1999, investigators found that a 72-year-old man had been living and working in Las Vegas for 20 years under an assumed identity, after obtaining an identity package for a reported $800. The package contained vital documents, including the social security number of a living person. This offender had also resided in Florida and California.¶

---

* Black, M.C., Basile, K.C., Breiding, M.J., Smith, S.G., Walters, M.L., Merrick, M.T., Chen, J., Stevens, M.R. 2011. *The National Intimate Partner and Sexual Violence Survey (NISVS): 2010 Summary Report.* Atlanta, GA: National Center. p. 39 for Injury Prevention and Control, Centers for Disease Control and Prevention.

† Standon, S. et al. 2014. Feds Say Sacramento Shooting Suspect Was Deported Twice, Had Drug Conviction. *The Sacramento Bee: crime–sacto 911,* October 25, 2014. http://www.sacbee.com/news/local/crime/article3368389.html.

‡ Spagat, E. 2014. *Suspected Cop Killer Luis Enrique Monroy-Bracamonte Had Multiple Identities.* Associated Press via HuffingtonPost.com, 10/27/2014. http://www.huffingtonpost.com/2014/10/27/cop-killer-luis-enrique-m_n_6053608.html.

§ Epler, P. 2011. Illegal Immigrant, Former APD Officer Facing 1 Year in Prison. *Alaska Dispatch News,* August 18.

¶ Benka, C, 8NewsNOW Web Team. 2011. Man Missing for 30 Years Found Alive in Las Vegas. Las Vegas, NV: *8 News Now,* http://www.8newsnow.com/story/15131101/man-missing-for-30-years-found-alive-in-las-vegas.

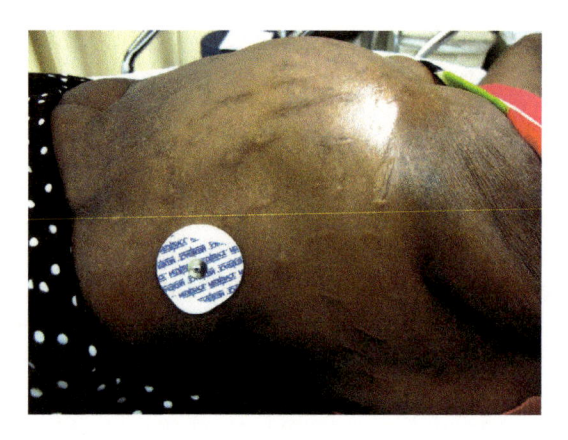

Figure 10.1 Unidentified decease identified with unique scars. (Courtesy of Detective Mark Czworniak (retired), Chicago Police Department.)

Today, identify theft is easier than ever due to data breaches involving retailers and financial institutions. In 2013, 43% of data breaches in the United States involved medical records that included social security numbers, addresses, employment histories, relatives' addresses, phone numbers, and more.[*] Due to the staggering amount of identity theft currently taking place and the severe consequences it imposes on communities and law enforcement, NGI was expedited to allow identification through the multimodal biometric confluence of fingerprints, the National Palm Print System, the Repository for Individuals of Special Concern (a mobile ID option for law enforcement), Rap Back (which identifies individuals in positions of trust who are involved in criminal activity), and the Interstate Photo System (which catalogues faces, scars, and tattoos [Figure 10.1]).[†] NGI implementation provides resources to MP/UP investigators that were once difficult if not impossible to implement in a coordinated and efficient manner when little else is available as is common in homeless victims (Figure 10.2).

Fingerprints, which are among the oldest forms of human identification, have a romantic aura like no other. In China, the thumbprint of the emperor was used for centuries to officially mark letters of state. The first emperor of China, Qin Shi Huang (ruled 246–210 B.C.E.) was the first to use such seals there.[‡] In 1858, Sir William Herschel used a fingerprint system as a means of

[*] Ollove, M. 2014. *The Rise of Medical Identity Theft*. Stateline, The PEW Charitable Trusts, February 7.

[†] Federal Bureau of Investigation. 2014. *Next Generation Identification: FBI Announces Biometrics Suite's Full Operational Capability*. 09/2/2014.

[‡] Lakshmi, R. 2013. *Annals and Essences of Dentistry*. Nellore, Andhra Pradesh, India: Department of Orthodontics, Narayana Dental College and Hospital, V(4), October–December 2013, p. 30.

Figure 10.2 Urban unidentified victim. (Courtesy of Detective Mark Czwornik (retired), Chicago Police Department.)

authentication in England.* In 1880, the fact that fingerprints could be used for criminal identification was brought to the attention of the English public by Henry Faulds. However, it was Francis Galton who gave fingerprint identification its scientific foundation between 1890 and 1895 by focusing on the minutiae (islets and forks) that provide their uniqueness.†

Public infatuation with forensic science was as pronounced in the 1880s as it is today. Mark Twain captivated readers of *Life on the Mississippi* (1883) when he described the use of fingerprints to identify a murderer, and with descriptions of fingerprint identification in "Pudd'n Head Wilson" (1893).‡ NGI has now taken fingerprints to the leading edge of human identification, as new resources are being placed in the hands of law enforcement officers so that they may more efficiently serve their communities.

The common wisdom that no two fingerprints are the same does not capture their complexity and differentiating minutiae, which still require a certified human print examiner to render an opinion for the purpose of identification. Before September 2014, fingerprints were sent by law enforcement to the FBI's Integrated Automated Fingerprint System (IAFIS) in hopes of finding a potential match among the millions of fingerprints on file in this criminal database. When queried, IAFIS would return a ranked list of potential candidate fingerprints that placed likely candidates near the top and less likely candidates near the bottom. An experienced certified fingerprint examiner would then render an opinion.

* Gundagin, S. 2007. Sex determination from fingerprint ridge density. *Internet Journal of Medical Update*, 2(2).
† Stigler, S. 1995. Galton and identification by fingerprints. In *Perspectives Anecdotal, Historical and Critical Commentaries on Genetics*, Crow, W. and Dove, J. (eds). Genetics Society of America 140, pp. 857–860.
‡ U.S. Marshalls Service. 2014. *U.S. Marshalls Service for Students.* http://www.usmar shals.gov/usmsforkids/fingerprint_history.htm.

The major latent print examiner certification requirements (excluding proficiency examinations) of the International Association for Identification are listed below

- Eighty hours (minimum) of certification board-approved training.
- Two years (minimum) full-time experience with the comparison and identification of latent print material.
- A bachelor's degree plus 2 years of full-time experience; an associate's degree plus 3 years of full-time experience; or 4 years of experience. The Latent Print Certification Board prescribes appropriate experience.[*]

The DHS developed a similar fingerprint database, Automated Biometric Identification System (IDENT), which was operated by United States Visitor and Immigrant Status Indicator Technology (U.S. VISIT) and houses fingerprints related to immigration and naturalization. In order to query IDENT, local law enforcement usually needed federal law enforcement to make the request on their behalf. Few MP/UP investigators knew about IDENT, which houses a significant number of fingerprints that are not contained in other fingerprint databases.

In September 2014, NGI replaced IAFIS. As a result, criminal database files, certain civil database files, and immigration database files may be queried instead of having to do separate searches in IAFIS and IDENT. The interoperability between multiple databases provides more effective and efficient fingerprint-search capabilities.

> **Key point:** NGI allows automated searching of much larger numbers of fingerprints with greater speed and better accuracy than ever before thought possible. Due to a history of territoriality among federal fingerprint databases, interoperability between them had not been successful.

In 2005, a man visiting the Texas Missing Persons Clearinghouse website found a sketch of an unidentified 1998 homicide victim who appeared to resemble his missing cousin. This man notified the clearinghouse, which then coordinated with a latent print examiner who obtained inked prints from the UD, who had been strangled, wrapped in plastic trash bags, and dumped on a roadside. When the thumbprints from the UD were compared to the MP's Texas driver's license records, a match was confirmed.[†] This case

---

[*] International Association for Identification. 2014. *Latent Print Certification Requirements*. http://www.theiai.org/certifications/latent_print/requirements.php.
[†] Davis, T. 2014. *Fingerprint Key to Identity*. Texas Department of Public Safety Annual Report 2005.

took nearly 7 years to be resolved. Today, however, the combination of NGI and simple, sound investigative strategies results in automated steps. All the examiner must do manually is confirm a match between a UD's fingerprints and fingerprints associated with an MP's driver's license.

In 2003, the thumbprints of an unidentified deceased John Doe were searched through the Texas Department of Public Safety (TXDPS) Automated Fingerprint System (AFIS) database without success. In 2007, the fingerprints were run a second time through TXDPS AFIS database and produced a candidate match.[*] Fingerprints and criminal history information are submitted on a voluntary basis to IAFIS (NGI)[†] but registration, which enables searching, is often delayed. IAFIS had searching access to various criminal fingerprint databases across the county that amounted to about 70 million fingerprints of individuals including past and present U.S. military and federal employees.[‡] NGI has now taken that number of records up to 100 million, and it continues to grow.

A single biometric should rarely be used to establish identification, as the Brandon Mayfield (Madrid bomber) case demonstrates. As described in Chapter 2, Mr. Mayfield was identified as the suspect on the basis of a fingerprint alone and several print examiners agreed. The spurious identification was soon revealed, however, when the real bomber was arrested and linked to an unknown print from the scene.

NGI includes various biometrics and metadata for multimodal identification support. Therefore, when a comparison is made between a known profile and an unknown profile and a hit occurs, a probability or a likelihood ratio is produced that provides a number that indicates the rarity of the profile based on a population study, at least one more confirming metadata identifier (dentals or NGI biometrics) should be utilized for confirmation. Starting 2014 the Texas Department of Public Safety had required driver's license applicants to submit fingerprint images of all 10 digits for identification purposes. Due to public outcry, it has returned to capturing only thumb prints. We must always be cognizant of public's concern for privacy is a major consideration in all public and private databases, medical/dental records and even missing person reports.

It is not unusual for an ME/C to submit fingerprints of a UD for NGI processing and for the returns to include multiple identities with different names and birthdates. In a 2012 study by DHS, 825,000 fingerprints were associated with different biographic data including different names and dates of birth.

[*] Austin, D. n/d. *Who Are You? Case Studies in Human Identification.* Tarrant County Medical Examiner District: Human Identification Lab.

[†] Federal Bureau of Investigation. n/d. *Integrated Automated Fingerprint System.* U.S. Department of Justice, Federal Bureau of Investigation Criminal Justice Information System. http://www.fbi.gov/about-us/cjis/fingerprints_biometrics/iafis/iafis/.

[‡] *Ibid.*

Most all of the hundreds of thousands of records were associated with data integrity (input) errors at the points of collection; in some instances, individuals had intentionally provided incorrect names and birthdates.[*]

In addition, through interoperational agreements, NGI can search fingerprint databases that were not previously available to local law enforcement agencies, such as IDENT (a subset of DHS's US-VISIT). These additional biometrics and metadata assist law enforcement in sifting through spurious hits. The identification of a John or Jane Doe may prove very challenging without NGI.

In 2001, a California sheriff's office established a link with IAFIS through the state DOJ. In testing the system, a latent print from a 1999 unsolved murder was submitted. Three possible candidates were returned. The sheriff's office latent examiner determined that one of the returned candidates was indeed a match and, 2 weeks after the murder in California, this submitted known print hit to an arrestee from Texas. The person of interest was located in the local area of the murder; when questioned, he admitted to meeting the decedent and agreed to provide prints. However, he could not explain how his fingerprints had come to be on a door frame at the murder scene, or how his palmprint had come to be on the dead man's face. Eventually, the person of interest pled guilty to homicide and received a 32-year prison sentence.[†]

This case was resolved, but initially the Texas arrestee's fingerprint could not hit the California offender's fingerprints because California's prints were not available in IAFIS. In this case, multimodal identification technologies (fingerprints and palmprints) supported and confirmed the identification. Additional metadata was also available for complementary support of the identification; this consisted of the suspect's admission of knowing and being with the deceased before death and the suspect's location in the same local geographic area as the deceased. Moreover, several law enforcement agencies collaborated and shared information in secure environments to achieve resolution for the victim and family.

This case is an excellent example of effective NGI informational flow between agencies. The same approach can be utilized in MP/UP investigations if prints are registered with the state bureau for submission to NGI. However, as previously explained, NGI is a tool that facilitates collaboration between law enforcement agencies. Investigators should therefore keep in mind that most law enforcement entities may only share their information through secure environments and with other agencies that have the ability to

---

[*] U.S. Department of Homeland Security. 2012. *US-VISIT Faces Challenges in Identifying and Reporting Multiple Biographic Identities (Redacted)*. U.S. Department of Homeland Security, Office of Inspector General. p. 3.

[†] Federal Bureau of Investigation. 2013. *Latent Hit of the Year Award: Fingerprint Tool Helps Solve 1999 Murder*. Federal Bureau of Investigation, Criminal Justice Information System, July.

access and contribute to NGI resources. These criteria often do not apply to criminal justice agencies, which do not have the investigative responsibilities that law enforcement agencies do. Sending fingerprints to criminal justice agencies that cannot utilize NGI resources as a single-source search effort is probably not a good strategy.

Fingerprinting a child is of particular concern in all states and to all investigators. The statutes differ from state to state, but their intent can be summarized by the following paraphrase (from the 2014 Texas Attorney General's *Juvenile Justice Handbook*):

> As a general rule, a child may not be fingerprinted or photographed without the consent of the juvenile court. Exceptions to the general rule include fingerprinting and photographing a child with a parent or guardian's voluntary written consent, or for the purpose of obtaining a driver's license or personal ID card, or for inclusion in the missing children information clearinghouse. [...] Once the child is identified (or if the child cannot be identified), law enforcement must immediately destroy all copies of the fingerprint records or photographs of the child... All law enforcement files and records concerning juveniles may not be disclosed to the public and must be kept strictly separate from adult criminal files and records.[*]

Because of these and similar rules, NCMEC is used in NamUs for handling child and adolescent MP cases. Investigators in every state may be impacted by strict regulations related to collecting, disseminating, and controlling juvenile biometrics. State clearinghouses should always be consulted before information related to a juvenile is released, due to the complexity, volatility, and subjective interpretations of statutes related to missing juveniles.

Various images of an individual are linked through NGI for identification purposes. In part, this is because eyewitness courtroom testimony has a tremendous impact on juries and prosecutors' ability to have offenders convicted and numerous studies have affirmed the fallibility of eyewitness identification. Dr. Marc Green presents an excellent article[†] on eyewitness identification that identifies several studies for additional in-depth study. Gordon Garrett's book *Convicting the Innocent* provides an extensive look at misidentifications of eyewitnesses and the impact on juries and prosecutors.[‡] Other studies and scientific literature have documented the poor ability of individuals whose occupations require them to verify identities with photographic identification (for fraud prevention) to confirm associations between

---

[*] State of Texas. 2014. *2014 Juvenile Justice Handbook.* Office of Attorney General State of Texas. Rev. 11/2014 pp. 9–10.
[†] Green, M. 2013. *Errors in Eyewitness Identification Procedures.* http://www.visualexpert.com/Resources/mistakenid.html (Accessed August 10, 2015).
[‡] Garrett, B. 2011. *Convicting the Innocent: Where Criminal Prosecutions Go Wrong.* Harvard University Press, Cambridge, MA. Chapter 3, pp. 45–82.

a photograph and an individual. Kemp, Towell, and Pike, 1997—demonstrated such circumstances according to an article in "Justice of the Peace" in January of 2008.* For example, in a 1997 experiment, cashiers performed badly when validating that the person who presented a photo-embedded credit card was in fact that person, even though doing so was part of their job description and they knew that their performance was being monitored. Half of the fraudulent cards were accepted, whereas one in ten were erroneously rejected. The cashiers' performance did not improve when they viewed photographs for establishing associations to the actual person.[†]

Perhaps these test participants did so poorly because they were not already familiar with any of the people they were asked to identify via image. According to one research team of psychologists, "[F]amiliarity is the key... The principle is straightforward. In the case of human performance, familiarity seems to be a natural consequence of increased exposure."[‡] In terms of cases registered in NamUs and filed with state clearinghouses, investigative leads that resulted in positive associations between an MP and UHR were developed not from strangers but from family members who saw images of UD and then contacted authorities to submit identification.

NGI will allow photographs to be submitted with arrest data and with civil records, and will accept photos in bulk format. In addition, Interstate Photo System (IPS) enhancements will be applied to facial recognition in the near future. National Institute of Standards and Technology (NIST) has reported that facial recognition accuracy software improved as much as 30% between 2010 and 2103.[§] It may not be long before biometrics may provide usable lists of candidates to assist in identifying UD.

Disseminating information about UD is handled differently than in MP cases. With UD, there is not the same expectation of privacy as is assumed for an MP (who is probably missing voluntarily). However, ME/C usually enjoy statutory immunity related to disseminating information that is necessary to locate MP or identify UD. For example, Minnesota Statutes 2014, 390.25 states:

> Nothing in this section shall be interpreted to preclude any medical examiner or coroner from pursuing other efforts to identify unidentified deceased persons, including publicizing information, descriptions, or photographs that may aid in the identification, allowing family members to identify missing persons, and seeking to protect the dignity of the missing persons.

* Kemp, R., Towell, N., Pike, G. 1997. *When Seeing Should Not Be Believing: Photographs, Credit Cards and Fraud*. Applied Cognitive Psychology. John Wiley & Sons, Ltd. Vol. 11, Issue 3. pp. 211–222.

† Jenkins, R., Burton, A. 2008. Limitations in facial identification: The evidence. *Feature of the Week: Justice of the Peace 172*, 5–12 January 2008, p. 4.

‡ *Ibid*. p. 5.

§ Brown, E. 2014. *NIST: Performance of Facial Recognition Software Continues to Improve*. NIST Information Technology Laboratory, NIST Tech Beat: June 3, 2014.

Most states have similar statutes. Therefore, ME/C can be of tremendous help to investigators in MP/UD cases. Nonetheless, important and wasteful disconnects can and do occur between ME/C and law enforcement.

For example, many ME/C maintain agency websites for UD and cooperate with other public and private databases to disseminate appropriate information about them. However, they often may not follow through to ensure information is sent to local or state law enforcement agencies and clearinghouses. In such cases, cooperating law enforcement agencies should offer to enter or register appropriate information in NCIC, NDIR, and NGI for continuous searching. In addition, upon identification, the ME/C may or may not notify law enforcement to remove the case from the various databases. Furthermore, the law enforcement agency of record may not think to search for outstanding warrants and wanted person records in NCIC that was entered by other agencies, thus causing tremendous waste of investigative resources by extending the investigation unnecessarily. When briefing/deconstructing closed cases I have found open warrants and active MP/UD records still active in NCIC.

Many ME/C and auxiliary death investigation entities do not have access NCIC or NGI. Others that are considered to be criminal justice agencies may have access to NCIC but may not have access to the Interstate Identification Index. Most states require fingerprints to be sent to a state law enforcement agency for entry into NGI for both state and national searching; however, in practice this does not always happen. Some larger ME/C offices can search local AFIS databases themselves and may voluntarily chose not send prints to state law enforcement agencies; they then lose the advantage of being able to locate UD fingerprints in outlying locations. Many agencies have AFIS systems of their own, but these may not be compatible with other AFIS systems that outside agencies could use to search their records. These problems are compounded in that the U.S. population is highly mobile and early life records may be places that are quite distant from where an MP was last seen or a UD was last known to be alive.

> **Key point:** There is no guarantee that all UD fingerprints will be available to law enforcement agencies that have the ability to access multiple local, state, and national NGI fingerprint databases; many may remain in local databases and ME/C offices.

As of summer 2015, the NGI IPS (Interstate Photo System) has not, as of yet, played a significant role in searches related to UHR. Facial images of MP have not been a major factor in NCIC or NamUs assisted identifications; however, facial images of decedents as well as their scars, marks, and tattoos have played a role in many UD identifications. Most of the related literature has noted that the best source of confirming an association between an image and an individual is someone who views the image has been in close, regular contact with the individual. A close family member would be most likely to be able to recognize a likeness and make an association. Mothers, for example, are so familiar with their children that they can often recognize them from even partial photographs or from how they walk or run in videos.

The NIST is aware that facial recognition software is impacted by several different attributes associated with an image. The following attributes of imaging software are very helpful to UD identification, depending upon the conditions of the remains when photos are taken.

- Absolute accuracy (quality of the photo as a result of environment or equipment).
- Accuracy ensured by the software developer and its proprietary algorithms.
- Ability to supply accuracy in spite of increasing population size (i.e., in spite of the existence of more people who have similar facial features).
- Utility of long candidate lists (more candidates means more similarities).
- Human adjudication factor (i.e., how many candidates a reviewer might actually examine).
- Accuracy by age (older individuals are easier to recognize and differentiate).
- Sketch recognition, which is especially applicable for UD.[*]

As is emphasized throughout this book, the foundational strategy for MP/UP investigations should widen from local to regional/state to surrounding states to national. This flow may be impeded, however, if local agencies do not submit all criminal fingerprints to state databases; in fact, this is not routine practice for some misdemeanor and juvenile offenses. Many states only submit serious misdemeanor fingerprints for inclusion in state and national searches. In addition, prints associated with juvenile and minor misdemeanor offenses are often inaccessible to outside agencies.[†]

All law enforcement agencies within two counties or a 150-mile radius around the county in which UHR are found should be surveyed and

---

[*] Grother, P., Negan, M. 2014. *Face Recognition Vendor Test (FRVT), Performance of Face Identification Algorithms, NIST Interagency Report 8009.* Information Access Division, National Institute of Standards and Technology, May 25, 2014.

[†] Capital News Service. 2006. FBI Expands Fingerprint Database to Misdemeanor, Juvenile Offenders. *Fox News Service*, September 26, 2006. http://www.foxnews.com/story/2006/09/26/fbi-expands-fingerprint-database-to-misdemeanors-juvenile-offenders/.

should receive UD fingerprints in a suitable scanned or electronic format for searching against their AFIS systems and paper files. The survey is a one-time query to ascertain what an agency requires in order to conduct a search quickly and efficiently, but it may be very useful in other types of criminal investigations. The radius of 150 miles was developed from my review of 44 cold hit (fingerprint and DNA) cases from across the United States that indicated the average distance between locations where bodies are found and the locations where UD were last known to be alive. The median distance in the reviews was approximately 49 miles, which means that half of the cases could have been resolved within distances of 49 miles or less between the locations where the bodies were found and the locations where the UD were last known to be alive. It is hoped that my case review findings, which supports the investigative anomalies of TXDPS first sixteen cold hit cases, will function as a catalyst more multiple in depth academic studies to increase our body of knowledge about unidentified human remains investigations.

Most agencies have some fingerprints on file that are not in a state database or that may be in a database that is not compatible or available for searching. As has been mentioned numerous times, not all AFIS systems are compatible with one another.

> **Key point:** In general, the utility of biometric data is impacted as much by human habit and behavior (historical factors) as by circumstances and policies (current factors). Investigative efforts should be directed toward local avenues, which offer greater opportunities for success, and also utilize alternate resources and systems to cover more distant areas.

Historically, agencies may not have had sufficient funding to buy new equipment. They may also have lacked sufficient manpower resources to reenter fingerprint records into compatible databases or send paper fingerprint cards to state agencies for entry into state AFIS databases. These factors can strongly impact cases, such as in 1978 when a 61-year-old male was murdered in Nebraska. Local police recovered prints from the scene, along with fingerprints and palmprints from a stolen vehicle thought to be associated with the murder. The investigators contacted all local agencies in 1978 and requested that they search their fingerprint records for a likely match; however, no confirming responses were received (IAFIS did not exist in 1978).

In 2008, the fingerprints were submitted to IAFIS because the case remained open. Within a few hours, a candidate list was returned that contained a confirming hit to an offender who was incarcerated in Illinois.

With this biometric evidence, investigators were able to get a warrant to obtain a DNA sample just days before the suspect was to be released. The DNA analysis supported the fingerprint identification. In 2011, the suspect was tried for murder and sentenced to 33 years in prison.[*]

In this case, multimodal biometrics were used in a complementary manner to confirm the identification of an individual. The prints from the scene were not matched when they were originally entered. However, the offender's fingerprints eventually were entered into IAFIS. When the latent fingerprints from the murder scene were also entered in to IAFIS, a candidate match was immediately returned. The moral of this story for investigators, as is emphasized throughout this book, is that the first order of business in an MP/UD investigation is to ensure that any useful fingerprints are digitalized and made available for NGI searching. This is particularly important because, as noted above, fingerprints are often retained at the local agency level and are not sent to state agencies for registration and IAFS searching. Despite the impression given by the CSI effect, searching UD fingerprints is very complicated and heavily dependent on how all fingerprints are stored and made available for searching.

The importance of registering all UD/UHR fingerprints with the sheriff's office of the county where the remains were found, and with state bureaus for NGI searching, cannot be overstated. These fingerprints should be audited annually via resubmission and searching in the following order:

- Local law enforcement agency with full NCIC access, including Interstate Identification Index (III) that is available to law enforcement agencies.
- Law enforcement agencies within a two-county or 150-mile radius of where the remains were found.
- State bureau AFIS and NGI.

As stated several times, an audit should return a hit to the previously submitted fingerprints; this indicates that the prints are still active and available for searching by other agencies. Fingerprints are the base identifiers in NGI; names, images, and other biometrics are linked to fingerprint records. Biometric information does not change but names can easily be changed. Investigators should keep in mind that although NGI replaced IAFIS in 2014, comprehensive searching of UD fingerprints in various fingerprint databases remains perplexing due to the discretion of law enforcement agencies,

[*] Federal Bureau of Investigation. 2012. *30-Year-Old Murder Solved: Fingerprint Technology Played Key Role*. Federal Bureau of Investigation, Criminal Justice Services, 9/11/2012 http://www.fbi.gov/about-us/cjis/cjis-link/july-2012/2012-latent-hit-of-the-year.

different practices by region, state, agency, and even opinions and behaviors of individual fingerprint examiners.

If fingerprints cannot be obtained from a UD, verbal descriptions and images of scars, marks, and tattoos should not be overlooked. If agencies do not routinely submit fingerprints to the state in a digital format to be searched via NGI, they may submit fingerprints and images to surrounding agencies (preferably working outward from where the remains were discovered). Accessing NGI should always be the first step, as the goal for investigators is have all biometrics entered and linked to NGI.

Rapid DNA Technology and Sentinel Events

11

Rapid DNA technology (RDNA), which can produce a viable STR DNA profile (see example: Figure 11.1) in less than 90 min, holds the key to the elimination of a significant number of the sentinel events that occur in routine criminal investigations as well as UHR investigations. A sentinel event in the criminal justice system has been defined by the Joint Commission on Accreditation of Health Care Organizations (JCAHO) as "an unexpected occurrence involving death or severe physical or psychological injury, or the risk thereof."[*] For the purposes of this book, it refers to a negative outcome that signals underlying weaknesses in an investigation or in the criminal justice system overall. Currently, the most notable sentinel event in the criminal justice system is a wrongful conviction, because it exposes all attendant parties to significant personal and institutional liabilities. As explained in previous chapters, sentinel events are likely the result of compound errors.[†]

The report on the Wrongful Convictions Summit released by the International Association of Chiefs of Police and the DOJ contained 30 recommendations to reduce sentinel events in the criminal justice system.[‡] The recommendations of the Summit Advisory Group (2013) in focused on preventing racial profiling, investigative biases, aggressive interviewing, faulty lineup protocols, false testimony, and eyewitness errors—all of which compound sentinel events. The public safety community has made little comment on the use of RDNA to prevent sentinel events, even though doing so fulfills the criminal justice system's mission of protecting the blameless while holding the blameworthy accountable. Even so, using RDNA technology before charges are filed may significantly reduce the incidence of sentinel events in the criminal justice system.

I find it useful to think of RDNA technology as the kind of sentinel that, in the words of James Doyle, "stands watch, [detects] the first signs of

---

[*] The Joint Commission. 2009. Facts about the Sentinel Event Policy. *The Joint Commission.* http://www.jointcommission.org/assets/1/18/Sentinel%20Event%20Policy.pdf.

[†] Doyle, J. 2013. NIJ's sentinel events initiative: Looking back to look forward. *NIJ Journal,* 273 (NCJ 244145).

[‡] International Association of Chiefs of Police, & Department of Justice, Office of Justice Programs 2013, August. *National Summit on Wrongful Convictions: Building a Systematic Approach to Prevent Wrongful Convictions.* International Association of Chiefs of Police Wrongful Conviction Summit, pp. 18–20.

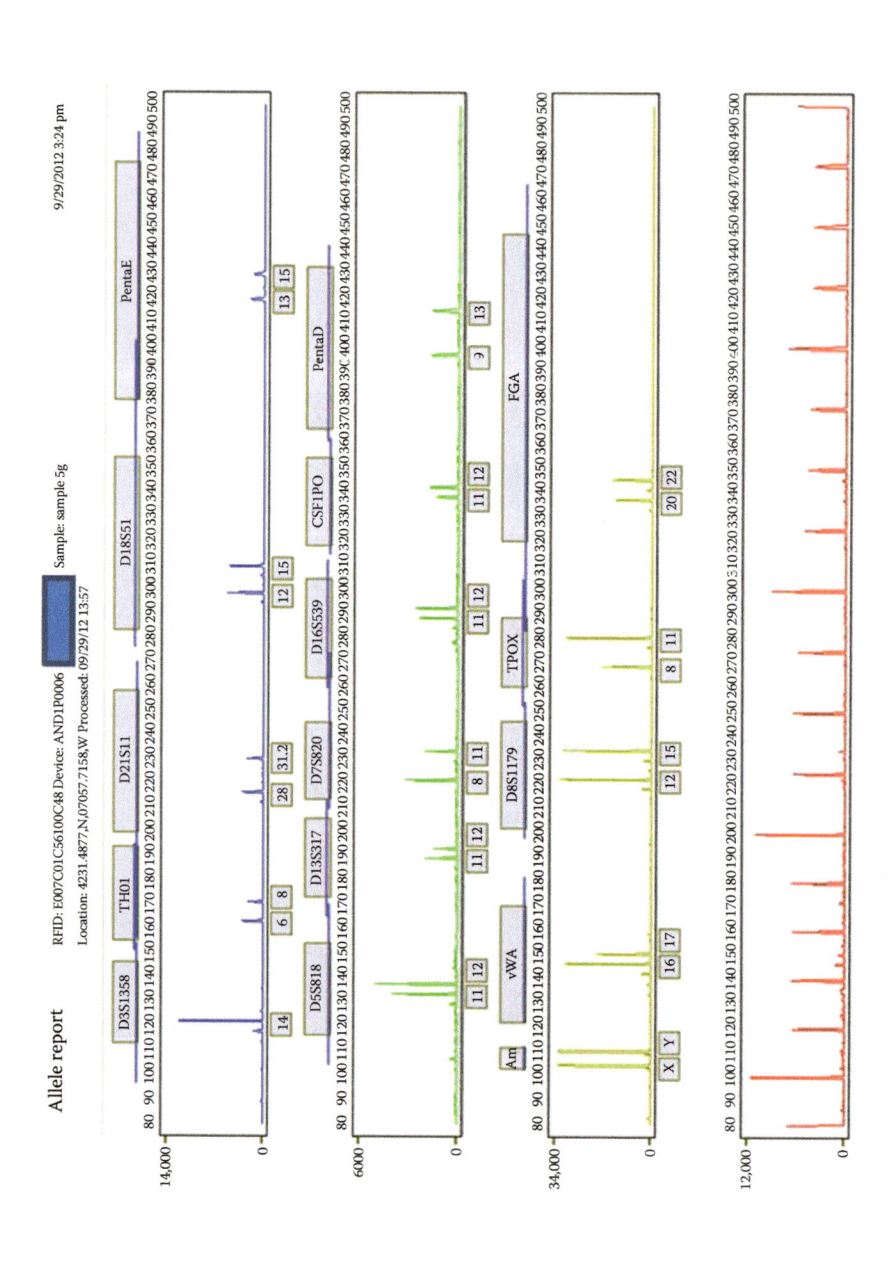

Figure 11.1 Allele report developed in less than 90 min utilizing GE's DNAscan rapid DNA equipment by George W. Adams.

a looming threat and sound[s] a warning that should not be ignored."[*] For those who take advantage of this guardian, a single-source biological family RDNA reference sample may quickly confirm whether or not a UD profile belongs to a particular MP.

The sentinel event initiative launched by the DOJ in 2014 takes its nonblaming approach to problem solving from the healthcare and aviation industries.[†] In the healthcare industry, as in law enforcement, a sentinel event is defined as a serious adverse outcome that includes the risk of or actual death or serious injury (physical or psychological). The word "sentinel" indicates the need for immediate response and action,[‡] which is also called root cause analysis (RCA). As previously emphasized, sentinel events are likely to be the results of compound errors. However, when properly analyzed and addressed, they may provide information that can be used to strengthen the system and prevent future adverse events or outcomes. Even near-misses can signal serious weaknesses in an investigative approach or wider system.[§] The healthcare industry term "never events" is also relevant to the criminal justice system. These are serious, preventable, and costly errors that should "never" occur.[¶]

Sentinel events in the healthcare industry involve serious situations, tragic outcomes that should never happen (never events), and high-risk circumstances (near-misses) that could have easily resulted in harm to a patient. A root cause analysis (RCA), which is immediately undertaken while all evidence is available and recoverable, functions to mitigate subjective interpretations in both the healthcare and aviation industries. By contrast, in the criminal justice system, sentinel event evidence is often unavailable, irrecoverable, and heavily dependent on subjective interpretations, years to decades later, of an officer's motivations and actions.

Sentinel event investigations in the aviation industry are focused on human factors such as errors and violations. Errors represent the mental or physical activities of individuals that fail to achieve their intended outcome. Given the fact that human beings by their very nature make errors, these unsafe acts dominate most aviation accident databases. Violations, which are much less

---

[*] National Institute of Justice. 2014. *Mending Justice: Sentinel Event Reviews* (NCJ 247141). Washington, DC: U.S. Government Printing Office. p. 1.

[†] Office of Justice Programs, National Institute of Justice. 2014. Mending Justice: Sentinel Event Reviews. U.S. Department of Justice, Office of Justice Programs, National Institute of Justice. NCJ247141. p. 10

[‡] The Joint Commission. 2011. *Sentinel Events (SE). CAMOBS Refreshed Core*, January 2011: Comprehensive Accreditation Manual for Office-Based Surgery Practices. http://www.jointcommission.org/assets/1/6/2011_CAMOBS_SE.pdf.

[§] U.S. Department of Justice, Office of Justice Programs, & National Institute of Justice 2014, February. *Research on "Sentinel Events" and Criminal Justice System Errors.* p. 3.

[¶] American Health Lawyers Association 2010, July. *Never Events.* Retrieved October 17, 2014, from http://www.healthlawyers.org/hlresources/Health%20Law%20Wiki/Never%20Events.aspx (Accessed October 17, 2014).

common, include willful disregard for the rules and regulations that govern flight safety.* The truth is that we are all human beings, prone to errors, violations, biases, and complacencies, and that our lives will contain some level of these and other factors no matter how hard we try to eliminate them.

RDNA technology, which can reduce the human factors that contribute to sentinel events in the criminal justice system, may be conceptualized as a lab in a box. Currently there are two major types of RDNA equipment: the DNAscan manufactured by GE and the RapidHit 200 manufactured by IntegenX. Usable results can be obtained in less than 90 min, which means that it is possible to go from sample collection to usable profile in less than 2 h.

Awareness of human factor contributions to a fatality probably began in the aviation industry with the September 17, 1908 crash of the U.S. Army's first airplane, which resulted in the death of Lt. Thomas Selfridge and serious injury to Orville Wright. The Board of Inquiry investigation into this crash highlighted the need for seatbelts and helmets. Over the years, the participation of medical examiners in aircraft investigations grew in order to more accurately determine the extent to which human factors contribute to fatal crashes. Although a multitude of factors were identified, intervention efforts were not successful.

Between October 31, 1964 and October 31, 1965, 122 fatal general aviation accidents occurred in the United States, with 206 fatalities. Globally in 2013 there were 16 fatal accidents and 210 fatalities, according to the International Air Transport Association (IATA).[†] "Of particular concern was the frequency with which family, friends, and local officials knew the habits and physical and mental conditions of the pilots and tolerated the situation."[‡] It is the same in the criminal justice system. This book's examination of forensic technology's black box demonstrates the same is true. In my 10 years of focusing on improving investigations of unidentified human remains, numerous human factor errors have been observed, as delineated in examples, but not made openly known to families and investigators. The healthcare and aviation industry comparisons are given to provide you a contextual understanding about human factors present in the criminal justice environment.

* Shappell, S., Wiegmann, D. 2003. *Human Error and General Aviation Accidents: A Comprehensive, Fine-Grained Analysis Using HFACS*. Retrieved October 18, 2014, from http://www.hf.faa.gov/docs/508/docs/gaFY04HFACSrpt.pdf.
† Allianz Global Corporate & Specialty. 2014. *Global Aviation Study: A Review of 60 years of Improvement in Aviation Safety*. http://www.agcs.allianz.com/assets/PDFs/Reports/AGCS-Global-Aviation-Safety-Study-2014.pdf. p. 9.
‡ Dille, R., Morris, E. 1966. *Human Factors in General Aviation Accidents (AM–66-27)*. Springfield, VA: Clearinghouse for Federal Scientific and Technical Information.

Humans are naturally prone to error; therefore, it should come as no surprise that human error has been implicated in a variety of occupational accidents, including 70%–80% of accidents in both civil and military aviation.[*] Clearly, more emphasis must be placed on the genesis of human error as it relates to accident causation if fatal errors are to be reduced.[†]

A 2013 report in the Journal of Patient Safety cites estimates from the Institute of Medicine that indicate (based on 1984 data) that 98,000 hospital patients die in the United States each year from medical errors; the true number of preventable adverse events (PAEs) is unclear. A review multiple studies from 2008 to 2011 was published in 2013 by Dr. John T. James with the following conclusion: "In a sense, it does not matter whether the deaths of 100,000, 200,000 or 400,000 Americans each year are associated with PAEs in hospitals.[…] one must hope that the present, evidence-based estimate of 400,000+ deaths per year will foster an outcry for overdue changes.[‡] A 2003 sentinel event alert issued by the Joint Commission on the Accreditation of Healthcare Organizations reported that, according to estimates from the CDC, nearly two million hospital patients per year in the United States develop infections, and about 90,000 of them die as a result.[§]

Regardless of the true numbers of annual sentinel events in the healthcare and aviation industries, one thing appears to be abundantly clear: the current approach, which is to deal individually with the various types sentinel events, is not working.

The definition of sentinel event used in this book (a significant negative outcome that signals an underlying weakness in a system or process, and is likely the result of compound errors) is also adopted by the NIJ. When sentinel events are properly analyzed and addressed, they may hold important keys to strengthening a system and preventing future adverse events or outcomes. Below are some examples of sentinel events in the U.S. criminal justice system

- Wrongful conviction or near-miss (innocent people brought to trial).
- Labeling of an individual during questioning by investigators.

---

[*] Shappell, S., Wiegmann, D. 2000. *The Human Factors Analysis and Classification: Final Report*. U.S. Department of Transportation, Federal Aviation Administration System–HFACS. Abstract, Item 16, www.nifc.gov/fireInfo/fireInfo_documents/humanfactors_classAnly.pdf (Accessed August 14, 2015).

[†] Wiegmann, D., Shappell, S. 2001. *A Human Error Analysis of Commercial Aviation Accidents Using the Human Factors Analysis and Classification System (HFACS) (DOT/FAA/AM-01/3)*. Springfield, VA: National Technical Information Service.

[‡] James, J., 2013. A new, evidence-based estimate of patient harms associated with hospital care. NCBI: PubMed.gov. Abstract. http://www.ncbi.nlm.nih.gov/pubmed/23860193 (Accessed August 14, 2015).

[§] The Joint Commission 2003. Sentinel event alert; Infection control related sentinel events (Issue No. 28). doi: January 22.

- Inaccurate eyewitness testimony.
- False statements by informants, victims, or witnesses.
- Overreaching by forensic subject matter experts.
- Exoneration outcomes that incur liability risk for criminal justice personnel and agencies.

The necessity for prophylactic applications to eliminate a significant number of sentinel events is demonstrated by the following:

- Between 20% and 25% of successfully litigated Innocence Project cases included false confessions.[*]
- The National Registry of Exonerations shows 1450 exonerations as of October 19, 2014.[†]
- The Beatrice Six (defendants who confessed to murder in 1989) were exonerated in 2012 when DNA evidence identified a suspect not associated with them; as a result, a 42 USC Sec. 1983 claim was filed against investigating parties.[‡]

As investigators seek justice for crime victims, they must perform due diligence when they establish grounds for bringing charges against a criminal suspect. Due diligence requires investigators to explore all leads; as they do so, they confirm probable cause in order to either move forward with or refute a particular lead. In law enforcement, probable cause is a reasonable suspicion by a prudent officer that an offense has been committed or may soon be committed; investigators may cite the lack of probable cause as a reason to not follow up on a particular line of inquiry or to end investigative efforts altogether.

When a UD investigation coincides with a homicide investigation, or becomes one, officers must follow up on all leads, regardless of their likelihood of producing viable results, to protect the case from challenges at trial and protect the agency and themselves from charges (currently or in the future) related to negligent investigation. The problem for investigators is how to clearly document their decisions to end these lines of inquiry (for the purposes of this book, this would occur because a suspect has been cleared by DNA evidence). Investigators must have physical, objective documentation to support their decisions so that they may justify/defend their actions

---

[*] Jenson, J.K. 2014. The dilemma and debate over confession evidence strategies. *Journal of Forensic Research Criminal Studies*, 1, pp. 1–10.
[†] University of Michigan Law School, & Center On Wrongful Convictions At Northwestern University School Of Law. 2014. October 19. *The National Registry of Exonerations.* http://www.law.umich.edu/special/exoneration/Pages/about.aspx.
[‡] Sheppard, Circuit Judge. 2012. Thomas W. Wilson v Richard T. Smith. No. 11-2884. http://media.ca8.uscourts.gov/opndir/12/10/112882P.pdf.

if wrongful conviction claims are brought by innocent defendants. These justifications and defenses may have to be presented in court years after the original trial.

The solution is surprisingly simple. Once DNA evidence is obtained from a crime scene or a sexual assault kit, a person of interest can be asked to voluntarily provide a buccal swab for RDNA analysis. The rapidity of obtaining a DNA profile in this way means that a person of interest may be eliminated with little inconvenience or loss of time, or reasonable suspicion may be established if the DNA profiles match. Furthermore, the DNA results may be immediately transmitted, by fax or email, to a subject matter expert for consultation.

Whether RDNA evidence provides elimination or probable cause to bring charges, the decision can be made quickly—which is necessary in the pursuit of justice for both victims and suspects. As in the healthcare and aviation industries, proactive intervention is far less expensive and more effective than corrections after the fact. Unfortunately, sentinel events in the U.S. criminal justice system may be repeated for years or decades in successive cases. Adding RDNA technology to investigative protocols can mute or even eliminate sentinel event factors.

During and after mass disasters, the identification of human remains becomes very challenging. Visual identification and circumstantial factors are often used to determine identification. For example, in 2010 two girls were involved in a severe car wreck in Arizona. The family of one girl was advised that their daughter had died at the scene. The other family was advised that daughter was in serious condition at a hospital. It was later discovered that the girls' identities had been conflated.[*] I have personally received calls from more than one ME who, after identifying a UD through papers found on the body, received a visit from the person who was supposedly dead.

Five factors severely impact human judgment and opinion, which can lead to sentinel events. These factors are complacency, bias, stress, time, and confusion. Current legacy DNA technology does not reduce any of them, not least because it may take months to provide urgently needed answers. With RDNA technology, positive identification or suspect elimination may be achieved in less than 2 h, regardless of physical distance between a UD and a reference DNA source or between a suspect and a crime scene.

In addition, RDNA can reduce the sentinel events that happen due to circumstances or lack of experience. For example, the condition of UHR (see Figure 11.2) after water accidents, automobile accidents, and fires often makes it difficult for ME to ascertain identity. When families are sure the

---

[*] *CBS News.* 2010. Mourning the Wrong Girl. http://www.cbsnews.com/news/mourning-the-wrong-girl/.

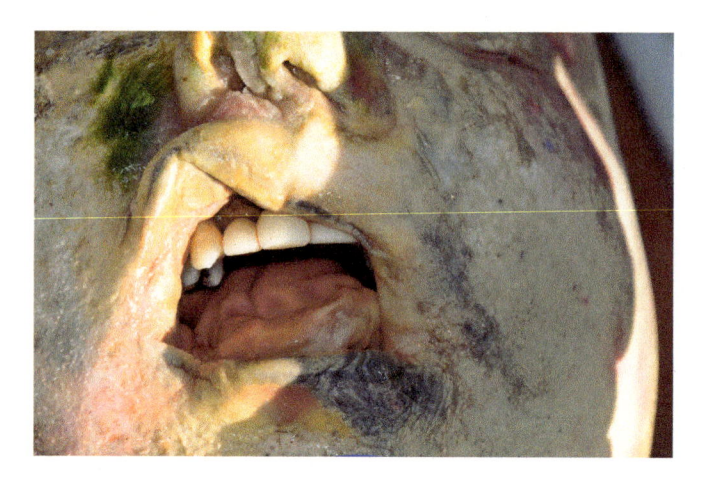

Figure 11.2 Conditions of human remains present challenging conditions for visual identifications. (Courtesy of Detective Mark Czworniak (retired), Chicago Police Department.)

UD is their family member, considerable pressure is placed on ME/C to defer to circumstances to establish identification. During or after natural disasters, RDNA use can help quickly reunite infants and young children with their parents. For all of these reasons, RDNA should become part of every investigator's toolkit.

Next-Generation Sequencing and Stable Isotope Analysis
12

There are multiple types of DNA that are used for different and complementary purposes for human identification, depending on circumstance and samples. Each type of DNA requires different processes and skills that are laboratory and analyst dependent with current legacy DNA technology.

Emerging technologies are now available to help identify UD whose remains yielded partial profiles or no viable profiles from current CE technologies used in most forensic laboratories. Those profiles reside at LDIS and SDIS labs across the country but cannot be effectively be searched as legacy DNA technology failed to produce full profiles. Next-generation sequencing (NGS) DNA acquired profiles supported with stable isotope analysis (SIA) may produce a full DNA profile for effective searching and to possibly locate a geographic area for a candidate match or association are discussed first in this chapter.

Mitochondrial DNA (mtDNA)

When degraded and skeletal remains fail to yield full nuclear DNA profiles, mitochondrial DNA (mtDNA) produced by a cell's organelles may, in some cases, be obtained from the remains; this process is very complex and labor-intensive. mtDNA is present in both males and females but is passed on only through the mother. Traditional mtDNA analytical methods, which are directed toward control regions HVS1 and HVS2, have limited discriminating power. In fact, they miss up to 70% of the mtDNA genome variation that may be available with NGS.[*] In October 2013, at the International Symposium on Human Identification in Atlanta, academic and government researchers along with practicing forensic scientists speculated that NGS will have replaced current mtDNA analysis in nearly all forensic mtDNA cases by 2018.[†]

---

[*] Templeton, J. et al. 2013. DNA capture and next-generation sequencing can recover whole mitochondrial genomes from highly degraded samples for human identification. *Investigative Genetics*. December 2.
[†] Melton, T. 2014. Digging deep: Next generation sequencing for mitochondrial DNA forensics. *Forensic Magazine*, 01/04/14. http://www.forensicmag.com/articles/2014/01/digging-deep-next-generation-sequencing-mitochondrial-dna-forensics.

Current standard typing techniques with mtDNA methods have several disadvantages. They are labor-intensive and complex; they consume significant amounts of valuable resources (chemicals and time); and they require multiple laboratory steps. The latter is particularly dangerous because multiple steps increase the risk of sample contamination.[*]

Low Copy Number (LCN) Analysis

Low copy number (LCN) techniques were originally developed by the Forensic Science Service (FSS) and have been in use since 1999.[†] LCN refers to any technique that exceeds manufacturers' recommendation for equipment used in nuclear DNA analysis. LCN techniques are regularly used to develop nuclear DNA from highly challenging or degraded remains. Although LCN approaches are expensive and fraught with difficulties similar to the mtDNA disadvantages mentioned above, they have proven very successful in facilitating associations and matches between MP and UHR. LCN techniques are not advisable, however, for DRS from objects that have come into contact with an MP such as toothbrushes, hairbrushes, or lipstick. This is because LCN magnifies the contamination from extraneous cells along with cells from the MP. LCN is best for sole-source samples such buccal swabs or actual remains.

Samples obtained by LCN were only authorized to be accepted at the NDIS level after January 31, 2015, as authorized in the NDIS Operational Performance Manual January 31, 2015 (Section 4.2.1.10, Version 1). Many laboratories at the LDIS and SDIS levels maintain LCN database indexes that may not be allowed to be sent forward to NDIS as the profiles were developed prior to NDIS approval. Searches of older LCN profiles may still be accomplished by exporting LCN profiles to an Excel file and then exchanging that file among cooperating laboratories for manual or keyboard searches. Manual and keyboard searches, which involve DNA searches of profiles without having to enter them into CODIS databases, can thus be done with LCN profiles without violating current or past NDIS guidelines.

Throughout this reference material, it has been stressed for investigators to have multiple modalities of identification and to know what actually takes place as opposed to assuming what is policy or what happens

---

[*] Templeton, J. et al. 2013. DNA capture and next-generation sequencing can recover whole mitochondrial genomes from highly degraded samples for human identification. *Investigative Genetics*. December 2.

[†] Caddy, B., Taylor, G., Linacre, A. 2008. *A Review of the Science of Low Template DNA Analysis*. University of Strathclyde, Cancer Research UK. www.gov.uk/government/uploads/system/uploads/attachment_data/file/117556/Review_of_Low_Template_DNA_1.pdf, p. 23. (Accessed August 14, 2015).

in one location occurs everywhere. An example to help drive home the point occurred in New York in January 2015 where the judge tossed out two types of DNA evidence (LCN and Forensic Statistical Tool) used regularly in criminal cases.* The decision may affect previously adjudicated cases. Remember in forensic science, which is prone to highly subjective review, what is true today in one locality may not be true in the future or another locality. It cannot be stressed often enough for investigators to have two separate (types and providers) modality as part of their investigative strategies.

Y-STR

Y-STR (a short-tandem repeat on the Y or male chromosome) is passed from fathers to male offspring. Despite mutations that occur fairly predictably, Y-STR remains the same from generation to generation. Thus it reflects the father's male bloodline accurately but is less discriminating than nuclear DNA. In other words, the Y-STR profile is the same in all brothers, uncles, fathers, and grandfathers from the same paternal line.

Y-STR profiles are extremely important in familial searching, which involves ranking nuclear DNA profiles by probability ratios and then reanalyzing them to extract a Y-STR profile. Because this approach is too expensive for analysis of a great number of profiles, laboratories limit the number of profiles they will analyze to produce a Y-STR profile. With current DNA technology, creating Y-STR profiles requires a separate skill set from analysts. Y-STR like mtDNA is not exclusive to a family's lineage. One thing that I have noticed in forensic conferences for investigators that tout the unique benefits of Y-STR and mtDNA is that the profile (Y-STR or mtDNA) derived with current legacy DNA technologies may match many families and many individuals within and outside the current sphere of investigative inquiry. In familial searching of arrestee and convicted offenders, it may be more beneficial to rank candidates by location rather than by probability. By location, I am referring to the distance from the crime scene to the location of arrest of the offender.

The FBI addresses many of these concerns in its article "Missing Person Comparison Request," which states "when limited genetic information is available, associations may not be possible through database searches. Circumstances that may prevent a database association from occurring

---

* Jacobs, S. 2015. Judge Tosses Out Two Types of DNA Evidence Used Regularly in Criminal Cases. *New York Daily News*, Monday, January 5, 2015. http://www.nydailynews.com/new-york/nyc-crime/judge-tosses-types-dna-testing-article-1.2065795 (Accessed August 14, 2015).

include: the DNA data has not been uploaded to NMPDD/NDIS; insufficient STR results obtained from the human remains; the resulting DNA data contains a mtDNA or STR (haplotype) that is relatively common in the relevant population; or there is diminished allele sharing between relatives and remains when first-degree relatives (e.g., parents, offspring, or siblings) are not available to provide a sample."[*] In my opinion, until NGS is implemented both Y-STR and mtDNA will experience limited utility for UD/UHR investigators.

Single-Nucleotide Polymorphism (SNP)

A single-nucleotide polymorphism (SNP) is a genetic variation within an allele at a particular locus. STR DNA profiles indicate the number of times a particular DNA base-pair sequence is repeated in the allele at a particular locus, but do not reveal internal mutations in these base-pair sequences. However, such mutations may provide enough discrimination to make an association possible.

Next-Generation Sequencing (NGS)

Currently, forensic DNA analysis in the U.S. centers on capillary electrophoresis based technology that consider the 13 core loci identified by the FBI.[†] In 2012, an NIJ special report summarized the DNA analysis landscape.

- DNA laboratory capacity continued to grow as a result of more automation, additional personnel, implementation of overtime hours, and improved operations.
- 10% more DNA cases were processed in 2011 than in 2009.
- The overall workload had decreased by 46.3% since 2009 levels because fewer samples were taken from convicted offenders and arrestees. However, the backlog of cases had increased by 16.4% since 2009.
- Hiring and retaining more DNA analysts, implementing new technologies, and altering business practices were recommended.[‡]

---

[*] Federal Bureau of Investigation. 2015. *Laboratory Services: Missing Person Comparison Request*. http://www.fbi.gov/about-us/lab/biometric-analysis/codis/missing-person-comparison-request (Accessed August 15, 2015).

[†] Illumina. 2013. *Targeted Next-Generation Sequencing for Forensic Genomics*. http://www.illumina.com/forensics. Pub. No. 770-2012-034, February 18.

[‡] Nelson, M. et al. 2013. *Making Sense of DNA Backlogs, 2012—Myths vs. Reality*. U.S. Department of Justice, National Institute of Justice. *NCJ* 243347.

The report also noted the stress experienced by forensic DNA laboratories that mainly used CE (capillary electrophoresis)-based DNA technology. For example, the requirements of human identification place higher demands on laboratories to run tests that involve first-generation sequencing approaches such as mtDNA, Y-STR, and SNP. The new technologies developed for DNA analysis have overcome the limitations of CE-based analysis, such as the inability to analyze multiple polymorphisms (types of DNA) in a single workflow, inability to utilize valuable genetic data from degraded samples, low resolution in analysis, and difficulties in mixture analysis.[*] These limitations are brought into sharper focus by the increase in demands for DNA testing, not only for MP identification but also for kinship testing, ancestry investigations, and other human identification applications. This increase in demand strains the fixed capabilities of CE-based methods.[†]

The NIJ gave a tremendous boost to UHR investigations in October 2014 by awarding the nonprofit Battelle corporation an $800,000-plus grant to introduce NGI across law enforcement operations. The Battelle study, which will conclude in early 2016, involves the Armed Forces DNA Identification Laboratory; the Bureau of Alcohol, Tobacco, Firearms, and Explosives; the California DOJ; the National Institute of Standards and Technology; Pennsylvania State University, and the Philadelphia Police Department.[‡] New instruments, laboratory materials, and software will be tested for the development of evidentiary samples. However, NGS is currently available and is being effectively utilized around the world.

The power of NGS lies in its ability to both produce profiles that are compatible with nuclear STR, Y-STR, and mtDNA, and to utilize additional capabilities with the same effort. NGS loci that can be simultaneously analyzed include CODIS autosomal STRs, worldwide autosomal STRs, CODIS Y-STRs, worldwide Y-STRs, full Y haplotypes, full X haplotypes, identity SNPs, ancestry SNPs, phenotypic SNPs, and mtDNA D-Loop/complete mtDNA genomes. In addition, NGS can reveal intra-STR SNPs that are not revealed by current CE technologies.[§]

With NGS results, physical anthropologists may be able to deliver analyses that pinpoint the ancestry of remains and also more accurately estimate secondary data such as height and skin tone. Artists may then be able to utilize this NGS data to produce more accurate sketches. Moreover, keyboard

[*] Yang, Y. et al. 2014. *Application of Next-Generation Sequencing Technology in Forensic Science.* Elsevier, B.V. on behalf of Beijing Institute of Genomics, Chinese Academy of Sciences and Genetics Society of China. p. 192.
[†] Illumina. 2013. *Targeted Next-Generation Sequencing for Forensic Genomics.* www.illumina.com/forensics. Pub. No. 770-2012-034, 18 February 2013.
[‡] Battelle. 2014. *Partnership with Severn Leading Labs Will Help Spur Use of Next-Generation Sequencing in Law Enforcement.*
[§] Ilumina, Inc. 2013. *Targeted Next-Generations Sequencing for Forensic Genomics.* http://www.illumina.com/documents/icommunity/article_2013_03_forensics.pdf.

searches can compare profiles obtained with NGS to CODIS profiles (as with LCN profiles that cannot be uploaded into CODIS).

In other words, it is now possible to identify decedents who could not be identified before the advent of NGS. The capacity to overcome legacy technology deficiencies means that LDIS laboratories will be able to increase the effectiveness of their LDIS databases for both NDIS-eligible and noneligible samples. CODIS administrators can create dispositions for a greater number of incomplete DNA profiles than ever before. All agencies can lower their costs, and families have greater opportunities to locate missing loved ones. NGS holds the potential to conduct all types of DNA analysis at the LDIS level so that the need for specialized DNA laboratories will not be necessary. The costs of DNA laboratory construction and operation validation may be greatly diminished, which in turn could allow for more DNA laboratories to be constructed and more positions for advanced forensic analysts. We will finally be able to fully support the contention that there should be no such thing as a cold case.

Stable Isotope Analysis (SIA)

It is the combination of NGS and SIA that may magnify the power of NGI and traditional identification forensic and biometric resources. SIA compares the isotope ratios for oxygen, carbon, and nitrogen derived from human remains with the isotope signature of a geographic area anywhere in the world. Entities that only process one or two of the three isotopes cannot narrow the possible geographic origination area or recent trajectories (travels and/or activities) of a decedent because the possible concordant areas are just too large. There are certified laboratories with extensive experience servicing the law enforcement community, especially with SIA-related analysis in unidentified decedent investigations: the Jim Hutton Institute in the United Kingdom and the Ehleringer/IsoForensics Laboratory at the University of Utah. Both institutions have conducted peer-reviewed research that is published and easily available for additional study. In my 10 years of research into cold case sentinel events involving unidentified decedent cases, it appears that the international community outside of the United States shines in the practical application of forensic science as DNA, anthropology, and SIA. It is my personal belief that stable isotope analysis will soon come to the forefront as the amplifier that helps all forensic science from human identification to drug trafficking to achieve results that would never be possible otherwise.

SIA is therefore extremely valuable; it helps to determine trajectories of UD during the last year of life as well as geographic birthplaces or early residences. By measuring isotopes in hair and nails, it may be possible to ascertain whether a UD was born or raised in the immediate geographic area where remains were found. Through SIA of bones, it may be possible to enhance NGS ethnicity-derived data and to make reasonable projections about where the UD lived early in his or her life. As SIA develops, it may even be possible to estimate, with a good degree of accuracy, the geographic areas for multiple periods of the decedent's life. This very valuable information can allow a death investigator to concentrate the search in the local area, thereby not only saving investigative resources but also increasing the chances of making rapid identifications, or to widen the investigation more quickly to outlying areas—including other countries.

Initial Strategies and Values-Based Leadership IV

The overall conceptual and foundational strategy for improving UHR investigations is presented in Section IV. This information, which has been gathered from cold hit identifications, illuminates why resolution may take so long even when solvability factors are abundant. In addition, case examples illustrate concepts that were discussed in previous sections.

Advocates for families of the missing may find much helpful information in Section IV. This is an important point because although systems such as NamUs are publicly accessible, only a few categories of people may manage case files that involve UHR. They must in all reality (though not currently the case as of January 2015) be law enforcement officers working on a specific case, medico-legal death investigators, ME/C with access to NCIC, members of a state clearinghouse, or other authorized personnel who have online access to NCIC.

Because information may not be shared from NCIC, NDIR, or NGI with other than authorized law enforcement or criminal justice personnel (certain information such as NGI and III may not be shared with criminal justice agencies—those CJA with an ORI ending with an alphabetic character), case managers must be able to access NCIC online in order to reconcile information between NCIC and NamUs. When discrepancies between NCIC and NamUs databases are observed, confirming information should be obtained from independent outside sources and shared with the ORI in NCIC or case owner in NamUs. NCIC and NamUs case owners/agencies may be different due to the concurrent jurisdiction phenomenon in the United States. In this manner, security of NCIC is still maintained and both systems are reconciled as is the desire of U.S. Congress as indicated in H.R. 5519, Section 4: Sharing of Information between NCIC and NAMUS. Unless the independent outside verification is undertaken and updated in both NCIC and NamUs, the cycle of errors is destined to continue.

It is not unheard of for various databases to contain different data, or incorrect data. Many states have restrictions on utilizing NCIC, NDIR, and NGI information. Nonetheless, external validation of the discordant information is necessary when data must be corrected and/or updated.

Chapter 14 addresses values-based leadership. In collaborative endeavors, such as the ones between families and investigators, the parties are constantly judging each other and must maintain trust if the partnerships are to be effective. This chapter can provide important guidance about working with people in all walks of life.

Initial Strategy Development 13

All of the previous 12 preparatory chapters were constructed and presented in preparation for Chapter 13, which will help investigators construct their own unique investigative strategy to resolve a UD/UHR case. As each UD/UHR case is unique, so is the strategy the investigator develops. The strategy is a reflection of the investigator's training, knowledge, and experience. The prudent investigator realizes that his or her strategy must encompass deficiencies in their training, knowledge, and experience. We all have deficiencies regardless of our work or education.

A strategy with a solid principle-based foundation is necessary to protect the case, insure justice for victim, family, and society, as well as provide protection for the case, investigator, and investigating agency, well after the case is resolved. There will be many pundits offering advice in service of their agendas that have no skin in the game (i.e., risk associated with investigating the case other than being wrong) who provide training and strategies based on celebrity cases, situational truths, and what-if scenarios. From my experience of listening and reading many such agenda-driven presentations over the years, it was obvious that many presenters have not worked wearing a badge, made an arrest, spilled a drop of their own blood in service to their community, or placed themselves or their families' physical and financial welfare in jeopardy. Both families and investigators, as is reinforced throughout this book, are just different sides of the same coin. Developing and communicating an effective transparent investigative strategy between family and investigator will go a long way in helping each understand that there is a common goal. A solid foundation built on simple unwavering principles is necessary prior to the consideration of developing any effective strategy for a particular case.

A foundation for a house or mansion serves special purposes—the same is true for criminal investigative strategies. A building's foundation serves to bear the load of the building (the case), anchor it against known natural such as earthquakes (witness or subject matter expert error), and to isolate it from ground movement (failure in other cases or circumstances that retroactively impacts a previously resolved case).[*] The same is true for criminal

---

[*] Layton, K. n/d. *Purpose of a Building Foundation.* eHow. http://www.ehow.com/info_8143249_purpose-building-foundation.html (Accessed August 17, 2015).

investigations to prevent an investigative failure during the investigation and after resolution. "If you were to construct a house, even a simple and ordinary one, wouldn't you take great care to lay a proper foundation? [...] If the foundation is not strong, the mansion of self-knowledge will not last long. It will soon collapse." Sai Baba Gita.[*]

I teach the following as foundational principles, which are very simple, few in number, and never changing (principles do not change):

1. Every forensic report is to be considered qualitative (subjective and opinion based in nature of its originator). Many forensic reports as DNA association, match reports, or anthropological analysis may appear quantitative in nature (measurements and number counts); however, all must be interpreted, which converts the quantitative data into qualitative results. A recent stunning example is the new $220 million Washington, DC lab that was closed with problems over interpretations. "Local prosecutors have ordered the review of 182 cases as a result of the errors they said they discovered problems in the lab's DNA results. Prosecutors, as well as the accreditation board, had problems with the interpretation in DNA mixtures cases, those in which more than one person's DNA is present in the evidence."[†]

2. Two separate confirmations or modalities of confirmation or identification should be the standard operating procedure in any case. One modality of identification may be impaired or encumbered by circumstances within or outside the control of the investigating parties. Examples: the chain-of-control may be compromised within the laboratory or property control; or events totally unrelated to the case that may have a historical impact. Just this year (2015), it has been reported that a Brooklyn judge threw out results of low-copy DNA testing as being so controversial that numerous of scientists who are experts in the field disagree. In such cases, it is not appropriate to place the evidence in front of a lay jury and expect them to be able to make sense of it.[‡] It is unclear at this time how other LCN cases

---

[*] Drucker, A. 1998. *SAI BABA GITA: The Way to Self-Realization and Liberation in this Age.* Atma Press Wisconsin Dells, WI, pp. 126–127.

[†] Alexander, K., Zauzmer, J. 2015. *Director of D.C.'s Embattled DNA Lab Resigns After Suspension of Testing.* Washington Post, April 30, 2015. http://www.washingtonpost.com/local/director-of-dcs-embattled-dna-lab-resigns-following-suspension-of-testing/2015/04/30/1c619320-ef80-11e4-8666-a1d756d0218e_story.html (Accessed August 15, 2015).

[‡] Javcoba, S. 2015. Judge Tosses out Two Types of DNA Evidence Used Regularly in Criminal Cases. *New York Daily News.* Online January 5, 2015. http://www.nydailynews.com/new-york/nyc-crime/judge-tosses-types-dna-testing-article-1.2065795 (Accessed August 15, 2015).

previously adjudicated or waiting in the wings may be impacted with the ruling.

3. When conflicting results come to light with any one modality of analysis, all modalities should be reexamined/retested by different subject matter experts not connected to the original subject matter experts. An *a priori* argument dictates that all modalities of identification point in the same direction.

For a decade now I have been exploring and questioning the reason for the existence of sentinel cold cases. By far the most common cause in my opinion is human factor error and lack of critical thinking challenges that could have prevented them, if only the above three principles would have been the foundation for the investigative strategies. The above three foundational principles are not purposed to be critical of forensic resources or criminal investigations, but rather, to recognize the shortcomings in what we call the human experience.

Cold cases involving UHR identifications are probably the most difficult cases for law enforcement to resolve. Many such cases remain unresolved because initial strategies have never been implemented or communicated to families, law enforcement officers, ME/C, and advocates for MP/UP. Families should be aware that subject matter experts and service providers may consciously avoid including the following initial strategies because of concerns about resources such as funding, manpower, and time.

1. As emphasized throughout this book, MP/UP investigations should begin at the location where the body was found and move outward: from local to regional/state to surrounding states to national areas to overseas.

2. Three core investigative metadata factors should be considered: distance, age, and time (Figure 4.3). No possible candidates should be eliminated based on any other metadata alone. Spurious eliminations may cause cases to go cold and become sentinel events.

3. STR DNA profiles should be processed at the nearest LDIS laboratory where an MP was last seen or a UD was found and uploaded to SDIS of that state. That LDIS laboratory should be listed as the primary contact in NCIC, NamUs, and any other database used by investigators.

4. Fingerprints acquired for MP/UP, should be converted to digital format, and registered with the applicable state law enforcement agency where the MP went missing or the UD was found so that the fingerprints can be used for NGI searches. If the fingerprints are initially rejected for quality reasons, they should be resubmitted after problem areas are corrected the images by a qualified latent print

examiner. For the best chances of obtaining a hit, a new NGI search should be requested after 90 days and at least annually thereafter. A hit, even if it doesn't pan out, ensures that the fingerprints will be available at local, regional, and national levels as long as the case remains unresolved.

5. Local or in-state subject matter experts and forensic service providers (anthropologists, dentists, odontologists, pathologists, ME) should be first choice if they are available. If they are not, families should know that qualified national subject matter experts are equally useful as a backup resource; local subject matter experts maintain networks in their specialties, as well as similar or related specialties, and stay in frequent contact with their peers. Local subject matter experts are preferable not only for the ease of communication with families and investigators but also because they may have more actual hands-on case experience under local conditions and know local statutes.

6. The case manager associated with the case in NamUs should have direct online access to NCIC in order to ensure NCIC and NamUs records are, and remain, reconciled. Records must be reconciled until a case is resolved.

7. A root cause analysis should be conducted immediately when any association is made that involves fingerprints or DNA at the national level; it is necessary to understand why the hit could not have been made at the state or local levels.

Follow-Up

Because few investigators have many opportunities to work a UHR cold case, little educational material is available for them. This book represents an attempt to correct that situation. One of the most important things investigators should know is that effective conceptual and foundational strategy centers on four basic investigational phases: preservation, triage, exchange, and correlation (PTEC).

All evidence should be preserved as though it has come from a murder scene. Although the ultimate goal is identification, investigative leads should be worked because there are no second changes to make things right. If evidence is properly collected, stored, and preserved with a good chain of custody (COC), even evidence that did not initially produce enough of a DNA profile for effective database searching may be reanalyzed with new technologies and in conformance with evidentiary rules of the court.

Triage refers to the process of determining what evidence may be available and the best entities to analyze it. Enough unidentified remains evidence should be properly collected for testing to be conducted independently at multiple laboratories, some of which will have more advanced equipment and use more advanced techniques than others. Viable results that cannot be obtained with currently available technology may become possible in the future or may already be possible. For example, the CE (capillary electrophoresis) technology now widely used to generate STR profiles is being replaced with NGS (next-generation sequencing) technology.

The process of exchange refers to transferring evidence from initial scene to property control to laboratories under a properly executed COC. Although samples are rarely lost, tracking is not only time-consuming but may not be possible as samples are forwarded from lab to lab. The investigator should always know exactly where all samples are located, the exact number of samples at a given location, and the specimen numbers of every sample at every location. This knowledge includes the new specimen numbers that are assigned when an original sample is split into multiple smaller samples for testing; when the original sample is also renumbered, or when samples are renumbered a second time after testing, this can be especially confusing. Sample remnants (aliquot or extracts) are stored for later use by all responsible laboratories and should be shown on the chain of custody. Investigators must know the location for every aliquot or extract of a sample or its disposition as it may become a key piece of evidence in the future. Should a laboratory be closed for any reason, the extracts and aliquots may be the only evidence remaining of a previously processed sample.

Information control is just as important as evidence control. Therefore, all aspects of sample movement and documentation should be recorded in NCIC administrative fields, as well as at the locations of analysis and evidence storage. Hard copies of investigative case files get lost, misplaced or damaged over the years; NCIC provides a permanent tracking record mechanism to record the location and details of those cases that may be retrieved for offline searches. Laboratory case files may also contain additional forensic reports or communications from subject matter experts, which may be unknown and undisclosed to investigators and be critical to the investigation.

Investigators should be careful to correlate the results (DNA, fingerprints, dentals, and anthropological analyses) from forensic service providers and to compare the outcomes to ensure consistency. The human tendency is to look for points of congruence and consistency; however, the truly objective investigator attempts to challenge or even discredit every aspect of the investigation. To the truly objective investigator, discordance does not imply incompetence. Instead, it provides opportunities for resolution that will, in turn, produce accurate and bias-free outcomes. I often refer to cold cases as bias free cases to stress the importance to produce bias free results. Just as DNA labs utilizing legacy DNA technology have difficulty in identifying and controlling contamination, investigators have difficulty in identifying and controlling bias in their investigations.

The logical process in UHR investigations is counterintuitive for people who habitually focus on developing support for the initial set of circumstances—in other words, for people who seek to affirm their biases rather than to demolish them. However, challenging every aspect of an investigation with critical thinking is logically very sound. If events have been correctly reconstructed or interpreted, and if identification is accurate, the outcomes of additional tests cannot discredit such analyses and/or opinions.

When test results contradict each other, investigators should reexamine evidence and what have been interpreted as facts and also request reanalyses of the test(s) in question by an independent party. Care must be taken to ensure that examiners/laboratories do not collaborate and are unaware of the results of the original tests. Most subject matter experts refer to all reports and crime scene information as they formulate their opinions. However, as discussed in Chapter 2, such knowledge makes their analysis vulnerable to bias. Along with being aware of the possibility of bias, investigators should do their best to make sure that individual laboratories and subject matter experts do not collaborate as they conduct tests and render opinions. In the end, neither the cause nor the outcome of an event can be proven with 100% accuracy. Human beings have to make do with what is known at the time, and must accept that if a cause or outcome cannot be disproved, it is probably accurate. We refer to this as inductive probability: the degree of belief which is rational to place in a proposition given the evidence.* All forms of UD/UHR identifications are made via inductive probability by appropriate statutory authority based on the degree of belief they place in what they see before them.

The CSI effect creates the illusion that all cases can be resolved, and success stories in the media focus on case resolutions that are reached decades after the original report is made. However, in reality, investigators and families have very limited access to educational resources about effective investigative strategies for UHR investigations. Most of the training currently available is aimed at professional scientists, which means that much of its precedents, principles, and vocabulary is unfamiliar to the public. In addition, many of the available educational resources for law enforcement and families are funded through grant initiatives for scientific research; therefore, the resultant programs tend to be agenda-driven rather than holistic. All too often, families and investigators are thus left with a hope and pray strategy in which they collect samples or evidence, get it tested/analyzed, and hope it is in the right database while praying that it hits something.

A new approach should be implemented that educates law enforcement and families, is objectively presented, and is tailored to audience needs. In the words of Peter Drucker, "Unless strategy evaluation is performed seriously

---

* Blumer, M. 1967. *Principles of Statistics*. Dover Publications Inc., New York, NY (electronic version), p. 48.

and systematically, and unless strategists are willing to act on their results, energy will be used up defending yesterday."[*] Here, "strategy evaluation" may refer to the critical thinking process and the phrase "energy will be used up defending yesterday" echoes Sir Francis Bacon's statement that "It is the peculiar and perpetual error of the human understanding to be more moved and excited by affirmatives than by negatives."[†] What we humans first see or hear, or what is first brought to our knowledge, carries the most impact; the longer it goes unchallenged or is repeated, the more factual we believe it to be.

It might be helpful to conceptualize initial strategy as a general contractor would view the framing of a new home. As the construction continues, interior layout may change within various parameters and exterior additions may be necessary. Analogously, as an investigation continues (i.e., as more becomes known or as strategies fail to produce results), it may become necessary to rethink and revise strategies—even cherished ones. Than, after resolution is achieved, the case must be debriefed/deconstructed to understand why certain things went wrong—particularly if those errors delayed resolution for months, years, or decades.

The following cold-case scenario could happen anywhere. A passenger is killed when the vehicle in which he is riding is involved in accident. His body ends up at an ME/C's facilities as a UP. Fingerprints are retrieved from this UD, and blood samples are sent to the state law enforcement agency, but no dental records are included and no medical abnormalities are noted. The case remains unresolved for 20+ years.

A few months before the accident, an MP report was filed with a local police department located well within a two-county radius from the site of the automobile accident in which the UP perished (and was brought into contact with the criminal justice system through the ME/C's office). Fingerprints of the MP were registered with the state bureau and the local police department, and the case was posted on numerous websites; the case files include descriptions of physical characteristics such as a tattoo and healed broken bones. When the fingerprints of this MP and the UD who died in the car accident are compared, a confirmed match is returned.

Contrary to popular notions, an investigator's work is not complete when a case like this one is resolved and the family of the MP/UD is notified. The positive identification has confirmed the case as a sentinel event (a case that stayed cold far longer than it should have).[‡] At this point, deconstruction of the case should begin with asking questions that help discover possible

[*] Whitesel, B. 2010. *Growth by Accident, Death by Planning: How Not to Kill a Growing Congregation.* Abington Press, Chapter 7.

[†] Bacon, F. 1561–1626. *Gaiam Life.* http://blog.gaiam.com/quotes/authors/francis-bacon/ 56895.

[‡] Doyle, J. 2013. *NIJ's Sentinel Event Initiative: Looking Back to Look Forward.* Office of Justice Programs, National Institute of Justice, *NIJ Journal,* No. 273.

disconnects in the critical thinking process. Critical thinking is "the intellectually disciplined process of actively and skillfully conceptualizing, applying, analyzing, synthesizing, and/or evaluating information gathered from, or generated by, observation, experience, reflection, reasoning, or communication, as a guide to belief and action."[*] When applied to sentinel events in forensic work, the process can be described as "looking back to look forward."[†]

RCA questions include

- Why did this case take so long to resolve?
- Were both the MP and UD cases entered into appropriate databases where they remained in as active records? If not, why not? If the case entered into NCIC, how often was an offline search conducted within a two-county radius?
- Were $.M (possible hit) messages generated by NCIC? Which agencies, if any, received the $.M messages? How were the $.M messages disposed? In light of the fact that automatic NCIC searches are conducted only when records are altered or updated, how often were the records updated in order to generate a new NCIC search?
- Were all known MP cases reviewed within 4 years of when the UD was found and the MP was last known alive?
- Were body markings and physical anomalies (in this case, tattoos and previously broken bones) noted in the MP and UD database records? If not, why not?
- Were the fingerprints in both the MP and UD files searched at both local and state levels? Were the prints of the UD searched every 6 months or every year by local and state agencies? Was a survey of all law enforcement agencies conducted within a two-county radius to ascertain if the agencies maintained fingerprint records not registered with the state? If records not registered with the state were maintained, how could requests have been made for searches of these records?
- Did the blood sample from the UD on the card sent to the state law enforcement agency contain enough blood to generate a DNA sample? Could a DNA sample have been generated for the MP?

It cannot be overstated that when sentinel events occur in a complex system such as the U.S. criminal justice system, they are rarely the result of

---

[*] The Critical Thinking Community. 2014. *Defining Critical Thinking.* http://www.criticalthinking.org/pages/defining-critical-thinking/766.
[†] Doyle, J. 2013. *NIJ's Sentinel Event Initiative: Looking Back to Look Forward.* Office of Justice Programs, National Institute of Justice, *NIJ Journal,* No. 273.

one individual's error. Rather, numerous small errors made by many people combine and are exacerbated by underlying weaknesses in the system.[*] It is also important to recognize when routine results indicate error or system weakness. For example, any time a fingerprint is found outside a local region via limited secondary databases other than NGI technology (meaning that a fingerprint was there all along but could not be detected), an investigative systemic failure should be assumed and a root cause analysis conducted.

The chances of sentinel event occurrence can be reduced by implementing the basic strategy design suggested in this chapter: preservation, triage, exchange, and correlation. As a case develops, this initial design should be adjusted whenever an anomaly is discovered.

In the first phase, preservation, there is only one chance to get it right; despite the impression given by the CSI effect, opportunities are almost nonexistent to correct what has been compromised, contaminated, or overlooked. As has been repeatedly stated in this book, every death scene should be treated as a possible homicide. Often enough, what appeared at first to be accident or suicide does turn out to have been murder—and it is imperative that a homicide investigation not be compromised. Assuming that a creature who walks like a duck, quacks like a duck, and looks like a duck, is in fact a duck demonstrates a deeply flawed logic that, unfortunately, continues to dominate the environment surrounding long-term UHR cases.

Below is an application of PTEC to a well-documented, publicly reviewed case that involved a fatal accident and a UD (this same case is also discussed in Chapter 2). As recounted in the *Texas Prosecutor*[†] and by media outlets around the world, a car was found in flames at the bottom of an embankment in central Texas on June 18, 2004. Texas Rangers were called to the scene. A body in the front seat of the vehicle was burned beyond recognition and all its limbs were missing; ultimately, only 12 pounds of flesh would be recovered. Two women who arrived on the scene claimed to be the wife and mother of the UD, one Clayton Daniels. The vehicle was registered to Clayton and his wife, Molly. No skid marks leaving the roadway were noted; the fire seemed to be very intense and appeared to have begun in the area of the driver's seat. At the scene, Molly Daniels identified the body as her husband, Clayton, from a tennis shoe, a button, and a pin. Arson investigators were called to take charge of the vehicle, and the 12 pounds of remains were sent to the local ME's office. All of the evidence was preserved because the case was recognized as a possible homicide.

[*] Holder, E. 2014. *Mending Justice: Sentinel Event Reviews.* U.S. Department of Justice, Office of Justice Programs, National Institute of Justice, NCJ 247141. p. 1.

[†] Starnes, J. 2005. Woman digs up corpse to fake husband's death. *Texas Prosecutor*, 35(5), 22–28, Texas District and County Attorneys Association.

During the triage phase, no fingerprints or dentals were available, but the ME observed a penis in the 12 pounds of flesh even though other investigators could not distinguish such. The autopsy named the deceased as Clayton Daniels. Suicide did not seem to be out of the question, because not long before the accident, Mr. Daniels had pleaded guilty to aggravated sexual assault of a child and had been placed on probation; in addition, his life was insured for $110,000.

In the exchange phase, one inconsistency became obvious: the visual observations of the remains made by law enforcement at the scene (i.e., that there was no penis) did not match the observations made at the ME's office (i.e., that there was a penis). To resolve this inconsistency, which also meant challenging the identification made by the ME, a sample of the remains was sent to a laboratory for DNA analysis. An FRS was collected from Mr. Daniels's mother and forwarded to the same laboratory.

The correlation phase began several months later, when the results of the DNA analysis excluded Clayton Daniels. Because Mr. Daniels was apparently not dead, investigators revoked his parole and placed his wife under surveillance. A man she met at a local fast-food restaurant turned out to be Clayton Daniels, who was immediately arrested.* Further investigation revealed that an 81-year-old woman, recently deceased, had been dug up from a local cemetery, placed in the car, and incinerated in the deliberately set inferno.

This story well illustrates that multiple modalities of identification are critical in UHR investigations. As history has shown over and over, what appears to be so may not actually be so. The circumstances, metadata, and subject matter expert's original opinion indicated that the remains belonged to Clayton Daniels. It was not until the second modality of identification (DNA) was exploited that investigators were able to uncover the inaccuracy of the circumstantial identification by the ME and the visual identification by Molly Daniels. The moral of this story for investigators is clear: Try, if at all possible, to avoid relying exclusively on any one modality for identification.

Working with fingerprints, in MP or UHR cases, provides another example of why investigators should use multiple modalities. As previously recommended, fingerprints should be registered in digital format with the state bureaus for NGI and searched in NGI on a regular basis. A matching candidate may not be initially returned, but in subsequent searches the prints should be expected to hit against the original submission wherever they have been registered. These hits show that the prints are active in various databases and are viable candidates for hits with NGI. Fingerprints that have been submitted to state and federal agencies and accepted by them may not be of sufficient quality to actually be searched. A good fingerprint examiner

---

* *Ibid.* pp. 22–28.

or contractor may be able to work with the prints to get them in suitable format to be accepted searched appropriately.

When considering the probability values in an association report (that is, reports that compare DNA from UHR and possible biological relatives) investigators should keep in mind that these probability values are less-desirable indicators than match reports based on DRS. Of course, the higher the probability number is, the rarer the profile is within the general population. However, the probability values derived from the same DNA data can vary from lab to lab and from analyst to analyst, depending on the assumptions made by analysts, the reference population databases they use, and the equipment in their labs. In addition, different labs and different analysts may use different algorithms to develop their probability numbers. When an association report states that "investigators may find it beneficial to submit additional biological family reference samples to improve the statistical probability numbers," investigators should realize that they may be at risk if the identification is incorrect—no matter when this error is discovered.

Unfortunately, reading and understanding forensic reports are often beyond investigators' training and expertise. In addition, it is up to laboratories to decide whether or not statistical probability is sufficiently high to issue an association report, or whether it is so low that their results are inconclusive and additional biological family member samples should be requested. The context in which these decisions are made may not be explained in the association report. Therefore, it is crucial for investigators to develop go-to independent resources for assistance in analyzing association and match reports as well as reviewing the laboratory file for the case. The question must now be asked, "Why did the problems with the Washington, DC lab, as mentioned previously in this chapter, not surface earlier? Had any of the 182 at-risk cases that were previously processed at the laboratory had their case files reviewed by independent experts as part of the case's investigative strategy, could the problems been resolved amicably early-on through collaboration and conversation for everyone's benefit?" Please understand that critical thinking challenges benefit everyone and every agency associated with a case. Interpretation of statistical probability numbers may differ between investigators and subject matter experts; the former may see a very rare probability whereas a subject matter expert may see a very low probability.

Understanding context in a report is as dependent upon the knowledge base of the reader as it is upon the knowledge base of the originator. Only the legal authority responsible for issuing a death certificate should determine that there is enough evidence to make a definitive identification. This person is usually an ME/C, not a law enforcement investigator. Nonetheless, any time an investigator receives an association report (meaning that a possible identification has been made) and another agency is involved in the case, he or she should contact that agency to correlate its investigations. Many times, only one agency actually receives the notification regardless of policies and procedures to the contrary.

These fundamental strategies may be applied to all forensic technologies associated with UHR investigations. A UHR investigation is really a probability game; identifications are more often made close to where the body was found than far away from where the body was found. Working outword from the location of the UD saves time and resources that may then be used for the more rare outlier cases. In addition, it cannot be overstated that investigators should not be afraid to change or alter initial strategies. Each UHR is unique and therefore may require different strategies.

Values-Based Leadership 14

Without leadership by families and investigators, effectively designed strategies for resolving MP/UD cases may be severely impaired. Due to the necessity of adjusting strategies in response to circumstances, UHR investigations require genuinely collaborative partnerships between investigators and families. Without transparency and mutual trust, leadership dies and contention is born.

Families that have not experienced what it means to wear a badge in service of a community may find it difficult to understand the sacrifice and anguish that investigators must endure: the memories of lost innocence that haunt our dreams and thoughts, carefully constructed lives that change forever after the death of a fellow officer, and the ghosts of past events that may drive us or drown us. Empathy is a two-way street that allows each to see and appreciate the leadership of the other.

Values-based leadership is about who we are, as communicated by our personal actions as we challenge the status quo and try to make things how they ought to be rather than allow them to stay as they are. This kind of leadership is crucial to MP, UD/UP, and UHR investigations. For example, participants in the National Missing and Unidentified Persons System advisory groups were chosen for their individual leadership qualities that supported the NIJ's mission for NamUs: "Bring hope to the families of missing and unidentified persons."[*] Values-based leadership is not about leaders or organizations, but rather who people are at the core.

> Values are like fingerprints. Nobody's are the same, but you leave 'em all over everything you do.
>
> **Elvis Presley[†]**

---

[*] U.S. Department of Justice, Office of Justice Programs. n/d. Bringing Hope to the Families of Missing and Unidentified Persons Program. U.S. Department of Justice, Office of Justice Programs, *News Center*. http://ojp.gov/newsroom/events/missingpers_photos.htm.

[†] Philosiblog. 2010. Values are like fingerprints. Nobody's are the same, but you leave 'em all over everything you do. December 17, 2012. On-line article. http://philosiblog.com/2012/12/17/values-are-like-fingerprints-nobodys-are-the-same-but-you-leave-em-all-over-everything-you-do/.pph.1 (Accessed August 15, 2015).

The most important question one must answer in order to form a lasting collaborative partnership is "Who am I?" If you do not know yourself, collaborators cannot know who you really are as a partner. Potential partners should not be misled by false perceptions; instead, they should observe others' actions as a reflection of their authenticity—and investigators and families should do the same. In *Principle-Centered Leadership*, Steven Covey describes the necessary principles as "self-evident, self-validating natural laws" that "apply at all times and all places"[*] and names the most fundamental one the Law of the harvest, which includes preparing, seeding, cultivating, watering, weeding, and harvesting.[†] In other words, we are that which we sow.

According to Covey, principles remain permanent and operate whether or not we have knowledge of them. Principles also stay the same throughout creation, where values are expressed as personal characteristics. Covey put everything into perspective for us when he characterized principles as objective natural laws and external[‡]; values, by contrast, are subjective and internal. We must hold ourselves accountable for the core values by which we are known but must also be careful, as the philosopher Epictetus warned, not to take oaths and if at all possible to avoid them.[§]

Others measure one's words against one's actions when judging the authenticity of one's leadership. According to a popular quotation often attributed to Tolstoy: "Truth, like gold, is to be obtained not by its growth, but by washing away from it all that is not gold."[¶] Perhaps Tolstoy is advising us to think critically and challenge the façade of rhetoric, in order to really know others. Perhaps he is implying that values are learned, or that they are forged in reality's kiln. In any case, values-based leadership is about us, individually, as we communicate them the world by our actions—however they may be construed.

Although everyone has values that we learn from our individual perceptions of reality, certain values may be shared. These are referred to as "core values." Shared core values allow us to collaborate and fulfill our missions. Noncore values may be described as attitudes. Partnerships and shared core values are the genesis of transformational relationships that can change the world over time, whereas attitudes allow us to enjoy the company of others, whether or not we are in partnership with them. Without self-validation and others' authentication of shared core values, collaborations cannot move forward. It is the heat of reality's kiln that provides the opportunity to express

---

[*] Covey, S. 2009. *Principle-Centered Leadership*. Rosetta Books, LLC Electronic Edition. Loc. 174.

[†] *Ibid*. Loc. 1947.

[‡] *Ibid*. Loc. 1346.

[§] Long, G. n/d. *Epictetus: A Selection from Discourses of Epictetus with the Encheiridion*. Ted Garvin, David King and the Online Distributed Proofreading Team.

[¶] Tolstoy, L. n/d. As quoted from Goodreads. http://www.goodreads.com/quotes/415634-truth-like-gold-is-to-be-obtained-not-by-its.

our leadership and core values. Values-based leadership does not allow others to stand in for us when reality challenges us to prove our honor.

Didactic lectures and checklists have not helped to fill the longtime leadership void in the criminal justice community. Perhaps Anthony de Mello provided some insight into this problem when he wrote: "People who want a cure, provided they can have it without pain, are like those who favor progress, provided they can have it without change."* In truth, despite tremendous advances in forensic science, more than 1400 exonerations have been pronounced, tens of thousands of untested sexual assault kits gather dust, thousands of UD languish in laboratories, and the homicide clearance rate is the lowest in decades.

We can fill that void through values-based leadership, but we cannot do it as individuals. Shared core values provide the basis for forming partnerships that can effect change, but even cooperation is not enough: positive outcomes require innovation, collaboration, and education. We must strive to learn about the latest research on forensic science resources and how to access the newest technologies. De Mello, in his book of parables, offers guidance with the line "You have yet to understand, my dears, that the distance between a human being and the truth is a story."†

I would like to share a story which shows that families and law enforcement have the same fears, anguish, and losses. The evening of Thursday, October 28, 1971, was expected to be uneventful. At that time, the Fort Worth Police Department's Four District was one of the most violent areas in the country. Its Unit 324 was my second home, from 3:40 p.m. to 2:40 a.m.—the second shift, Thursday through Sunday. This was a one-man unit until the third watch came aboard. When friends asked what 324 was like, I told them "It's like going deer hunting four days a week, except the roles are reversed."

The Electric Circus nightclub, at the corner of Berry and Riverside, drew pimps, prostitutes, thieves, drug dealers, and fences every weekend. Standing orders were for officers not to set foot on the property unless dispatched. During a recent traffic stop, we had taken down the primary Southeast Fort Worth LSD supplier along with his inventory and ledger.

Eddie Belcher, an academy classmate, worked third shift. A beautiful family supported his work as a police officer as he attended college to become a social worker; he loved serving others first. Eddie was normally assigned to the kinder, gentler side of Fort Worth. On that fateful night, however, a complainant reported a disturbance at Riverside and Berry and patrol was short that evening in the "Four District." When dispatch called 1000 Calvert, the

---

* De Mello, A. 1986. *One-Minute Wisdom*. Image Book by Doubleday, Dell Publishing Group. E-book Loc. 713.

† *Ibid*. Loc 234.

assembly point for patrol, to see if a third-shift officer had arrived early, Eddie was there, studying as usual before his shift. He answered the call himself.

At the scene, Eddie met Ron Turner, our academy class president along with other officers. As Eddie and Ron stood outside their cars talking, however, no disturbance could be detected in or near the Electric Circus; seemingly, someone wanted an officer to be at that particular place at that particular time. Suddenly, a rifle shot ripped through the air as officers looked on, frozen in shock. Eddie's skull exploded and pieces struck Ron. Both went down. It would be Eddie's last watch; Ron would stand his last watch a few years later during a single-car accident in the wee morning hours.

The events of that evening had to be reported to me by officers on the scene. I was not present because I was enjoying my first comp-day, ever, which I had requested in order to be introduced to my wife's grandparents (they had arrived from Germany with the sole intent of meeting their granddaughter's American husband). We relished each other's company and shared stories about Germany well into the evening as we planned the next day's activities, but these were disrupted by the morning news.

An arrest and conviction were made in short order, but the shooter walked free within a few years.* Although the rifle was recovered, and witnesses appeared, there was no DNA testing in 1971; even today, the outcome may have been no different because of the difficulties associated with DNA mixtures and LCN DNA in forensic cases. Hardly a day goes by that I do not remember Eddie and feel guilt over his sacrifice and that of his family. I hear about the same feelings from victims, their families and our communities. It is the active commitment to values-based leadership that will bring forth the innovation, collaboration, and education that are necessary to correctly identify criminals as well as missing and unidentified persons. With families and officers working together for the common good of their communities, we may have a chance to change outcomes for many people. Organizations cannot fulfill leadership responsibilities; it is their membership, and the families of members, who must deliver the leadership to bring about victim-centered approaches in MP/UP investigations.

A cursory review may give one the impression that values-based leadership is the latest fad in leadership literature. But it has have always been here; we just need to brush off that which obscures our view. History seems to support Covey's concept of principles that "apply at all times and all places." Similarly, transparency, trust, and collaboration are the gold nuggets in all organizations and all communities.

When people come together in relationships to interlink their core values and empower leadership, they establish beliefs that give substance and

---

* Hinz, D. 2009. *In Search of FWPD History.* Signal 50n 1st Quarter 2009, Fort Worth Police Officers Association. p. 11.

character to the organization's mission and vision statements. Relationships interlock values and leadership; values are interlocked with the individual; leadership is then interlocked with reality.

If leadership is about mutual empowerment among partners, it cannot be seen as a hierarchy or process of ascendency. Instead, leadership is the successful collaboration among partners where the concept of "leader" actually becomes blurred through interactions that are acknowledged, improved, and redirected through critical thinking processes. This interdependent quality of effective leadership manifests itself through mutual trust, integrity, respect, and security between partners as they serve the other.

When Covey speaks of "self-evident, self-validating natural laws," he is telling us that leadership is a personal action in which the individual validates his or her own outcomes and accountability. In light of today's vacillating values, which seem to be based on circumstance, weakness is perceived by victims and families when the leader's (investigator's) actions do not match his or her rhetoric. Instead, families become uncertain of the leader's (investigator's) judgment under the stress and frustration of the investigation. Weakness and uncertainty begin the decomposition process in an organization, not just around the investigator; critical thinking, the primary tool for constructing successful collaborations, falls into disuse. Values-based leadership is about mutual empowerment of relationships, and there can be no empowerment or leadership in the presence of active and rhetorical dissonance.

NamUs was designed to be a facilitator of collaborative, mutually respectful, and effective interactions between investigators and families. As Einstein wrote in 1934, "Without creative personalities able to think and judge independently, the upward development of society is as unthinkable as the development of the individual personality without the nourishing soil of the community." Without partnerships between families and investigators in victim-centered investigative approaches, the chances of resolution are limited and relationships often turn toxic.

We need to remember those who are no longer with us to ensure that we are building communities that blend in harmony and unity, for everyone's security and prosperity.

Final Thoughts

15

Not many people have had the magnificent opportunities to occupy the positions I have since February 2005, when I first became a program coordinator at the UNT Center for Human Identification, and later when I became the Director for the National Missing and Unidentified Persons System (NamUs). These positions allowed me to witness the evolution of missing and unidentified decedent investigations from multiple perspectives. My adventure started after the first cold DNA hit was made through CODIS, in the Donna Lisa Williamson case. The excitement and emotions at that time could only be described as ecstatic. New technologies involving nuclear DNA and mitochondrial DNA analysis were being applied to MP/UD investigations. Families finally had hope of resolution in their searches for their long-lost loved ones.

Although I tried, I failed to shield myself from the families and support law enforcement agencies to resolve their cases. There is nothing more determined than a mother caring for her child, present or missing. Jan Smolinski, in her search for her son Billy, was among the first to reach me on a foundational level. She opened not only my eyes but also my heart and soul to the anguish of the families.

From that first call, from an unknown caller that I thought at first was a police officer, I have hesitated to press forward with all I can do for families that are suffering both needlessly and for too long. Jan's call revived the thoughts and feelings I experienced when I learned that my old classmate and current comerade Eddie Belcher was assassinated on a corner of my beat.

A stoic façade is often presented as a characteristic of police officers, but the truth is that we feel and cry at night just like everyone else. That night after Jan's call, and for several nights after that, I was no different. Why the sentinels of our communities have to be sacrificed, I do not know. Why our children and spouses are murdered, I do not know. Families and police officers may appear to be very different, but when officers remove their façade we are exactly the same. If you have ever hugged a beloved family member, knowing that this will be the last time you will have such an opportunity, you can understand that the same feeling represents the lives of families with missing loved ones and the lives of police officers.

The evolution of forensic technology is occurring at such a rapid rate that what is known one year is often obsolete by the next. This book was written for officers to welcome a new era in MP/UP/UD and criminal investigations as legacy technologies evolve. It was written for investigators to take advantage of this new era. And it was written for families to help provide the answers they desperately seek.

Chapter 12 describes emerging technologies that are available, now, to help identify the STR, mtDNA, and LCN profiles that are currently residing in LDIS labs across the country but cannot be searched or compared because they are ineligible for NDIS entry due to incompleteness or technological incompatability. Despite next-generation technologies, the numbers of such cases may grow as databases grow, the number of potential matches increases, and the administrative workloads become heavier. In addition, use of the new technologies is actively discouraged in some jurisdictions under the guise of the results not being useful as evidentiary samples or not being compatible for uploading to CODIS.

LCN-derived samples that were once in CODIS have had to be removed from CODIS/NDIS, and as January 2015 LCN samples are once again allowed into CODIS/NDIS from single source samples, it is unclear if the older samples will be allowed to reach NDIS. Nonetheless, LCN comparisons have been used for years, shared between labs, and have helped to make hundreds if not thousands of associations. Many mtDNA samples cannot be used for identifications on their own, but are used in conjunction with STRs to help define a higher level of statistical probability. If mtDNA use was not restricted to a very narrow range of mitochondria variation as with current legacy DNA technology, its stand-alone performance would improve dramatically. The benefits of implementing new technologies far outweigh the benefits of continuing to resist their implementation. They are here, they are effective, and they should be used in developing investigative leads that can rapidly and efficiently help end the suffering of thousands of families.

As you discuss the contents of this reference material with others, there may be the criticism that multimodalities of identification and separation of forensic service providers are too expensive. I would just like to point out that regardless of where we find ourselves, we are still part of nature and nature will guide us by time-tested principles from the beginning of time. Please indulge me by listening to one of my observations.

I work from home a good portion of the time writing, reading, and reviewing articles as a peer reviewer for several international publishers. To keep my focus, I take a brief respite every couple of hours and enjoy a cup of coffee or tea in the backyard where we have a giant pecan tree that houses several families of squirrels, a host of birds, and multicolored lizards. In late summer and early fall, the squirrels are busy burying pecans in the yard all over the place one by one. In the winter and early spring, they are busy digging up their stash. They do not bury all of their pecans in one spot, but rather individual hiding places. They know that if something happened to one large stash, they would perish in the winter. The same is true of your case if you have only one forensic service provider or one modality of identification. There are no shortcuts in developing effective strategies in unidentified human remains cases.

Index